FOUNDATIONS OF GROUP ANALYSIS
FOR THE TWENTY-FIRST CENTURY

To Marilyn,
(my therapy sibling!)
with my best wishes.
Hope the strength that she
gained in 'our' group will
stand her in good stead.
Jason
21.1.2015

NEW INTERNATIONAL LIBRARY OF GROUP ANALYSIS
Series Editor: Earl Hopper

Other titles in the Series

Contributions of Self Psychology to Group Psychotherapy: Selected Papers
  Walter N. Stone

Difficult Topics in Group Psychotherapy: My Journey from Shame to Courage
  Jerome S. Gans

Resistance, Rebellion and Refusal in Groups: The 3 Rs
  Richard M. Billow

The Social Unconscious in Persons, Groups, and Societies.
Volume 1: Mainly Theory
  edited by Earl Hopper and Haim Weinberg

The Social Nature of Persons: One Person is No Person
  A. P. Tom Ormay

Trauma and Organizations
  edited by Earl Hopper

Small, Large, and Median Groups: The Work of Patrick de Maré
  edited by Rachel Lenn and Karen Stefano

The Dialogues In and Of the Group: Lacanian Perspectives on the
Psychoanalytic Group
  Macario Giraldo

From Psychoanalysis to Group Analysis: The Pioneering
Work of Trigant Burrow
  edited by Edi Gatti Pertegato and Giorgio Orghe Pertegato

The One and the Many: Relational Psychoanalysis and Group Analysis
  Juan Tubert-Oklander

Listening with the Fourth Ear: Unconscious Dynamics in Analytic
Group Psychotherapy
  Leonard Horwitz

Forensic Group Psychotherapy: The Portman Clinic Approach
  edited by John Woods and Andrew Williams
  (joint publication with The Portman Papers)

Nationalism and the Body Politic: Psychoanalysis and the Rise of
Ethnocentrism and Xenophobia
  edited by Lene Auestad

The Paradox of Internet Groups: Alone in the Presence of Virtual Others
  Haim Weinberg

The Art of Group Analysis in Organisations: The Use of Intuitive and
Experiential Knowledge
  Gerhard Wilke

The World within the Group: Developing Theory for Group Analysis
  Martin Weegman

Developing Nuclear Ideas: Relational Group Psychotherapy
  Richard M. Billow

FOUNDATIONS OF GROUP ANALYSIS FOR THE TWENTY-FIRST CENTURY

Edited by
Jason Maratos

KARNAC

First published in 2015 by
Karnac Books Ltd
118 Finchley Road
London NW3 5HT

British Library Cataloguing in Publication Data

A C.I.P. for this book is available from the British Library

ISBN-13: 978-1-78220-112-0

Typeset by Medlar Publishing Solutions Pvt Ltd, India

Printed in Great Britain by TJ International Ltd, Padstow, Ltd

www.karnacbooks.com

CONTENTS

PART I: HISTORICAL FOUNDATIONS

PART II: GROUP-ANALYTIC THEORY

PART III: PSYCHO-ANALYSIS AND GROUP-ANALYSIS

ACKNOWLEDGEMENTS

The Trust Board of the Institute of Group-Analysis (IGA) entrusted me with the task of editing a book which would contain some of the most influential contributions by its members in the 40 years since it was founded. One of the objerctives of the book is to celebrate the contribution of the Institute of Group-Analysis.

Following this "instruction," I contacted a number of group analysts and asked them for their suggestions, pointing out that they were free to mention their own work, if they so wished. I have taken account of their suggestions and am grateful to them for making them, although the final responsibility rests with me. I am, of course grateful to Marion Brown, the Chair of the Trust Board and all the members for giving me this important and highly enjoyable task.

Dr Earl Hopper deserves a special mention as he has been of exceptional support to me, both through his presence and his ideas. Mrs Dorothy Brown has helped with the thoughts about the all important title. The office of the IGA and particularly Mary Ellen Cairns was the main person seeking release of copyrights.

The publishers of the original texts have released the copyrights for the purpose of this publication as have the authors where the copyright reverted to them after publication. I am grateful to the authors and to Sage Publications, Routledge and Kegan Paul, the Royal College of Psychiatrists and Karnac Books. The exact reference to the first publication is cited with each chapter.

PERMISSIONS

The chapters in this book were previously published as the following:

Chapter One
Foulkes, S. H. (1946). Principles and practice of group therapy. *Bulletin of the Menninger Clinic, 10*: 85–89.

This paper was previously published in *Bulletin of the Menninger Clinic* in 1946 and is reprinted with kind permission of the Menninger Clinic.

Chapter Two
Foulkes, S. H. (1948). *Introduction to Group-Analytic Psychotherapy*. Heinemann: London.

This paper was previously published by Heinemann: London in 1948 and is reprinted with kind permission of the publisher.

Chapter Three
Foulkes, S. H. (1973). The Group as matrix of the individual's mental life in group therapy. In *Group Therapy—An overview*. ed. L. R. Swartz & E. K. Wolberg), Stratton: New York.

This paper was previously published by Stratton: New York in 1973 and is reprinted with kind permission of the publisher.

Chapter Four
Foulkes, S. H. (original in 1948). *Introduction to Group-Analytic Psychotherapy: Studies in the Social Integration of Individuals and Groups*. Maresfield Reprints: London. Part 1: General Introduction—The individual as a whole in a total situation. pp. 1–11.

   This paper was previously published by Maresfield Reprints from the original of 1948 and is reprinted with kind permission of Karnac Books.

Chapter Five
Fuchs, S. H. Book review: Oberschichten des Abendlandes. Academia Verlag, Prag (Advance Copy) 1937: *The Civilising Process. Vol. 1: The History of Manners*. By: Norbert Elias. Translated by: Edmund Jephcott. Blackwell, 1978. £8.50 Group Analysis 1979 12: 78.

   This paper was previously published by Group Analysis in 1979 and is reprinted with kind permission of Sage Publications.

Chapter Six
Foulkes, S. H. (1971). My Philosophy in Psychotherapy. In *Selected Papers. Psychoanalysis and Group Analysis*, (ed. Foulkes S. H.).

   This paper was previously published by in S. H. Foulkes, Selected Papers in 1971 and is reprinted with kind permission of Karnac Books.

Chapter Seven
Garland, C. (1982). Group-analysis: Taking the non-problem seriously. *Group Analysis, 15*: 4–14.

   This paper was previously published by Group Analysis in 1982 and is reprinted with kind permission of Sage Publications.

Chapter Eight
Roberts, J. P. (1991). Destructive Phases in Groups. In *The Practice of Group Analysis*, (ed. J. A. P. M. Roberts), pp. 128–135. Routledge: London.

   This paper was previously published by Routledge in 1991 and is reprinted with kind permission of the publisher.

Chapter Nine
Pines, M. (1978). Psycho-analysis and group analysis. *Group Analysis, XI*: 8–20.

   This paper was previously published by Group Analysis in 1978 and is reprinted with kind permission of Sage Publications.

Chapter Ten
Brown, D. (1979). Some reflections on Bion's basic assumptions from a group-analytic viewpoint. *Group Analysis, 12*: 204–210.
    This paper was previously published by Group Analysis in 1979 and is reprinted with kind permission of Sage Publications.

Chapter Eleven
Hopper, E. (2012). The theory of Incohesion: Aggregation/Massification as the fourth basic assumption in the unconscious life of groups and group-like social systems.
    This paper was previously published by Karnac in E. Hopper (Ed.), *Trauma and organisations*. London: Karnac Books.

Chapter Twelve
James, D. C. (1994). "Holding" and "Containing" in the Group and Society. In *The Psyche and the Social World*, (ed. Brown, D. and Zinkin, L.), pp. 60–79. Routledge: London.
    This paper was previously published by Routledge in 1994 and is reprinted with kind permission of the publisher.

Chapter Thirteen
Hopper, E. (1982). Group Analysis: The Problem of Context. *Group Analysis, 15*: 136–157.
    This paper was previously published by Group Analysis in 1982 and is reprinted with kind permission of Sage Publications.

Chapter Fourteen
Schlapobersky, J. (1994). The Language of the Group. In *The Psyche and the Social World*, (ed. D. Brown & L. Zinkin), Routledge: London/ New York.
    This paper was previously published by Routledge in 1994 and is reprinted with kind permission of the publisher.

Chapter Fifteen
Brown, D. G. and Zinkin, L. (1994). The psyche and the social world. In *The Psyche and the Social World*, (ed. Brown, D. G. and Zinkin, L.), pp. 232–252. Routledge: London.
    This paper was previously published by Routledge in 1994 and is reprinted with kind permission of the publisher.

Chapter Sixteen
Nitsun, M. (1991). The anti-group: destructive forces in the group and their therapeutic potential. *Group Analysis, 24*: 7–20.

This paper was previously published by Group Analysis in 1991 and is reprinted with kind permission of Sage Publications.

Chapter Seventeen
Dalal, F. (2012). Specialists without spirit, sensualists without heart: Psychotherapy as a moral endeavour. *Group Analysis, 45*: 405–429.

This paper was previously published by Group Analysis in 2012 and is reprinted with kind permission of Sage Publications.

Chapter Eighteen
Stacey, R. (2001). Complexity and the group matrix. *Group Analysis, 34*: 221–239.

This paper was previously published by Group Analysis in 2001 and is reprinted with kind permission of Sage Publications.

ABOUT THE EDITOR AND CONTRIBUTORS

Dennis Brown, psychiatrist, psychoanalyst, and group analyst, devoted much of his working life to the development of group analysis, theoretically and practically. He was twice President of the Group Analytic Society and was a valued member of the Institute of Group Analysis. Dennis was one of the pillars of modern Psychotherapy and contemporary Group Analysis. His publications, his teaching and supervision along with his generous support and, for many, his sensitive therapy have had an impact which is valued by many therapists and teachers of psychotherapies today. His was an important contribution to the early development of the European Association for Transcultural Group Analysis. His lifelong enthusiasm and interest in literature and the arts constantly enriched his writing. His collected papers, *Resonance and Reciprocity*, edited by Jason Maratos, give evidence of the range and clarity of his thinking.

Farhad Dalal, PhD, is a psychotherapist and Group Analyst in private practice in Devon. He also works with organizations. He was Associate Fellow at the University of Hertfordshire's Business School. Currently, he is Visiting Professor at the PhD School, Open University of Holland. He has been studying and writing on the themes of discrimination, equality and diversity for over 25 years. He has published three books, *Taking the Group Seriously: Race, Colour and the Processes of Racialization*, and his most recent book *Thought Paralysis: The Virtues of Discrimination*, is a constructive critique of the Equality movements.

Siegfried Heinrich Fuchs, soon after migration to the UK known as **S. H. Foulkes** (1898–1976). Starting from medicine, psychiatry and psycho-analysis he moved on to become a true pioneer in Group Analysis. He was founder of the Group Analytic Society, and the Institute of Group Analysis (IGA), London and their first publication (GAYPAC) which developed into the journal *Group Analysis*. Foulkes published and lectured widely. No biographic note can do justice to the enormous impact that he had on the practice of mental health services world wide.

Caroline Garland is a consultant clinical psychologist and psychoanalyst, who founded the Unit for the Study of Trauma and Its Aftermath in the Adult Department of the Tavistock Clinic. She has worked for over 15 years with a number of colleagues specialising in the theoretical understanding and the psychotherapeutic treatment of trauma.

Earl Hopper, PhD, is a psychoanalyst, group analyst and organisational consultant in private practice in London. He is a supervisor and training analyst for The Institute of Group Analysis. Formerly a Lecturer in Sociology at the London School of Economics, Cambridge University and University of Leicester, he is associated with the Tavistock and Portman NHS Trust, the Anna Freud Centre and the Faculty of the Post-Doctoral Program at Adelphi University. He is a former Chairman of the Group of Independent Psychoanalysts of the British Psychoanalytical Society, and a former President of the International Association for Group Psychotherapy and Group Processes. His special interests include the study of social issues and of personal and social trauma. An internationally renowned lecturer and teacher, Dr Hopper is the author of many books and articles in psychoanalysis, group analysis and sociology. His most recent publications include: Hopper, E. & Weinberg, H. (eds) (2011) *The Social Unconscious in Persons, Groups and Societies: Volume I: Mainly Theory*; and Hopper, E. (ed) (2012) *Trauma and Organisations* (London: Karnac Books). He is the Editor of *The New International Library of Group Analysis*.

Colin James (1937–2008) was a psychoanalyst (Member of the Independent Group of the British Psyco-Analytic Society) and a prominent contributor in the world of psychotherapy and Group Analysis. As consultant at the London Hospital, The Maudsley, the Tavistock, and later at Cambridge, he supervised, educated and enlightened his juniors (the present editor being one of them). He is known internationally through his publications and held in special respect in Denmark where he taught in a Group Analytic supervision Course; in recognition of his contribution, he was made a professor of psychotherapy at Copenhagen University.

Jason Maratos is a Training Group-Analyst and a Fellow of the Royal College of Psychiatrists. He is a Consultant in Child and Adolescent Psychiatry and works clinically and as an Expert Witness appearing in the High Court and County Courts in family matters and trauma. In a recent publication, he explored ways in which the legal process can be less traumatic and potentially therapeutic. He is the Medical Director of PPCS and Responsible Officer. Dr Maratos has published chapters in books and papers in peer-reviewed journals in English, Italian, Greek and Czech and has lectured/taught in various courses in the UK, Italy, Greece, Brazil and Hong Kong. His publications reflect his interest in research, Self Psychology, Attachment Theory and Psychoanalysis. He has challenged the notion of the Death Instinct ("Thanatos; Does it Exist?") and expanded on the Oedipus Complex ("The Laius Complex") by exploring the psycho-pathology of the father and its impact on the emotional and cognitive development of a child. He edited a collection of papers by the late Dennis Brown (*Resonance and Reciprocity*).

Morris Nitsun was born in South Africa and has lived in the UK for 45 years. He is presently a consultant clinical psychologist, psychotherapist and group analyst in Camden and Islington NHS Foundation Trust and formerly head of psychology and psychotherapy for 30 years in the North-East London NHS Foundation Trust. He is a training group analyst at the Institute of Group Analysis, London. He convenes a new course at the Anna Freud Clinic in London, the "Diploma in Innovative Group Interventions," which is aimed at facilitating group work in the widespread NHS initiative "Improving Access to Psychological Therapies." He was for 12 years an Associate Member of the Group Analytic Practice, and works since 2001 at the Fitzrovia Group Analytic Practice in central London. He is a widely published author, best known for his books, *The Anti-group: Destructive Forces in the Group and Their Creative Potential* (1996) and *The Group as an Object of Desire* (2006), both of which have been described as classics in the field. "The Anti-group" is due for re-issue in 2014 together with the publication of his new book *Beyond the Anti-group: Survival and Transformation*, which is a collection of essays on group analysis in the twenty-first Century. He lectures and runs workshops in countries across the world and has many times been invited to present keynote lectures and workshops at national and international conferences. He is also a practicing artist, having had regular one-person exhibitions in London and several private commissions.

Malcolm Pines is one of the pillars of the Group-Analytic movement. He has published, lectured and taught widely to the extent that many group-analysts across the world feel proud and privileged to have been his students or to have known him. He is a psychiatrist, psychoanalyst (analysand of Dr Adrian Stephen and, after his death, Dr S. H. Foulkes) and a Group-Analyst. Dr Pines has been consultant psychotherapist at the Maudsley Hospital and at the Tavistock Centre for Human Relationships. He was one of the prominent partners at the Group Analytic Practice and experienced the death of Dr Foulkes as he was present in that fateful group meeting. He is the past president of the International Association of Group Psychotherapy, and of the Psychiatry Section of the Royal Society of Medicine and a member of the American Association of Group Psychotherapy. He edited the International Library of Group Analysis (Jessica Kingsley) and the journal *Group Analysis* for 16 years. His book *Circular Reflections* has been an significant influence in Group Analytic thought. His *Collected Papers* are due to appear in the near future.

Jeff Roberts trained in medicine at Lincoln College Oxford and Kings College Hospital London. At Oxford he took a special interest in neurophysiology and neurohistology. After qualifying he quickly specialised in Psychiatry and trained as a psychodynamic psychotherapist and later as a group-analyst at the IGA. His first consultant post was at the Ingrebourne Centre where he served as Medical Director for 6 years. He then moved to complete his NHS service as Consultant Psychotherapist at the Royal London Hospital and retired from this post in 1993. He is now completing his career as a member of the

Group-Analytic Practice, which he first joined in 1983. Jeff began this career hoping to understand consciousness and its part in our lives. In many ways he has accomplished this, to his own satisfaction, and in his final therapies finds himself amazed by the capacity of any individual consciousness to adapt to any stressor through the processes activated by EMDR procedures. He will retire from medical practice in 2014.

John Schlapobersky, BA, MSc, is a training analyst at the Institute of Group Analysis, London. He serves on the organisation's teaching staff, was Vice Chair of its Curriculum Committee, helped to design its teaching curriculum and edited its Training Handbook. He is responsible for supervising and evaluating dissertations on its Masters Degree programme at Birkbeck College, University of London. In the UK he teaches at other training institutes and university departments and is a Founding Member, British Society for Psychoanalytic Couple Psychotherapy. Internationally, he conducts a regular Workshop for the American Group Psychotherapy Association at their Annual Meetings that provides a Trans-Atlantic Dialogue between North American and European clinicians and he conducts an annual master class for senior psychotherapists in Israel. He was a Founding Member of the European Group-Analytic Training Institutes Network and its first Secretary. John was Programme Director for the 15th Annual Symposium of European Group-Analytic Society (International). He is in private practice working with individuals, couples and groups. He was an Associate Member of the Group-Analytic Practice for many years and then established the Bloomsbury Psychotherapy Practice in 2009. He has a special interest in creativity and caters for a number of creative artists. His other areas of special interest include relationship problems and trauma. He was a Founding Trustee of the Medical Foundation for the Care of Victims of Torture where he established their Group Work Programme and was a Consultant Psychotherapist there and at the Traumatic Stress Clinic, University College, London. He edited Robin Skynner's selected clinical papers and is the author of *From The Couch To The Circle: The Routledge Handbook of Group-Analytic Psychotherapy* due for publication in 2014.

Ralph Stacey is Professor of Management at the Business School of the University of Hertfordshire in the UK and a Member of the Institute of Group Analysis. His professional background is in management and organizational research. His work experience of more than 40 years covers working as an economist in the steel industry, director of corporate planning in the construction industry, investment strategist in the finance industry, management consultant, group therapist and academic focusing on teaching, research and research supervision in relation to organizations and their management. He is the author of a number of books and articles which include *The Tools and Techniques of Leadership and Management: The Challenge of Complexity* (Routledge, 2012) *Complexity and Organizational Reality: the need to rethink management after the collapse of investment capitalism* (Routledge, 2010), *Strategic Management and Organisational Dynamics* (6th edition, Pearson, 2011), *Complexity and Group Processes: a radically social understanding of the individual* (Brunner-Routledge, 2003), *Complex Responsive Processes in Organisations* (Routledge, 2001), *Complexity and Management: Fad or radical challenge to systems thinking* (with Griffin & Shaw, Routledge, 2000), *Complexity and Creativity in Organizations* (Berrett-Koehler, 1996), *Managing the Unknowable* (Jossey-Bass, 1992), *Chaos Frontier* (Butterworth-Heinemann, 1991). He is a co-editor of the book series *Complexity and Emergence in Organizations* as well as the series *Complexity as the Experience of Organizing*.

SERIES FOREWORD

It is an honour to provide this Foreword to a two volume collection of previously published articles and chapters written by group analysts in celebration of the founding of the Institute of Group Analysis. Most of these papers have been recommended by the members of the Institute in response to a query from the editor Jason Maratos, DPM, MPhil, FRCPsych, MinstGA: What articles have been the most important to you in the development of your identity as a professional group analyst? Although colleagues could recommend their own work, most recommended the work of others.

It will readily be seen from the Table of Contents and the biographies of the authors that whereas the founders of Group Analysis were white males from Europe, several women were prominent in the generation who succeeded them. Although it is likely that in 40 years time the authors of such a set of papers will include a larger number of women and perhaps people of colour, I suspect that there will continue to be an over-representation of immigrants into the United Kingdom. Somehow, the experience of immigration and perhaps of social trauma is at the core of the professional identity of a group analyst. It is also noteworthy that as the profession has developed it has attracted fewer colleagues with a background in medicine and certainly fewer psychoanalysts and analytical psychologists. Perhaps these trends will stop, if not reverse.

These contributions convey some of our foundational ideas in the work of S.H. Foulkes and his colleagues and associates in the United Kingdom. They also convey the main elaborations of these ideas by their professional offspring. Some readers will miss their favourite contributions to the field, but very few will not have been influenced by those that have been selected. Their quality is self evident.

This celebration of the life of the Institute of Group Analysis, first in "London" and now in the United Kingdom as a whole, and of the substantial contribution that it has made to the mental health professions, does not detract from the contribution by colleagues who have been trained elsewhere. Nor should this publication be taken as a devaluation of other forms of group psychotherapy and their institutional support. There continues to be a fertile exchange of ideas and techniques of clinical practice within a global network of psychotherapists who are committed to the continuing development of clinical work in groups. The Institute of Group Analysis has strong collaborative relations with the European Group Analytic Training Institutes (EGATIN) and the International Group Analytic Society, and many of its members participate in the activities of the International Association for Group Psychotherapy and Group Processes (IAGP) and the American Group Psychotherapy Association (AGPA).

These volumes might well be read along with those in the original International Library of Group Analysis, first edited by Malcolm Pines and Earl Hopper,[1] and then by Malcolm Pines[2] and the New International Library of Group Analysis edited by Earl Hopper.[3] *The Evolution of Group Analysis* edited by Malcolm Pines (1983) is especially relevant. Group analysis has developed in connection with several key themes, or perhaps foci, for example: clinical work in groups, including family therapy; consultation to committees and their organisations; convening constructed large groups; and the development of the field theory of the social unconscious with its emphasis on sociality, relationality, transpersonality and collectivity within the context of a transgenerational perspective, and with an emphasis on social trauma. Providing a wide ranging and unique record of the literary history of group analysis in England, *Group Analysis for the 21st Century* is a valuable resource for the study of its key concepts and applications in non-clinical settings, as well as the changing network of colleagues who have shaped our discipline.

Now, a few lines about Dr Jason Maratos, who not only initiated this project, but who has also taken special responsibility for it. At the beginning of his career, in the late 70s, as a junior psychiatrist at Bart's, he introduced group psychotherapy into an acute psychiatric unit, and studied its outcomes in a scientific manner. Having seen Dr Robin Skynner's video-recordings of couple therapy at the London Hospital, where Dr Maratos was a junior doctor, he was deeply impressed by Skynner's positive regard for his patients and by the way he looked at the "relationship" rather than only at one individual within it, which offered a new perspective to psychopathology within the family. Dr Maratos then saw Dr Skynner with a view to becoming his patient. Skynner recommended group analysis to him. Eventually, Dr Maratos applied for training in the Qualifying Course at the Institute of Group Analysis. In other words, he began as a patient and then moved on to the training, not the other way around!

Having qualified, Maratos applied group analysis in his work as a consultant in the National Health Service. He and his colleagues initiated numerous groups for parents, adolescents, children and for staff of family centres, children's homes, and for teachers and heads of special units which functioned within schools. Acknowledging their need for supervision, this team invited Dr Sabina Strich, who was a "Foulkesian," to conduct private group supervision for them. Having become a monthly "Group-Workers Workshop" they had further consultation with Isabel Menzies-Lyth, who was a "Bionian," for help in reflecting on their own group dynamics.

Jason's many publications start with his research interests in clinical outcomes, but move on to the study of attachment theory and self-psychology. He has provided sceptical discussions of some of the premises of classical psychoanalysis, in particular the theory of the death instinct and the universality of the Oedipus complex. He continues to be interested in inter-professional consultation and in the subject of combined therapies.

Dr Jason Maratos has been my friend and colleague for many years. He has played an important role in the development of group analysis in the United Kingdom, in Europe and elsewhere. I am grateful to him for providing this altogether fitting tribute to the Institute of Group

Analysis, to group analysis as a profession and to group analysis as a continuing clinical project.

Earl Hopper
Series Editor

Notes

1. The International Library of Group Analysis published in London by Routledge.
2. The International Library of Group Analysis published in London by Jessica Kingsley Publishers.
3. The New International Library of Group Analysis published in London by Karnac Books.

Reference

Pines, M. (Ed.) (1983). *The Evolution of Group Analysis*. London: Routledge.

INTRODUCTION

Πόλεμος πάντων πατήρ ἐστί, πάντων δέ βασιλεύς, καί τούς
μέν θεούς ἔδειξε τούς δέ ἀνθρώπους, τούς μέν δούλους ἐποίησε
τούς δέ ἐλευθέρους.

Ἡράκλειτος

*War is the father and king of all, and has created some as gods and some
as men, and has made some slaves and some free.*

Heraclitus (544-484 BCC)

Although Heraclitus did not state the above in praise of war (nor does
the present editor wish to do so) his maxim is relevant to the origins
and development of Group Analysis which was born in a military
hospital treating survivors and psychological casualties of the second
world war. It is, of course, not the abstract concept of "war" that creates "some slaves and some free" but the interaction between events
and actual people. No one is invulnerable to trauma but neither are all
people helpless victims. In our practice, as therapists, we come across
people who have become "enslaved" by traumatic events, and others
who are able to free themselves and even become enriched (and help
others) by the experience.

xxv

This was exactly true of Foulkes. He and his family were traumatised but far from being "enslaved" to the trauma, he used his experience not only to help others in his lifetime but also to create a system which has benefitted many others after his death.

The First Part contains a few of the articles which form the foundation of Group Analysis. Foulkes published his first thoughts on the development of Group-Analysis while he was still a major in the Royal Army Medical Corps (in itself a positive development for one who was classified as an "undesirable alien") and we are opening this volume with this landmark contribution to our field (Chapter One) (Foulkes, 1946). It is not readily accessible. The paper is impressive, it is written in plain language without obscure terminology. The reader of it can witness the birth of a radically different form of thinking and practice.

The second chapter (Foulkes, 1948) follows naturally from the first as it goes beyond the neonatal period of Group-Analysis into its "adolescence" as it begins to be more secure in its identity and anticipates the challenges concerning destructive elements. Surprisingly, it introduces, almost in passing, the enormously important notion of "mirroring." The politically correct reader may cringe at some aspects of the language used (as the reference to "Neurotics" with capital N, and to "these people"); before dismissing the author as a person who unconsciously discriminates against the very people he is supposed to help, he should read on and accept Foulkes' own explanation that these are "people just like you and me." Foulkes uses the language of the time of his writing in order to connect with his readers and in the process challenges the prevailing discrimination (conscious or unconscious). This section also includes Foulkes' own original statement of the "Basic Law of Group Dynamics." (Foulkes, 1990b)

It is easy to underestimate the revolutionary nature of the paper on the Group as Matrix (Chapter Three) (Foulkes, 1990b). This is where Foulkes challenges individualistic thought with the notions of group mind, network, transpersonal, complexity and, of course, the foundation and dynamic matrix. It is brilliant in its depth, originality and in its ability to weave together individual psycho-analysis and group analysis and to do so in impressively plain language. This article is the basis of the resolution of numerous (as he called them) "pseudo-problems"— referring to false conflicts and false dichotomies between the inner and the outer, the personal and the social, the somatic and psychic as well as so many others. One could argue that this paper represents the cornerstone of group analytic thinking. This article has no references (!) and, I believe, that this is a mark of its originality.

In the next Chapter (Four), (Foulkes, 1948), after an excellent exposition of a psychosomatic case, asks "What does all this have to do with Group Analysis"? In reply to his own question, he introduces the converse thinking: what does Group Analysis contribute to psychosomatic medicine? How does group analytic thinking help us overcome the false dichotomies that he initiated in previous publications, and how does group-analytic thinking lead to a more comprehensive understanding of the person with the disease in their context, instead of a simplistic and unrealistic confrontation of an isolated chemical reaction.

I consider the following article (Chapter Five) (Fuchs, 1938) of cardinal importance. It is a publication in Foulkes' original name and it is published in a (possibly the only, at the time) psycho-analytical journal. It also demonstrates Foulkes' awareness of the power of society, the context, and of the "group" in the most extensive meaning of the term. It also demonstrates how "seriously" he took the group and society in formulating his new theory. This is all in 1938 (!) before the war and before Northfield. The article manifests Foulkes' charismatic capacity to integrate diverse theories which (then as is often now) were seen as incompatible or in conflict and a contradiction.

The Second Part contains some fundamental contributions on the theory of Group-Analysis. The chapter on Foulkes' philosophy (Chapter Six) (Foulkes, 1990a) contains his basic beliefs in Group-Analysis; he expresses metaphysical—in this cases meta-psychological—as well as moral views or beliefs, though he could have also included the aesthetics of analysis. Foulkes makes thirteen enumerated points covering the central issues of transference, developmental psychology and psycho-pathology as well as his belief on the primacy of the group and his "theory of mind." In advocating that "we look *seriously* at the group as the essential frame of our reference" he anticipates some of his later critics who after many years implied that he did not. Paradoxically, some of his later critics who implied that his belief in the importance of the group represented a sort of manic defence will find reading about his belief in the destructive forces, to be illuminating. Foulkes, however continued to believe in the existence of the death instinct about which I (Maratos, 1994) have expressed misgivings.

The chapter by Caroline Garland (Chapter Seven) created a justifiable stir when it was published, as it legitimised and threw light on one group phenomenon about which there were conflicting opinions: the preoccupation of therapeutic groups with matters other than their presenting symptoms. Garland claimed that such work is not only a defensive avoidance but needs to be considered as important part of group therapy. Garland goes beyond this point and claims that adhesion to the presenting problem may, in itself, be a defensive practice. But the article offers a lot more by integrating concepts from family therapy, systemic thinking and the pioneering ideas of Winnicott on play and reality.

No theoretical overview of Group-Analysis could be complete without reference to the destructive potential of (even therapeutic) groups. This is the aspect that the article by Dr Roberts (Chapter Eight) (Roberts, 1994) is called to fulfil. The article is brief, to the point and contains descriptions of actual destructive phases of groups conducted by five different group-analysts. Roberts concludes, paraphrasing Foulkes, that such forces can lead to "destruction of the group, by the group, including the conductor."

Part III focuses on contributions which connect psycho-analysis and group-analysis. No student of Group-Analysis can afford to be unaware of the enormous contribution of Malcolm Pines; the editor of this volume was strenuously exercised in performing a selection of only one of Pines' papers for inclusion. The chapter on linking Psycho-analysis and Group-analysis (Chapter Nine) is written with the erudition and clarity that have made its author one of the giants of the theory in the field. Although Pines refers to numerous authors, he fails to provide a reference list; only a pedantic reviewer will consider this as a shortcoming as, rather than referring to particular articles, Pines refers to the work of great minds as a whole. Choosing one article by, e.g. Kohut would be reductionist when Pines builds on the work of the founder of Self Psychology as a whole and links it to the development of contemporary Group-analysis.

The serious student of Bion and group-analysis will do well to read the book edited by Pines and in which D. Brown has contributed an extensive article (Pines, 1985). However the article included in this volume (Chapter Ten) was written previously; it has the freshness with which he expresses and develops his ideas. The views of Bion are explored in this volume by other contributors in different contexts (such as Hopper and James).

In the next chapter (Chapter Eleven) Earl Hopper develops Bion's theory of basic assumptions through his conceptualisation of Incohesion as a fourth basic assumption stemming from traumatic experience and the fear of annihilation. Drawing on his Foulkes' lecture in 1997, he attempts to connect group-analysis with the work of Independent psychoanalysts in Britain.

Colin James uses his article on Holding and Containing (Chapter Twelve) (James, 1984) as a platform to explore not only the mutual enrichment of our understanding of an individual through object relations theory and group-analysis but also to expand on the misgivings that Foulkes had about the former. This exploration clarifies complex notions. James refers to the individual both in isolation and as a member of a wider group—"the citizen"; moves from the internal worlds to the relationship with "the other." James clarifies the significance and separate identity of these two concepts and explores their affinity to the Foulkesian matrix. The reader of this chapter will be alerted to the fact that all thinking is not a defensive intellectualisation but a process inseparable from the processing of emotions. The analytically working therapist would do well to be mindful to promote thought and, at the same time, be aware if intellectualisations which need to be worked through.

Part IV addresses the connections between Group-Analysis and Society. The reader of this volume who has reached this point will be better placed to understand the development of *individual* work based on group-analytic principles. Group-analysis is a whole system of thought which leads to a different approach of the individual and to its psychotherapy (or analysis) even on the one-to-one basis.

The section of Group-Analysis and Society could not be better opened than with the lecture by Dr Hopper about the problem of Context (Chapter Thirteen). Dr Hopper gives us an opportunity to learn from his experience of one group-analytic session at many levels: from the deepest counter-transferential to the (seemingly) external and contextual. The detailed description of one session is almost cinematographic and we can think and feel like the members of his group—including the conductor. The reader will find the conclusion of this paper, which contains a series of recommendations for good practice, particularly useful.

John Schlapobersky is one of the important contributors in the new generation of group-analysts—the generation that followed the founders. His paper on the Language of the Group (Chapter Fourteen) explores and develops the modes of communication (of monologue, dialogue and discourse) and connects them to complex psycho-analytical concepts, such as those of transference, countertransference, projection and projective identification. Schlapobersky makes these concepts more accessible through the use of description of actual communication between members of groups that he experienced first hand. In this way he enables the reader to have a dialogue with the author.

The chapter by Brown and Zinkin (Brown and Zinkin, 1994) is unique as it integrates the wide spectrum of theories represented in the volume they edited (which carries the same title as the chapter); it derives its rich content from analytical schools (including the Jungian perspective) to attachment theory, to systems theory to sociological viewpoints. The authors demonstrate not only how group-analysis benefits from them but how it contributes to the understanding of the individual as well as the group.

The final Part (Part V) represents some of the challenges and developments of the theory of Group-Analysis.

One of the major challenges to Foulkes' concept of group-analysis (and directly "ad hominem" to Foulkes himself, who is presented as unrealistically optimistic, expressing naive views and to be using primitive defences of denial and idealization) is the exploration of destructive forces by Nitsun (Chapter Sixteen). It is relevant that the author, in his elaboration of these initial thoughts (Nitsun, 2002), felt necessary to add a reference to the "Creative Potential" of the destructive forces.

Farhad Dalal (Chapter Seventeen) is one of the original and prolific thinkers of contemporary Group-Analysis. He has written on the relational nature of individuals and on race. In the paper we include in this volume he moves into the territories of moral philosophy and builds on the work of Gaita and Wittgenstein. In the process, Dalal challenges epistemological foundations and goes beyond the material person and reaches for the "soul."

This volume is appropriately concluded (Chapter Eighteen) with the excellent integration by Stacey (Stacey, 2001) of contributions of complexity theory, the philosophical notions of Herbert George Mead and the insights on infant development by Daniel Stern. Stacy illustrates how his thoughts (which at the same time challenge and complement Foulkes' theory of the Matrix) can be applied in the way one understands and conducts and analytic group. This is an admirable achievement which connects the thinking of the nineteenth to that of the twenty-first centuries.

I hope that this volume demonstrates some of the major foundations and developments in the thinking and practice of group-analysis.

This collection inevitably leaves out some contributions which played a major role in the development of our discipline as we know it today. Many works by Pines, Hearst, Kreeger, Brown and others, who are indeed too many to mention, have been excluded—after considerable agonising by the editor. Nevertheless, no volume can be "the complete works" of Group-Analysis. We hope that the reader of this volume will form a view of the road that group-analysis has followed since its inception and feel inclined to continue on this path retaining what they consider valuable and also challenge and even reject aspects which, like in any science, prove to be dated, epoch-dependent or frankly harmful. This volume is partly a foundation and partly a stimulus for thought, as each paper included here has been at its time.

References

Brown, D. G. & Zinkin, L. (1994). "The Psyche and the Social World:" In *The Psyche and the Social World*, D. G. Brown & L. Zinkin, eds., London: Routledge, pp. 232–252.

Foulkes, S. H. (1946). Principles and Practice of Group-Therapy. *Bulletin of the Menninger Clinic*, 10, 85–89.

Foulkes, S. H. (1948). "General Introduction. The Individual as a Whole in the Total Situation," *In Introduction to Group-Analytic Situation*, Maresfield Reprints ed. Foulkes S. H., ed., London: Maresfield Reprints, pp. 25–33.

Foulkes, S. H. (1990a). "My Philosophy in Psychotherapy.," *In Foulkes S. H. Selected Papers. Psychoanalysis and Group Analysis.*, Foulkes E., ed., London: Karnac Books., pp. 271–280.

Foulkes, S. H. (1990b). "The Group as Matrix of the Individual's Mental Life," *In Selected Papers. Psychoanalysis and Group Analysis.* Foulkes E., ed., London: Karnac Books. pp. 223–233.

Foulkes, S. H. (1948). "General Introduction; The Individual as a Whole in a Total Situation," *In Introduction to Group-Analytic Psychotherapy*, Maresfield Reprints ed. Foulkes S. H., ed., London: Heinemann., pp. 25–33.

Fuchs, S. H. (1938). Book review of "UBER DEN PROZESS DES Z,IVILISATION 1st Vol.: Wandlungen des Verhaltens in den weltlichen Oberschichten des Abendlandes. Academia Verlag, Prag (Advance Copy) 1937." *Int J Psycho-Anal*, 19, 263–265.

James, D. C. (1984). Bion's "containing" and Winnicott's "holding" in the context of the group matrix. *International Journal of Group Psychotherapy*, 34, 201–213.

Maratos, J. (1994). Thanatos—Does it Exist? *Group Analysis*, 27, 37–49.

Nitsun, M. (2002). *The Anti-Group: Destructive Forces in the Group and their Creative Potential.* London, Routledge.

Pines, M. (1985). *Bion and Group Psychotherapy.* London, Rouledge.

Roberts, J. P. (1994). "Destructive Phases in Groups," *In The Practice of Group Analysis,* J. Roberts & M. Pines, eds., London: Routledge, pp. 128–135.

Stacey, R. D. (2001). Complexity and the Group Matrix. *Group Analysis,* 34, 221–239.

PART I

HISTORICAL FOUNDATIONS

CHAPTER ONE

Principles and practice of group therapy*

S. H. Foulkes

Instead of sitting alone with one individual patient, the therapist may call a number of them together and talk to them. In a military hospital, for instance, there are many things which he may wish to convey to all his patients together, or to a whole ward. In such a situation he would talk differently than when talking to a patient alone. At the same time, if encouraged, they will talk back and also to each other.

One of the first things the therapist will notice is the general atmosphere. His patients may appear obediently or curiously expectant, bored and apathetic, good humoured or tense with anxiety, adversity and hostility. The conductor will become aware of their predominant attitude towards himself. He will sense, for instance, whether and in what way his presence influences the picture. This may be due to the sort of person he is, what he may or may not do, what he has to say and how he says or does it. He will be observed by the group, scrutinized and summed up, quickly and precisely, as by common consent, yet by intangible ways of perception and communication.

*This chapter was previously published as: Foulkes, S. H. (1946). Principles and practice of group therapy. *Bulletin of the Menninger Clinic, 10*: 85–89.

Meanwhile his own observation of the group becomes more detailed also. The patients are not a uniform body. Sometimes they are in good agreement, sometimes sharply split and clashing over an issue only to march in perfect unison a few minutes later. They may be with him, or against him. Many of them stand out from the main body, and gradually all of them acquire individual characteristics. Some are absent altogether and others keep out of range choosing their seats behind the therapist. Some sit aside in isolation; some are at ease while others are tense and preoccupied. Some are attentive while others talk, and here and there is a man persistently unconcerned about what is going on, while another is restless and fidgety. A man, sitting in a corner, suddenly, as if awaking from sleep or out of a dream, makes a sarcastic remark or voices violent opposition, or shoots-off at a tangent; another, who had not spoken yet and remained undefined, unexpectedly sums up a whole discussion humorously, follows this up by one or two constructive proposals and alters the whole situation.

The group functions

The psychiatrist listens and mentally registers. His "patients" have become alive, acting in a reality which he can share with them, under his own eyes. He need no longer rely on their own accounts and descriptions, based on self-observation and introspection, with all their fallacies, but can see for himself how they behave, feel and react, where they fail or are hampered by their disturbances. If he is in a position to check this against other observations, he can convince himself of the significance and reliability of this display. He is then fully justified in attaching importance even to the smallest detail observed. Frequently a patient shows up quite new-facets, which the psychiatrist can follow-up with further observation and inquiry.

Thus a first contact is established. It is a mutual contact. The therapist need not be afraid of this searching test, unless he could be credited with bad intentions. All he need be is honest. Pretence and acting would not go far. Nor is there need for them for the group psychotherapist is not concerned with making a good impression, with being liked or disliked. By this first mutual contact a community of feeling has been experienced by the patients among themselves, as well as in relation to the therapist, and in addition embracing the whole little community, therapist and patients together. The importance of this cannot be overrated. While in itself a potent therapeutic agent, in particular against a background of the usual pre-existing apprehensions and misapprehensions, it is the indispensable matrix for other therapeutic steps. If the therapist is open and sensitive to this contact, meets his men more often and regularly in this way, he can learn to play on them at will, as on an organ, and could on this basis alone lead them almost anywhere, if that were his task.

The art of leadership

This, however, is not his task in a psychiatric hospital where the patients' difficulties are essentially of such a nature as to prevent them from standing on their own feet and grappling with their own problems. If the psychotherapist resists the temptation to be made a leader, he will be rewarded by their growing independence, spontaneity and responsibility and personal insight into their social attitudes. It happens in exact proportion to the psychiatrist's art of making himself superfluous. He can, however, resign only from something which he is strong enough to possess, and if there are doubts as to his capacity for leadership, he had better accept this function offered to him until such time as he is quite certain and secure in it. He must not hesitate to lead when the situation demands it.

The ward is the patient's temporary home and surround, his refuge from that strange and bewildering turmoil, the hospital. Here he meets his pals with whom he is to share the ups and downs of his present life and, more or less intimately, the experiences of the past and the worries at home, his and theirs. These are the people with whom he will talk on lonely walks and after "lights out" at night. The spirit which permeates the ward, and which the psychiatrist must foster, *is* thus of the utmost therapeutic significance. The ward has another function: that of a bridge between the patient and the hospital. It occupies a definite place and has an active, responsible and powerful part to play in the hospital. As a member of the ward, the patient shares in this, he begins to realize that the hospital is his, is what he makes out of it, that he is the hospital.

The psychotherapeutic group

More is needed, however. The patient needs insight i.e. insight into his own inner condition and life, insight into his present feelings, behaviour and reaction. Therein lie the limitations of a large meeting (30–80 men): The patient's reactions, cannot be brought to light, voiced, described, realized or brought home to him by others. For this a more intimate setting is essential. Seven or eight people at a time have proved a good number. They meet regularly about once to three times a week, for a set period of 1–1½ hours, in the presence of the psychiatrist, in order to discuss anything they wish. Strong interpersonal relationships develop and features of an organismic structure become more and more evident. This type of meeting we call a psychotherapeutic group. The psychiatrist leaves the lead to the group, acting mainly as a catalyst and observer. The individual participant produces himself or his ideas for the group, acting also as receiver and audience when he takes an active interest in the others' problems.

If the conductor sees to it that each member participates as fully as possible in these various functions and does not neglect to watch and treat the group persistently as a whole as well, it will soon become a self-treating, self-propelling and progressive body. He will be better able then to observe and steer the group unobtrusively—more towards this problem or that, towards one patient or another's needs, and generally towards psychological levels which he deems desirable or for which he feels fit. In such a group the individual is thrown into high relief and the greater the psychiatrist's experience and skill, the less will he find it necessary to relegate so-called personal problems to supplementary individual interviews.

Selection factors

No particular selection of patients is necessary for this type of group, but all sorts of selective principles can be interestingly and usefully applied. All that is desirable is to avoid too striking a disparity in such factors as intelligence, age, past Army experience and prospective disposal. It is equally undesirable to put individuals into a group who from certain factors are bound to be sharply separated from the group's other members. Where possible, a common general background is desirable. Such a group can be left "open": that is, as older patients leave the hospital newcomers take their place in the group. It is desirable that there should always be a representative number, say two-thirds, present who have been together for at least four weeks, if continuity is to be maintained. Alternatively, once established, it can be conducted as a "closed" group, keeping its composition unchanged until disbanded. This has many advantages, especially if the same group undertakes a group project together as well, and if the time of stay in hospital is altogether short. The stronger bonds thus established outweigh the possible disadvantage of inbreeding, and weaning especially as in spirit and orientation every group should be "open."

Many of the socializing and therapeutic factors become operative in the same way in the groups which have been extensively developed at this hospital to carry out group projects. Indeed they form their essence. But unless a skilled observer can be always present with the "Selected Activity" group and report to the psychiatrist concerned, these forces operate blindly and there is not the same opportunity, as there is in the therapeutic session, to make the patients aware of what is going on.

The therapeutic session is, in a sense, a "Selected Activity" as well: that of learning to talk, express and listen to opinions, discuss matters of interest and so forth—an important social activity. The relationship and mutual penetration of these two fields of observation, artificially separated as *psychotherapy* and *social therapy*, is a fascinating study as well as of great practical importance. It could be said that a group has boundaries like a membrane of variable permeability. If the hospital milieu is opposed to the spirit prevailing in the group, if the osmotic pressure is high, these boundaries harden and become more selective; if the spirit inside and outside is in harmony, they may almost or completely disappear. This is another most important and more specific link between the hospital and the patient, and the more the hospital as a whole becomes a therapeutic field, the more can it become the main function of the psychotherapeutic group to activate and prepare the patient for the impact of the hospital community upon him and in turn to work out with him the stimuli thus received. This puts the emphasis of treatment not upon past history but upon the immediate present—a desirable shift where time is short—and one of the most important aspects of this approach.

Group dynamics

As far as the individual is concerned in group-therapy he finds himself in others and others in himself, by similarity and contrast, thereby regenerating to some extent his ego and its boundaries. At the same time the group is a potent modifier of the superego and a modifier of the id, symbolizing, as it does, the community, and in the last resort being unconsciously understood by the group in its archaic significance. Group dynamics are not within the compass of this paper. They are manifold and seem to work with great precision. There is no doubt that they can be used as therapeutic vectors of great potency. Much of this is still empirical and intuitive, but one cannot escape the impression of a quasi-mathematical precision, best perhaps to be expressed in terms of Field Theory.

It has been possible within this framework to assign a number of psychiatrists and practitioners, without selection and for the most part without much preparation, to groups, or rather, assign the groups to them, without doing any harm, to say the least of it. There is general agreement that it does them, as well as their patients, a lot of good. With increased knowledge, the framework becomes more and more precisely adapted to the purpose. It leaves the individual conductor free to choose a style and range of group psychotherapy appropriate to his experience, skill, and the degree of rigidity in his own make-up, etc. His approach will in any ease be reflected in the group, and as he is himself thrown into the group as well, this acts as a mutually self-regulating procedure. This has helped matters a great deal, since our task at North-field Military Psychiatric Hospital is to devise methods as simple as possible so as to be applicable, as broadly as possible. A note of warning may be permitted here: not to-connect "Group Therapy" and such with a notion of mass production. It is not a sausage machine! Within a different framework and with more ambitious aims, it is an instrument so delicate and yet so powerful, that its skilled handling demands more from the therapist than the most difficult individual analysis.

One of the ways in which the individual psychiatrist's position tells, is expressed in what he feels he can handle in a group or individual session respectively (and here again he will choose the right proportion for himself). Individual sessions are partly supplementary, partly antagonistic to the group, at least as long as the approach is not "wholistic" in the therapist's mind.

The writer's practice at Northfield, from considerations both of experiment and expediency, has been increasingly towards putting the group into the centre, even in the individual interview where necessary, and shifting the emphasis from the smaller group of the consulting room towards the ward and the hospital as a whole, and in the last resort—from all levels—towards the community. This was possible since the hospital as a whole became more and more a therapeutic field and since he knew that, while digging a tunnel from one end, he would be met halfway by workers from the other end—in other words, that the general hospital activities were directed with the same basic idea and identical intentions.

CHAPTER TWO

Introduction to group-analytic psychotherapy*

S. H. Foulkes

General introduction

The Group Analytic Situation. All these considerations have an immediate bearing on Group Treatment and Group-Analysis in particular. For the Group Analyst, too, there are intrinsic reasons apart from practical ones, why Group Analysis has to be carried out under controlled conditions. At Northfield I could practise and observe Group-Approach in unorganised and spontaneous life situations, life, that is, of soldier-patients in a military hospital; free, semi-organised groups under all sorts of conditions, brought together by their chance participation in a particular form of occupation or activity, or by having been selected for a particular function or project, or organised themselves spontaneously for such, say a Netball or Football team. I could see this side by side with the working of group analytic, or I should rather say group analytically oriented sessions.

Some samples will be presented in later chapters to illustrate the mutual interactions and delimitations of these various approaches

---

*This chapter was previously published as: Foulkes, S. H. (1948). Introduction to Group-Analytic Psychotherapy. Heinemann: London.

within the different situations. This was possible under the conditions of a hospital community, with "inpatients," and with the Psychiatrist living in as well. Under ordinary conditions, when both the patient and the Doctor pursue their own private lives and meet only for the purpose of treatment, this is not possible. Now, to use an analogy; a photographer, to catch certain aspects of his client, might like to take a picture of him in his own home or garden. He will, nevertheless, on the whole prefer to have studio conditions for more ambitious attempts at a portrait. In the same way, the Group Analyst could not undertake to work to the full in the midst of the turmoil of life, but needs the more controlled conditions of the studio, his consulting room or similar room. The Psychoanalyst must remain undefined as a person, in order to enable the patient to project upon him, as on a screen, the unconscious images of his innermost self, to relive with him the vicissitudes of his long forgotten emotional relationships with his paternal figures and other persons of his past life.

The patient thus establishes a relationship of the utmost intensity and intimacy with a strange person. The participant in group analysis also meets with strangers, *with* whom he can mutually experience those relationships in particular, which are fraught with difficulties in life. In an unmodified life group situation he would prefer to avoid these difficulties, perhaps without even knowing that he does, or let his projections operate without check or correction, or defend himself by all manner of means against the experience of these difficulties. Under the conditions of the group-analytic situation he must face them, but he can also express his thoughts and feelings much more freely than would be possible under ordinary conditions and thus recognise these difficulties and correct them. He can find himself in others, and others in himself, and in this way free himself from old prejudices, as it were, and develop a more mature, creatively adaptable character. This is only one of the ways by which Group Analysis takes effect. For this to be possible, the group-analytic situation must have its own particular features, its own special rules of behaviour, its own code of what is permissible or not. This is very different from life under ordinary conditions. We will have to say more about this in detail presently. One can call such a situation "artificial" if one likes. In fact it stands halfway in artificiality between the analytic situation and spontaneous life situations, or perhaps somewhat nearer the latter. But one should not connect a modicum of reproach with this notion of artificiality or else one might

equally well blame the surgeon for operating under the artificial conditions of the operating theatre. It is a situation of life under special conditions; some people are troubled by something beyond their control,
they are called patients, and they consult another person, the physician
or doctor because they believe or have been told, or profess to believe,
that he can help them, "cure" them. If the doctor believes that too, or
professes to believe it the roles are cast, the play can begin and nothing
much happens. If he does not profess that, however, something very
essential does happen—but we come to that later.

Meanwhile the Group Analyst wants to create a situation which is
best suited to deal with the problem in which he and the group find
themselves, that is all. There is nothing further "artificial" about it. If
he is wise he follows the Group's hints in this. That is what I have done
and continue doing. Thus one arrives best at the most suitable arrangements in any particular circumstance. In this way the Group-Analytic
situation comes into being. It cannot be standardised, but is fairly well
defined. By following the Group I do not mean that I fall in with everything the Group wants. If the Group's tendency is towards the solution
of its problems, I follow it. If it is away from that solution, I counteract
this tendency by counter arrangements. That is what I mean by "following the Group's hints."

Two Questions.—Before we say more about this Group-Analytic situation, the reader, I hope, will want to have an answer to at least two
urgent questions. He has guessed by now, that in such group treatment
there are a number of patients together. I imagine now he will raise
these two questions:—

(1) How is it that these patients don't make each other worse? From
     what I have heard of Neurotics, they are full of imaginary com-
     plaints, terribly suggestible, weak characters in search for ever new
     excuses for escape. And on top of that, you treated even soldiers like
     that! They had nothing in mind but to invent or exaggerate their
     symptoms, so as to shirk their duties and work their ticket home.
     They quite deliberately spent their time in hospital to exchange
     experiences and learn tricks from each other to that end. I know that
     such a Neurotic is a damned nuisance and very difficult to treat and
     cure, and I sympathise with the Psycho-Analysts who spend years
     of their lives with a handful of these people. I suppose they must get
     some kick out of it, or else they wouldn't do it. I couldn't do it for

anything! And yet you take on even a number of them together, all at once, I don't know how many at a time, how can that work?

(2) How can these people possibly talk about their intimate, personal private affairs, thoughts, feelings and phantasies, in the presence of a number of others, total strangers at that? I understand that you can't cure them by talking about the weather. You have repeated, yourself, already this Freudian stuff about children's sexuality, repressions, dreadful unconscious phantasies and so on, so I suppose you expect them to talk about that, too. Do they? Can they?

I can't complain about your questions, as I have made you ask them myself. That is unfortunate, because I would be inclined to tell you: have patience and read this book first. But first of all, I am doubtful whether you would be satisfied even then, because in order really to answer these questions I would have to write a whole book on them alone, and I could not expect you to read that. Secondly, I am not suggesting that this happens "just so," that the Therapist has not a lot to do with it. These things are not easy to do, more difficult to teach, and most difficult to describe. So on the whole, I think I get out of it better, if I give you at least some answer straight away.

In some ways, I agree with what you say about the Neurotics, and also about the Analysts—but only up to a point. These Neurotics are, after all, people like you and me and part of our annoyance is due to the fact that they show us our own weaknesses in a mirror, like a caricature. They also tax severely our own balance and threaten it, if it is at all precarious. They also teach us a lot, because they have retained alive what so many of us have forgotten, or don't dare to face. Besides, if you are a Doctor, it may make you uncomfortable to meet with patients who know so much more of their condition than you have been taught.

Let us take the first question first. My first answer to both your questions is not an explanation, but a mere statement of fact, which you must take on trust for the moment:—

(1) No, these people do not make each other worse and they do not infect each other with their symptoms, but they improve together. Strange as it may seem, they even act as therapists towards one another. Perhaps it helps for the moment if I use a simile, which for some reason always occurred to me in this connection. If you want to wash a dirty shirt, and you have clean water and soap, the matter seems straightforward, there is no problem. But, suppose you

have to wash a number of dirty shirts together, and the water is not even clean and perhaps you have not even soap? You see my comparison, because you will agree that even then you can get the shirts reasonably clean, albeit you add dirt to dirt, by using them for mutual friction upon each other. This is a crude, but fair, analogy.

(2) Yes, these people can talk to each other—within certain limits—about their own very personal affairs, they really move all over the place, it is astonishing. These limits, barriers, are much further out than you would expect, and they are constantly moved and some of them even removed altogether. It depends on all sorts of things, the conductor's courage amongst others. But you must not think that they are going to the other extreme, and celebrate orgies of Exhibitionism in these groups. If the conductor has good sense, the group tends to keep a very reasonable balance between these extremes. It depends, of course, what group it is—a group of Neurotics behaves significantly different from Psychotics or Psychopaths, or Perverts, or Delinquents, and so on. But this is an over simplification. They don't all behave according to their psychiatric labels. That is why I don't group them according to these labels. I turn it the other way round and say: if I see people in a group, I can tell you best what they are like, and wherein they are disturbed. That belongs to what is called in scientific language: The Group Situation as a Diagnostic Test. There is more to it than that, we will come to it in time. We may have to alter our labels one day.

Now I will try and give you some explanations for my answers. Let us take the first question first.

A Basic Law of Group Dynamics.—(1) The deepest reason why these patients, assuming for simplicity's sake Psycho-Neurotics, can reinforce each other's normal reactions and wear down and correct each other's neurotic reactions, is that *collectively they constitute the very Norm, from which, individually, they deviate.* That is not really surprising, once it is understood. The community, of which they are a miniature edition, itself determines what is normal, socially accepted behaviour. It happens like this: each individual is to a large extent a part of the Group, to which he belongs. This collective aspect permeates him all through—as we said before—to his core. To a smaller extent, he deviates from the abstract Model, the Standard, of this "Norm," he is a variant of it. Just this deviation makes him into an Individual, unique, which he is again all through, even to the finger prints. One could picture him, crudely, as being submerged in a common pool, but sticking his head out of it. Now each such Therapeutic Group, like any other Group, has much more in common than it knows at first. It is struck by its differences, which provoke curiosity, hostility and fear. As it proceeds, it finds more and more of common ground, and less and less contradiction between individuality and community. The sound part of Individuality, of character, is firmly rooted in the Group and wholly approved by it. The Group, therefore, respects and supports the emergence and free development of individuality, and Group treatment has nothing to do with making people uniformly march in step. Quite on the contrary; good Group treatment—by developing a good Group—makes both processes go hand in hand: the reinforcement of the communal ground and the freer development of the individual differences. Like a tree—the firmer it takes root the freer it can display its individual characteristic beauty above ground. Now, neurotic peculiarities, symptoms, are relieved just as much, as they can be retransformed, by Analysis, from unshareable to shareable experience, from uncommunicable experience to communicable experience. This is just what Analysis, individual or in Groups, does. In a recent article, Theodore M. Newcomb (Newcomb, 1947) has expressed very similar views. He makes a number of statements of relevance for Group Therapy, and contributes many clear formulations throwing light on this problem. Neurotic symptoms disappear into the common pool as soon as they become communicable, and their individual ingredient is now free for group-syntonic, socially acceptable, employment. That is the reason, why neurotic behaviour tends to diminish in a Group and normal behaviour to be supported. Does the Group know that? Not consciously, but it is forced to act in this direction by the very fact that it can only grow by what it can share, an only share what it can communicate, and only "communicate" by what it has in "common"—e.g., in language—in common, that is, on the basis of the community at large. However, what the community supports, quite blindly and instinctively, is determined by its life conditions, historical and present, by its survival value. It calls it, at any given time, by special names, at present it calls it: "Normal" or "Natural." In this sense, the Group is always the ultimate frame of reference, in whatever setting "treatment" takes place.

The answer to the second question depends fundamentally on the same argument. Because the Group is bound to agree on what is compatible with itself, it sets the boundaries for communication accordingly. As the Group agrees in this with the standards of the larger group, of which it is a part, these standards are automatically the same as in life "outside." The Group's emphasis is more on the present than on the past, it is more progressively oriented than retrogressively. Accordingly it need not deal in so many words with the infantile, instinctive eroticisms and the concomitant details of intimate sex life perversions, excretory activities and so on. It can therefore express its problems sufficiently within the acceptable boundaries. Where this is not sufficient for any one individual, it is a sign that deeper, earlier, regressive levels are too active. This significantly, coincides clinically with the need for individual interview, where these manifestations of regression can be worked through, or calls for individual Analysis.

It is significant that this decision, the indication for individual treatment, arises out of the Group situation. In ordinary life also it is in the last resort the community, who decides the need of any given individual for treatment. Either he cannot carry on within the Group; the Psychoneurotic; or the Group cannot carry on with him; the Psychotic, Psychopath, Delinquent. If we cannot treat him successfully, we call his condition "constitutional." The Group Situation is the vantage point for Diagnosis and Prognosis and the primary locus for treatment.

The following schematic representation illustrated the interrelationship between these different situations:—

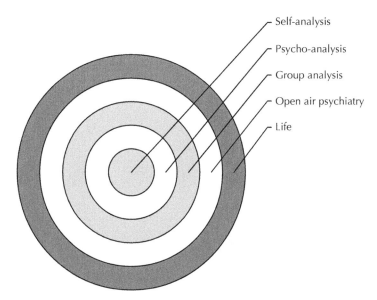

Figure 1. Interrelationships between life situations.

"Open Air" Treatment takes place under ordinary Life Conditions, but is concerned with a particular Group or Group situation, for instance a Group of Business Managers in a big concern, or, in terms of North-field, a Group of soldiers working in a project in the Carpentry Hut.

The three inner circles, represent selected and controlled, semi-arti-ficial, semi-experimental, conditions. "Group Analysis" at Northfield would have to be visualised towards the outer border of zone three, and *the "Open Air"* Groups towards the inner border of zone four, so that the boundary between three and four was less pronounced than indicated here, at Northfield.

One can readily visualise the dynamic interrelationships in between these different fields. They are all operative at the same time, but vary in degree according to the position of the individual and the Analyst's handling of the situation. The vantage position of Group Analysis can be well seen, it occupies a central position and is open in both directions.

Reference

Newcomb, T. M. (1947). Autistic hostility and social reality. *Human Relations*, 1: 69–86.

CHAPTER THREE

The group as matrix of the individual's mental life*

S. H. Foulkes

Defences against a comprehensive view

It seems difficult for many at the present time to accept the idea that what is called "the mind" consists of interacting processes between a number of closely linked persons, commonly called a group. Already when two people form a relationship, they create a new phenomenon, just as when two people play chess with each other they create a new phenomenon, namely, the game of chess which they produce. When a group of people, by which for our purposes I mean a small number of persons, form intimate relationships, they create a new phenomenon, namely, the total field of mental happenings between them all. In this context I have spoken of "transpersonal processes," that is mental processes which, like X-rays in the bodily sphere, go right through the individuals composing such a "network."

This totally new phenomenon which they create I usually refer to as the "context of the group." I do not talk of a group mind because

*This chapter was previously published as: Foulkes, S. H. (1990). The group as matrix of the individual's mental life. In: *Selected papers: Psychoanalysis and group analysis*. (ed. Foulkes, E.), pp. 223–233. Karnac: London.

17

this is a substantivation of what is meant and is as unsatisfactory as speaking of an individual mind. The mind is not a *thing* which exists but a series of events, moving and proceeding all the time. The difficulty that people still have, in and outside the field of psychotherapy, in accepting my hypothesis as a basis for understanding and for action, can be partly explained as the usual inability and unwillingness to learn anything new. To learn something new entails changing one's whole attitude to a number of things, to oneself and to the world in which one lives. I believe, however, that there is quite a specific resistance against accepting mental processes as multipersonal phenomena, a resistance based on the very personal as well as general consequences if we accept this truth. These resistances appear to be comparable to those found by Freud against the recognition of unconscious mental processes in the individual.

The reasons for this personal bias will become clearer, I hope, in what I shall have to say later. However, I will at least indicate them at this point. We can best study these mental networks in psychopathology: what we know of them, we know mostly through our patients. If our patients are not seen to be in need of help entirely for their own sake, but are in fact part and parcel of a whole network of interacting individuals, it follows that in certain respects they are merely the victims or scapegoats, or otherwise symptoms of changes and upsets within the intimate network of their human relationships. It can be observed that when patients in treatment begin to change seriously, they will, as a rule, get into trouble with others in their network. The whole equilibrium and the psychopathology of the network had been based on our patients being just as they are, and therefore the others' own equilibrium is now threatened.

Any change in any individual part of such a network upsets the whole balance inside it. As this is as true for psychologists, doctors or psychoanalysts as for everybody else, there exists a built-in interest against its being uncovered, for this would entail taking far greater notice of what happens in their patients' networks, as well as the doctors' own. Ultimately it would mean that the whole community must take a far greater responsibility for outbreaks of disturbing psychopathology generally. There is therefore a very specific defensive interest at play in denying the fact of the interdependence which is here claimed; the cry "but each is an individual" and "surely the mind is a matter for the individual" means, in this sense, "each for himself, I am not to blame for what happens to the other person, whether he is obviously near to me, or whether I am involved in concealed ways, or even quite unconsciously."

Communication: psychoanalysis and group analysis

All phenomena in an analytic therapeutic group are considered as potential communications. This dynamic way of putting it eliminates the need for the usual concept of the repressed unconscious, defences, and so forth, which is necessitated in a psychoanalytic orientation. Needless to say that it in no way contradicts or denies these observations. It may be useful to compare and contrast briefly at least the view arising from the psychoanalytic two-person method regarding these processes and those arising from group-analytic observations. Ultimately they must belong to a consistent theory of the human being as seen in various situations.

In comparing the psychoanalytic and the group-analytic points of view of the individual and of individual processes, the analogy of a differentially magnifying microscope is useful. The psychoanalytical view takes the individual mind as the unit of observation and tries to understand all mental processes in terms of this individual mind. This makes it particularly useful for its special purposes, namely the vertical analysis of the individual in a chronological, historical sense. Seen from the psychoanalytical approach, new relationships are brought about essentially by transference, and counter-reactions by the transference of the other people concerned act as modifiers on these now different relationships. Ultimately this means that they can be understood as results of the original family relationships of each individual.

By contrast, the group-analytic view would claim that all these interactional processes play in a unified mental field of which the individuals composing it are a part. It is therefore the method of choice for the observation and for gaining effective influence in the horizontal sense—this means in view of the present participants" different characters and reactions, and in the here and now of present life. The point I wish to stress is that this network is a psychic system as a whole network, and not a superimposed social interaction system in which individual minds interact with each other. This is the value of thinking in terms of a concept which does not confine mind, by definition, to an individual.

As group analysts we do not share the psychoanalytical juxtaposition of an "internal" psychological reality and an "external," physical or social reality which, for psychoanalysis, makes good sense. What is inside is outside, the "social" is not external but very much internal too and penetrates the innermost being of the individual personality. The "objective" external "reality" is inseparable from the being, animal or human, and indeed the individual whose world it is and therefore is part of the "psychological" reality as well. It can be in full harmony with the latter, or compensatory or contradictory—for example, by such polarizing processes as projection—but is never unaffected by it. On the other hand, the psychoanalytical point of view should also be seen as a deliberate abstraction, the individual being deliberately abstracted and considered isolated from his context. (Instead, it is very often considered as an absolute truth, as a simple, true account of observation that each individual has a mind to himself). The two considerations are therefore not incompatible with each other; they are, on the contrary, complementary. Which is the preferred one depends on circumstances or on the purpose of the observation and the indication for the action required. Personally, I believe that the multipersonal hypothesis of mind is nearer to the true nature of events.

Just as I do not doubt the phenomenon of mind, I do not doubt the existence of the individual person. The individual person not only exists in his mind and in our own experience, but his body is undoubtedly an individual coherent entity. In this way in our groups, too, the individuals react to each other, show their individuality, develop their own ideas and phantasies about the group, about the therapist, about certain co-members and so forth. Nevertheless, my own studies and experiences in group-analytic groups led me to see the existence of a suprapersonal mental matrix, and to speculate and theorize about this. I can put this quite simply: I thought to myself, "What an enormous complexity of processes and actions and interactions play between even two or three of these people, or these people and myself, or between two in relation to another three, and so on. What enormous complexity, quite impossible to perceive and disentangle even theoretically all at the same time. How is it they can nevertheless understand each other, that they can to some extent refer to a shared and common sense of what is going on? They move in a meaningful way from point A to point B. And the same applies to me myself."

So I thought: "What is really happening here, what am I really doing?" I found that the old theory of perceiving this in terms of individuals and their interaction as individual minds enclosed in each skull, interacting in the most complicated fashion with the others, that this theory acted as a great barrier to my understanding. Moreover, it set up many pseudo-problems to which there are therefore no satisfactory answers. Instead, I have accepted from the beginning that even this group of total strangers, being of the same species and more narrowly of the same culture, share a fundamental, mental matrix (*foundation matrix*). To this their closer acquaintance and their intimate exchanges add consistently, so that they also form a current, ever-moving, ever-developing *dynamic matrix*.

I do not want to enlarge on the concept of matrix here, except as a construct useful for seeing all the different processes I have described—as, for instance, location or figure-ground formation—as they operate in this interactional communicational network, the matrix. This enabled me to say that it is mental processes, not persons, that interact. I want to say a few words in order not to be misunderstood about this. Mental processes *per se* cannot interact, but no one would doubt that—to use a simple example—one homosexual recognizes the other before they know anything of each other, instinctively, as we say; nor that a sadist and masochist interact, complement each other and respond to each other in a certain affinity, before they know it themselves. This still does not mean, except in theory, that one can abstract these processes or forces (and they are far more complex than the ones indicated), as independent entities with actions of their own. It is ultimately always whole persons who interact with whole persons.

What I mean by saying that mental processes interact is the selective interaction that goes on impersonally, instinctively, intuitively, basically unconsciously, in accordance with the inner constellation and predispositions of those concerned and which determine their interaction. The highly interesting and important specificity, the interlocking of these processes, which in fact contain the whole of psychopathology in living action, I refer to as "resonance." Sometimes this is consciously acknowledged by the individual. The total interactions of the individuals are in fact the result of affinities or disaffinities of individual instincts, emotions, reactions of all sorts, character predispositions, for example. There is at the same time an unconscious interpretation of these reactions on this same basis. Essentially this gives the group coherence and meaning for each of the participants, even if each is far from conscious of this, or from understanding it in any way intellectually.

Group context

To understand and describe further what I am doing, and what are the thoughts and ideas that guide my actions, I speak of the group context. It is important to note that in the usual, standard group-analytic group, the individuals are the foreground, and the group context is the background on which we base our interventions and interpretations; the individual is in the centre of this procedure. Looking in this way at the total goings-on in the group leads to frequent misunderstandings concerning the neglect of the individual. The concept of group context holds no such threat. The truest account of what I do is that I analyse in the interest of each individual, but in the group context. For this purpose I use not only the processes as they reach me but as they reach everyone, that is to say, the total processes operating in the group. To do justice to the fact that this mental field of operation very much includes the individual but also transgresses him, I have used the term "trans-personal processes." These processes pass through the individual, though each individual elaborates them and contributes to them and modifies them in his own way. Nevertheless, they go through all the individuals—similar to X-rays in the physical sphere.

Perhaps it may not be inappropriate to illustrate this view with a simile from biology. Cells do exist. Cellular pathology is meaningful, and we can look at the goings-on from the point of view of this cellular pathology. If the cell in our case represents the individual, then the way I am looking at it would correspond more to molecular biology which transgresses each individual cell, which is not to say that the individual cell does not behave receptively and creatively in the total process.

Psychology is thus neither "individual" nor "group," except by abstraction. We cannot speak about the individual without reference to the group, nor about a human group that does not consist of individuals. Both are, therefore, abstractions as far as the psychology of the total person is concerned.

In order to see something whole we have, I believe, to see it in relation to a greater whole, so that we can step outside of that which we want to see. For instance, a larger group can be seen only in reference to still larger communities, or perhaps in reference to its leaders or its task.

Smaller groups can be seen whole only in relation to other groups. This is what I have in mind when I say that in our therapeutic groups, the group itself is the horizon. The group as such can only be understood from inside itself. Insofar as we also are included, we cannot strictly speaking see it as a whole either, except in relation to ourselves, nor should we habitually address it as a whole. A situation in which it is meaningful to address the group as a whole is, for example, when the conductor, the analyst, wishes to point out some response to his function or any shared responses in relation to himself or to some other member. The therapeutic group on the small scale, optimally of seven to nine persons, is the situation of choice to see the *individuals* composing this group really as a whole, in the round. However, as pointed out, this group situation highlights the internal interaction, transgresses the boundaries of the individual, of what is usually considered internal, intrapsychic, and shows it to be shared by all.

When speaking of psychology or psychopathology we would do better to have in mind the composite total which embraces and contains all psychological processes in any given situation of study. We can focus on the group as a whole or on any one individual or individuals in their specific interactions: all that happens is meaningful from any point of view, and the different meanings dovetail. It is not the case that the one viewpoint is right and the other wrong. It is rather as if we took photographs from various positions. One picture may be better for certain purposes and the others less good, but all of them show what is true from the position from which they are taken. However, the total process must always be defined from the total field. The relationship appears to be best understood in terms of figure and ground, as already mentioned. Figure is that which we choose particularly to observe, that on which we focus, or what in impartial observation forces itself into the foreground.

Group-network theory

I have spoken of the intercommunicational, interactional network in which the individual is embedded, and of the group network theory of neurosis. I do not identify this concept entirely with that of the family for reasons I will presently explain, though I operated with and studied family networks before family therapy as such existed. The original family is indeed the primary network in which the personality of the future individual is decisively formed; the whole of psychoanalysis has borne that out beyond reasonable doubt. This family network, seen as a group, acts as a whole complicated formulation. It has as it were a vertical axis pointing to the past, to the parents, to the parents' own childhood, to the parents' relationship to their own parents, all of which enter into the innermost core of the forming child.

We know that these events are covered by infantile amnesia and are in that sense dynamically unconscious, especially in regard to the instincts concerning infantile sexuality. However, the core of the ego and super-ego thus formed—formed in my view from the very beginning—are also in their essential parts equally unconscious, although not repressed. They are unconscious because the values imbued, the whole relationship to the world, and to objects, the whole way of expressing oneself, of breathing, of sleeping, of waking, of being amused, of speaking, the individual's total behaviour has been decisively shaped by the original family group. The individual is unconscious of this in that he is normally convinced that his way of feeling, of thinking, is the natural and right one, that his language *is* the language one speaks. I would like to remind you of a passage from Mark Twain. "Are the French human?" one of his characters asks another. The other replies: "Oh, yes, they are human." Then why don't they speak like humans?"

Thus it is one of the great advances in an analytic approach to individuals in groups that they begin to see for themselves that other people laugh about different things, feel different, are different—and yet that there is no reason to judge one kind of behaviour as better or more normal than the other, except again for reasons valid in the greater community of the total culture in which these people live. In what people differ, therein lies their true individuality.

As to the way in which the human person thus developed behaves later in life, we know that his early influences continue quite normally, as I have just explained, but also as disturbances, insofar as there are unresolved longings or traumas expressed respectively in transference and repetition-compulsion. This is true and remains true whether people lie on a couch, sit on a chair opposite you or sit around in a circle. Later, we find the individual's life in our type of Western culture lived in small as well as somewhat larger groups corresponding in size very much to the old tribal community of a few hundred people. These life—or current—networks of people prove significant for each individual. When one approaches these living current groups, as they operate, they will be found to overlap with the family, though they are not necessarily identical with it. They will include friends, rivals, superiors, inferiors, animals and even inanimate objects.

In one of my groups, after the mother's death, the cat she had left to the daughter, my patient, became an extraordinarily important object.

When examining such life groups, the people with whom the patient currently lives—and we all live our immediate life in such groups—we find that only a relatively limited number of persons are more or less persistently significant, and a limited number, perhaps not quite the same ones, are selectively significant for particular conflicts. If we examine these as they stand, either in our consulting room or in life itself, we treat them as a group in a particular way into which I cannot enter here in detail.

Essentially such a family or group network treatment of the natural group itself is extremely powerful and can be very successful. On the whole I have found, however, that it is only too often obvious that such a group as a whole cannot be sanitated. The conflicts and the complications are too great. The limitations lie in the resistance which the various members of such significant networks offer to change in any one of them, particularly in the designated patient, consciously and unconsciously. More often than not they are quite disinclined to being frank and open with each other and to revealing their secrets. In short, therefore, this natural life group, important as it is, is perhaps of the greatest value as a diagnostic and prognostic instrument as regards psychotherapy of an analytical kind.

Such a group is by definition treated as a group even if seen diagnostically a few times. So is a functioning group of people, a group with a task, if they are to be treated as a group for their group function's sake. Such examples of the group becoming the foreground are a football team or a group of managers in an industrial concern. Yet it is true that though the individuals become the background under these conditions, if we are successful in improving the total life and atmosphere in such a group, the individuals composing it change and benefit too, often surprisingly so.

However, the third type of group, the group-analytic group in the specific sense, is the one of choice if we wish to apply an intensive form—and a very effective form it is—of an analytic approach to the individuals in the round and through each other. This group is composed of strangers with no reality relationships whatsoever, totally abstaining from forming such relationships, and altogether under analytic conditions.

To mention at least two of the most interesting results of my investigations in this field: (1) I am satisfied that, as one would expect, the network theory holds good for any individual whatsoever, for any of our patients, if we take the trouble to take note of it. (2) The three group situations or group networks mentioned seem best to be studied in their interaction in the group-analytic group. Of special interest is their intertwining and particularly also the way in which the current network enters into the treatment process, while we go along.

CHAPTER FOUR

General introduction: the individual as a whole in a total situation*

S. H. Foulkes

Life is a complex whole. It can only artificially be separated into parts, analysed. Such isolation becomes necessary when we want to know what a particular set of forces contribute to the total phenomenon or, to put it more precisely, how the whole is affected by the absence or altered function of any one part.

This is of immediate importance in dealing with disturbances, as, for instance, in the field of Medicine, with so-called diseases. Disease has been defined as life under changed conditions.

The healthy organism functions as a whole and can be described as a system in a dynamic equilibrium. Dynamic means that it is never in a state of rest, has constantly to adjust actively to the ever changing circumstances, milieu, conditions in which it lives.

Such adaptation, however, does not take place mechanically, following physical or chemical principles merely. There is always a creative element present, even in the simplest forms of adaptation.

---

*This chapter was previously published as: Foulkes, S. H. (original in 1948) Introduction to Group-Analytic Psychotherapy. Studies in the Social Integration of Individuals and Groups. Maresfield Reprints. London Part 1. General Introduction. The individual as a whole in a total situation. P1–11.

The organism acts as if it knew its aim and had a choice as to the means to achieve this aim. It chooses those means which suit best all the prevailing conditions, inside itself or outside itself. If we want to say that we are aware of this and need to take into account all these factors in order to describe and understand what happened, we speak of the "total situation."

On the highest levels creative activity seems to be an inevitable ingredient, the hallmark of healthy life. Dynamic equilibrium therefore means: the active and creative maintenance of a good balance. From the point of view of the person such a state is described as being well, healthy, feeling happy, contented.

Disturbed function is due to disturbance in the equilibrium of the total situation. But we cannot and we need not take all factors in the total situation into account all the time. Some factors are more responsible than the rest for a disturbance and we must get them into focus.

Everything depends on whether we find the best perspective, the most adequate point of view, in approaching a disturbance. This includes that we concentrate on the right sector, make the right cut out of the whole. Sometimes one sees more under a microscope, another time more with the naked eye. If we know the problem already, this is easy enough. But if we don't know, we cannot find out before we find the correct approach, we cannot get the right answers before we ask the right questions. But worst of all, if we don't know but we believe that we do. Then we are hopelessly fixed to an inadequate approach, and land in a maze of pseudo-problems, and pseudo-solution defended by a host of theories. In such a case it is best to stand back and look afresh with the naked eye on the totality of the situation, with a mind as keen to observe and as free from prejudice as we can possibly muster.

Let us have an example: suppose a man suffers from lack of vitamin X. What do we find? A highly complex picture of disturbances, in the beginning stages probably only discernible on the mental plane, and on the other side the absence of a minute single ingredient of food. If the condition is known to us and if we know our stuff, we should be able to diagnose this condition from the nature of the patient's complaints and the mental disturbance alone. No examination of the patient alone, however, no matter how thorough, how subtle, could lead us to discover the specific factor—and here one could almost say the "cause"—as long as vitamins were unknown. What abstractions were necessary and adequate for the solution of this problem?

(a) We separated the person from the surrounding world, made a split between "inside" and "outside."

(b) The isolating scientific method, so characteristic of the nineteenth century, without which the vitamins could never have been discovered.

(c) We separated the physical from the mental.

(d) We applied to the problem the categories of cause and effect.

Thus we find: an outside, material factor (the absence of vitamin X) causes an inside psychological disturbance.

This fits in perfectly with the classical scheme of scientific medicine:

Examination—Diagnosis—Treatment.

Treatment here obviously consists in the replacement of the missing vitamin and is, therefore, causal, not symptomatic, and—if all goes well—curative. Symptomatic treatment would have been if the doctor had prescribed tablets to alleviate the patient's headaches. Such a treatment would have been inadequate and in the presence of better knowledge, wrong.

Our abstractions in the face of this problem were adequate and correct. This is the type of disturbance where the classical scientific abstractions have their heyday. The trouble starts when they are applied in principle to every "disease," where they are inadequate and out of place and where quite different sets of abstractions, quite a different point of view, become necessary.

The whole development of Medicine, and similar of other Disciplines, in the last half century, in a nutshell, is the gradual realisation of the fact, that this scheme is not sufficient in the great majority of disturbances and that—to do them justice—one must take the whole personality and its life situation, past and present, into account. This can only be done in terms of Psychology. The vantage point for the observation of the person as a whole is his own mind.

Let us see what kind of "case" sets people thinking on these lines, still taking an example, schematic and oversimplified, very much from the extreme end of a scale, still near enough a sphere, where the classical categories could operate.

A man has a duodenal ulcer. A clear cut and well-known disease, or at least syndrome. The pains and complaints are typical, it can be deduced from physical examination and to crown it all its signs can be clearly seen under the X-ray. Here it is. The diagnosis is clear. But what is the cause? A certain anatomical configuration of the stomach. Yes; there are a greater number of people with this configuration amongst ulcer patients than is the statistical average. But—by no means all of them ever develop an ulcer and most of the people who do have no such configuration. It can't be the cause; may be a contributory cause. Hyperacidity? Same argument and, besides, why the hyperacidity? Other causes—Hypermotility, irregular meals and—Psychology creeps in—worries, anxieties, mental strain, overwork, etc. A set of causes, co-operating, seem to fit into a new scheme: constitution, predisposition and accidental unfavourable external influences. But Psychology is an uncomfortable newcomer; once allowed entrance it uses its elbows, rudely asking question, not at all fitting to the medical upbringing. And the worst is still to come, we have not yet talked about Psychoanalysis. What does it asks for instance, about these worries and anxieties? You call them "external," but I can show you that they are very much" internal," I can show you that this person would not have worried at all over his, say, financial impasse if it had not been for his whole character. I can show you that this character itself is the result of his early experiences, can show you in detail that the worries he told you about are only a screen, a red herring, covering up deeply buried passionate longings and fears, buried maybe since his earliest years. However, he himself believes in these present-day worries and is quite unconscious of the war which is going on inside his own mind, even though I can show the most precise and detailed links between them and his unconscious mind, and also how and why it has to disguise itself almost beyond recognition. Moreover, I can almost—not quite—trace the links between these unconscious struggles and the stomach itself. I am nearer the stomach anyhow from "inside" than you, even with your X-ray and microscope.

Now stop, says the Doctor, this goes too far. Are you telling me that you can find out what is in a person's mind, which even he himself does not know? This is nonsense, phantasy, speculation! Precisely, says the Analyst, but the nonsense and phantasy are in the patient's mind, and very highly charged and very real too, and not in mine. Thanks to Professor Freud's discoveries, I have a Method of access to the unconscious mind, so that the patient himself can find it all out with my help, and there is a great deal of knowledge now to make it intelligible. However,

it is a very lengthy business and a long story and we can't go into all
that now. But I can tell you something else—you think of constitution
as organic, but studies by trained observers show, in this case most sys-
tematically in Chicago, that persons who develop ulcers belong to a particular, well-defined personality type. Anyhow, seen from this angle, the
ulcer itself is only a sideshow, an incident, so to speak, in a long chain of events.
If I ask you, for instance: Why did this patient develop an ulcer just now?
you could not give an answer, but the odds are that if I analysed him
I could. By the way, what about treatment and cure? In a good number of
people this condition will not heal under the usual dietary regime, and
the reason is that the underlying conflict has not been resolved. Do you
propose that every gastric ulcer, or every patient for that matter, should
be analysed? No, I don't, but we can't go into all that now.

This was at least reassuring to the Doctor that his colleague has not
altogether abandoned reason and common sense. But he wondered; he
had often noticed that some people with the "same condition" made a
good recovery and others went from bad to worse under the "same treatment" or even died. It had never occurred to him that "psychological"
reasons could be responsible for this—there might be something in this
Analyst's ideas, however incredible they may sound. Should artists
and writers know better than men of science? It came back to him that
he had read Thomas Mann's "Zauberberg" and the "Buddenbrooks."
He had represented the crisis in young Hanno Buddenbrooks' scarlet
fever—when he died—as a deep inner decision between will to live and
will to die … there might be something in it ….

We will leave this imaginary discourse between the Physical and the
Mind Doctor, but must remark that this was an unusually good Doctor,
not typical for the way the average responds.

What has all this to do with Group Analysis? It will soon become
evident.

The Problem.—It will have become clear that our classical scheme is
not applicable any more to the same degree.

In the case of an infection the cause is well defined, a bacillus. Without this and the organism's characteristic response to it, the condition
could not develop in its particular form. But this tells us very little as to
the real meaning of the event for the patient's life and its bearing upon
the future.

At first sight an accident seems to be only a matter of a motor car
and a patient's bones—a concern of the surgeon. But it has been shown

that to be run over can be far from accidental. There is a whole scale: from the person who may commit deliberate suicide in this way, to the far greater number of those to whom it happens while they are quite unaware of the dark powers inside themselves, which drive them into some such catastrophe, from deep, desperate, insoluble conflict; and finally those, who know peculiar, frightening, fleeting impulses to throw themselves under an oncoming train, which puzzle and bewilder them. Some persons never have an accident, others whole series of them, a great many during their lifetime. The latter have been shown to belong to a recognisable type of personality (Dunbar, 1935). They are "accident-prone" and become involved in a very much greater number of "accidents" than the statistical average. They have no conscious intention whatever for doing so. Don't we all know this and express it in so many superstitions?

Wise physicians always knew this. You must always treat the patient and not the disease, they say. But the advent of modern scientific medicine has made this more and more difficult to maintain. The more one learned about the details, the more one lost sight of the whole. Now, under the impact of modern scientific Psychiatry, it is being rediscovered. In some ways, the old pre-scientific idea that people are sick because they have fallen victims to evil spirits and ghosts, have become obsessed, invaded by them, was nearer the truth. So-called primitive people, not yet capable of rationally disciplined thinking, blame the transgression of taboos or the anger and revenge of restless ancestors for such occurrences.

What a dilemma! Is this the end of scientific medicine? Or is the pendulum just swinging? Neither. This is where Psycho-Analysis steps into the breach. It has shown that while it is not possible to ignore the truth in these primitive beliefs, nor the extent and power of the mind, it is possible to admit them without abandoning the ground of science and its principles. Psycho-Analysis has furnished the key which opened up this sphere to scientific investigation and, through this investigation, made it known and intelligible. It has done so in the first instance in such disturbances, which are either frankly psychological or for those physical symptoms the physician finds nothing to account for on purely physical grounds, the so-called Psycho-Neuroses.

Psycho-Analysis the key.—The contributions which Psycho-Analysis has made have inaugurated an epoch in the understanding of the human mind. It will take another half century until the momentum of its impact has reached its climax. We are witnessing the beginning of this process. Here these contributions must be condensed to a few statements. The total personality and total situation in their interaction could not be approached from the vantage point of Psychology as long as one was dependent upon introspection on the one hand and experiment on the other. There was no psychology which took everyday life and its meaning for the individual on emotional and instinctive levels into account, at least scientifically. Only the great philosophers and in particular true artists had been able to make their contributions. Psychology as a natural science, based on Biology, did not exist before Freud. Psycho-Analysis opened this territory up by developing three major tools:

(1) A method of investigation called free association. The Analysand is instructed to relate everything in his mind, as it occurs, resisting the urge to make a choice.

(2) A mode of understanding the full, unconscious, meaning of conscious thoughts, motives, actions, and the relationship between the two spheres of mind. It made clear that why, and how the most powerful motivations of human behaviour had often to be concealed from the person's own awareness, had to be excluded from consciousness, repressed. More than that—they had to be subjected to a barrage of transformations, distortions, such as symbolisations, sublimations, substitutions, displacements, perversions, condensations and other defensive mechanisms, before they were admitted to self-consciousness. The grammar of all this, a kind of deciphering code, is contained in Freud's "Interpretation of Dreams."

(3) Psycho-Analysis created a new situation, the analytic situation, between the Analyst and the Analysand. The essence of this situation lies in the fact that it is a transference situation. The Analysand tends to revive all those earlier relationships to other persons, which are still active in his mind, because they have not come to a satisfactory conclusion. While doing this he imbues the Analyst with all the features of his mind's images, allocates to him the roles of the most important persons of his earlier life, down to infancy. His most passionate love and hate, acutest anxiety, panic, despairing remorse and guilt come into play. If the Analyst allows it to happen, that is! If the Analyst would take the patient's reactions up as a real person in the present reality only, a Doctor in a consulting room, he would

force the Analysand to return on his part to the present, and to abandon this transference. The Analyst does not want to interfere with this transference process, however. He knows that by way of repetition his patient thus experiences and communicates his most vital and most unconscious conflicts. In fact, there is no other way of expressing these conflicts. They are not only forgotten, but could never be directly recalled to memory, because the had never been experienced in articulate language. The Analyst therefore allows the patient to manoeuvre him exactly as the patient's own unconscious mind dictates. This is where the possibility of Self-Analysis ends and the social situation, the other person, becomes indispensable. If the Analyst were himself conflict-ridden or anxiety-laden as to his own primitive instinctual reactions, he would be forced to keep away from this sphere and put up a resistance on his own, albeit unconsciously, against the patient's transference reactions. In the technical language of today this implies that the Analyst himself should have undergone a thorough analysis in his own person. Transference thus becomes the corner-stone of psycho-analytic procedure. It can be experienced and explored fully only in the analytic situation. Psycho-Analysis, as a therapeutic procedure, does not consist of a repetition of transference alone. The Analyst does both: he allows his patient to regress as far as he will, to make out of him what he likes, but also recalls him to the present-day level, represents present, mature reality for him. The art of the Analyst, his good technique as it is called, consists in fulfilling both these parts in the right proportion and at the right moment. Thus he enables the Analysand to link up his past with his present life, to bring his conflicts up-to-date, so to speak, and achieve a better integration.

Without these three tools, which we have outlined, free association, the knowledge of the unconscious and the analysis of the transference situation, no Analyst can work. The last mentioned, however, has gained more and more in importance. It must be mentioned that in its pure form it can only be experienced in a highly intimate social situation—an intimacy unprecedented and unparalleled—between two people. It should also be noted that this situation can be established only under exceptional circumstances, because the preconditions on the part of both the Analyst and the patient are dependent on highly selective factors.

In addition, it is a time-consuming process, necessitating daily sessions for a number of years.

With these tools Psycho-Analysis has, as we said before, made it possible to open up the total personality and the total situation for operation. Indeed, it revealed that the present personality and the present situation, even in their totality, are inseparable from the past—that of the individual and the race—and the future. It has stressed the unexpected importance of sexual life, its newly discovered pre-existence in the life of the infant, and the crucial significance of the Oedipus Conflict. It has established beyond doubt the formative nature of early childhood experiences not only for later life and its conflicts, but for the genesis of the person's "ego" and character itself. Through its concept of conflict as of paramount pathogenic importance, conflict, that is, "between innate impulsive instinct and restricting authority and limiting reality, it has allowed for the basic nature of man as a social animal. Moreover, the mental topography evolved by Psycho-Analysis, assigning certain functions of mind to an "Id," "Ego" and "Super Ego," has done justice, theoretically, to the fact that the "outer" world becomes internalised, that man's inner dynamic world is a microcosmic reflection of the whole world, at least his whole world. It has, in fact, allowed man's social nature to be represented in man's innermost structure.

Explicitly, however, Psycho-Analysis has not as yet allotted to this social side of man the same basic importance as it has to his instinctual aspect. For Freud, and for the majority of Analysts at the present day still, the social nature of man is a derivative from sexual love, or a reaction formation against incompatible destructive impulses. The infant is thought to be solipsistic, knowing nothing but his own instinctual urges, learning of the "outside" world only by a painful trial and error method. This is quite true from the infant's own point of view, and not only from the infant's, but from that of every individual. But it becomes wrong as soon as we want to build up the "world" and "society" or even the family from the sum total of such intricate complexities of "individual" interactions. It is the same mistake, as it was, to consider the whole as the sum of its parts. From a mature, scientific point of view, the opposite is true: each individual—itself an artificial, though plausible, abstraction—is basically and centrally determined, inevitably, by the world in which he lives, by the community, the group, of which he forms a part. Progress in all the sciences during the last decades has led to the same independent and concerted conclusion; that the old juxtaposition of an inside and outside world, constitution and environment, individual and society, phantasy and reality, body and mind and so on, are untenable. They can at no stage be separated from each other, except by artificial isolation. Freud's own concepts were, of course, in this respect determined by his epoch, and if he had lived fifty years later he would have been one of the first to correct them. He has, as it is, given sufficient evidence for this assumption.

Reference

Dunbar, H. F. (1935). *Emotions and Bodily Changes; A Survey of Literature on Psychosomatic Interrelationships 1910–1933*. Columbia University Press.

Book review: *The Civilising Process. Vol. 1—The History of Manners,* by Norbert Elias*

S. H. Fuchs

We refer to our mode of living, habits, customs, moral standards and so on as civilisation. What is considered as "civilised" behaviour is, however, subject to constant development. Its standards are by no means absolute but change from one country to another and from one period to another in the same country. This standard is always set by the ruling class in each society and shows a similar curve of development in the Western European countries. In some epochs the change is a more rapid one than in others, and its repercussions are therefore more obvious to the consciousness of the contemporaries. It is a process, the nature, causes, direction and means of which we are just now beginning to realise.

Here is a work approaching this subject, not by means of more or less vague and speculative generalisations, but by concrete and sober data. The author, who has seen what seems to be the general direction of this process, puts representative documents of each epoch on the stage

---

*This chapter was previously published as: Fuchs, S. H. (1979). Book review: *Oberschichten des Abendlandes. Academia Verlag, Prag (Advance Copy) 1937: The Civilising Process. Vol. 1: The History of Manners. By: Norbert Elias, Translated by Edmund Jephcott. Blackwell, 1978. Group Analysis, 12: 78.*

and lets them speak for themselves. He produces examples of the actual behaviour in situations which have not hitherto usually been made the object of historical research. We are shown how, in different countries, people in polite society behaved at table, in speech, what their attitude was towards sexual matters, defecation, urination and other similar activities, as for instance, spitting, blowing one's nose, etc. This evidence is collected under the headings of such natural functions and, as centuries march past, the curve of the development of the social taboos emerges only the more clearly, as under time concentration. This curve shows the same general characteristics in all the fields under review. Contrary to what we would perhaps expect, there is an ever increasing severity and specification of these social restrictions.

The reasons for this will be dealt with in a second volume to the present work. Obviously they are to be found in the ever increasing difficulty and complexity of social life. They cannot be of a primarily psychological nature because that would mean that a tendency in a definite direction is inherent in the psyche itself, an assumption which we, as natural scientists, see no reason to make. On the contrary, what forms the content and object of our mental life (and, for that matter, of psychology) is of necessity being constantly modified by these "external" circumstances. This statement might surprise psychoanalysts for the moment and even shock them, until they understand that psychoanalysis alone holds the key position for a scientific understanding of this process (which key position is fully realised and conceded to psychoanalysis by some modern sociologists, such as Elias) namely, in showing how the restrictions which society demands are communicated to the growing child until they become second nature, and why and in what way the prohibitions accumulated in history become transferred to each new generation. What the author is able to show is that the regulations which had to be forced upon the individual by the living conditions of society gradually became more and more internalised. What has been an external conflict (a "real" one), becomes an internal one. Originally the individual is much more at liberty to give vent to his aggressiveness, but at the same time much more at the mercy of his fellow beings. Life, therefore, is far more insecure and there is much more reason for fear from external dangers.

More and more, however, the application of crude physical force and violence is monopolised by the State. Correspondingly aggressive impulses have to be directed towards the inside and fear becomes internalised as well. At the same time the former personifications of inner fantastic anxieties are displaced from the outside world into the inner world of the person and become attached to the internalised objects (and into the "unconscious"). All this, it should be noted, can be shown to take place in historical times and there is no need to jump at once to hypothetical assumptions of prehistoric life. In short, this material is relevant for us as a contribution to the historical understanding of ego and super-ego formation. The fact that the individual has to arrive (and at an ever earlier age) at the level of civilisation reached by its surrounding society, thereby passing through phases similar but not identical to the historical stages, is described as "sociogenetic principle" (sociogenetisches Grundgesetz). The author calls his mode of approach as a whole "sociogenetic."

Psychoanalysis has hitherto tried to trace the sources of the all-important super-ego formation in the human species mainly in two directions: firstly, the phylogenetic, as a precipitation of pre-history (Oedipus complex); secondly, the psychogenetic, as an outcome of the history of the individual (in particular in this country). In addition to these two modes of approach we seem to get gradual access to material which opens the way for a third, and perhaps not less important, one, namely the sociogenetic (historical). It need not be said that any one of these modes of approach cannot be meant to supersede, but only to supplement, the others, nor that there is no hard and fast line between them and that they are all the time linked up with each other and in a state of interaction. In fact they meet in the field of psychoanalysis, with its commanding outlook on every sphere of the human body and mind. Psychoanalysis is indeed indispensible as a link between them, but this our position, which we rightly value so highly, brings with it an obligation for the analyst at least to know what is behind the doors he may help to unlock. At the same time, the analyst is only human and must be economical with his time. Because the present reviewer can be credited with a full appreciation of this, he hopes it may be taken for more than a phrase when he says that every analyst who is at all aware of the importance of an understanding of social and historical processes should read this book for himself. He will find in it a wealth of information and an abundance of stimulation. Moreover, he will find it pleasant and compelling reading. It need scarcely be said, therefore, that for the benefit of the English reader an early translation of the book is highly desirable.

PART II

GROUP-ANALYTIC THEORY

CHAPTER SIX

My philosophy in psychotherapy*

S. H. Foulkes

My "philosophy" is, of course, contained in my various writings. Here I will confine myself to some observations on a few aspects, especially controversial ones. My background consists of 40 years as a fully qualified psychoanalyst, 25 as a training analyst. My interest in the method and theory of group-analytic psychotherapy led me to quite new views concerning the whole of psychopathology and psychotherapy, including psychoanalysis. More recently, psychoanalysis has moved in similar directions, though slowly, and it will probably continue to do so.

(1) In my own practice as a psychoanalyst, I have, in the course of the last 20 years, become slightly more active, personal and deliberate. Therapeutically, I have found this method more effective. Psychoanalysis is indispensable as a method of training, but it is not, all considered, the best method of psychotherapy. Group analysis is far superior as a form of psychotherapy and the best method to study the theory of psychotherapy. Personal experience with it—as a patient—is indispensable for the future group analyst.

---

*This chapter was previously published as: Foulkes, S. H. (1971). My Philosophy in Psychotherapy. In: *Selected Papers. Psychoanalysis and Group Analysis*, (ed. Foulkes, S. H.).

(2) Psychotherapy is always concerned with the whole person. The human being is a social animal, he cannot live in isolation. In order to see him as a whole, one has to see him in a group, either that in which he lives and in which his conflicts arise or, on the contrary, in a group of strangers where he can re-establish his conflicts in pure culture. The group is the background, the horizon, the frame of reference of the total situation.

(3) Psychoanalysis sees the individual as a background. It highlights processes emanating from the body and those resulting from precipitations of early "object" relations, or even inherited prohibitions and taboos. The patient gets to know the meaning of everything that affects him in terms of his own desires, fears, phantasies, as the primary source. This view inevitably supports the idea of the individual as the elementary unit, who must form relationships with others in a roundabout, often very complicated way. He is forced to do this by his needs, for which the others are "objects." As we have each our own body, our own eyes, our own brain, so we have our own mind. The mind is inside us, everything else is outside us. Only by projecting back into primordial times can it be admitted that the group was, after all, there before the individual. It will be seen that I was led to a very different image of the nature of mind.

The fundamental discoveries that we owe to this psychoanalytical way of looking at ourselves are infantile sexuality, unconscious processes and transference. The topographical or structural viewpoint has given us an extremely valuable means of orientation in this dynamic scheme of the workings of the inner person. The possibility of thinking in terms of an unconscious ego and superego—charged with destructive energies—and of unconscious defence mechanisms, is of inestimable value for all psychotherapy.

Transference and countertransference

(4) Transference is the unrecognized transfer of unresolved experiences in early childhood into other people, and in particular the analyst. The delusion that they belong to the here and now is complete. Countertransference is the same process on the part of the therapist in relation to his patient. This should not often occur.

(5) The importance of transference necessitates specific precautions. Here belongs the avoidance of all contact with the patient outside the

consulting room. It is best to keep to this even when not working under strictly analytical conditions. Another precaution is the avoidance by the patient of any decisions with vital consequences, such as marriage, divorce, change of profession, of residence or country. This should be extended for a period after the termination of treatment—say, a year of quarantine. Almost invariably, when the analysand reverts to life, he carries with him a central neurotic unresolved problem which forms the nucleus of his neurosis for his further life and can more or less ruin it, even after quite a long time. One cannot overestimate this risk. I have seen it in innumerable cases—not just my own—where in the long-term psychoanalysis has done more harm than good. Answer: vigilance, reduce the duration of treatment, but consider the period after its formal ending as an important part of it.

(6) I do not think that the answer is the excessive concentration on transference in the analysis, which is fashionable. This is the specific answer of the "neurosis" against the curative threat of analysis and the victory of the neurosis. Theoretically, the thorough and shared analysis of the transference-countertransference neuroses should be the answer (see, for example, the very interesting "Notes on transference"), (Bird, 1972). In practice, this cannot often work out. The closely related enhanced personal participation on the part of the therapist removes the procedure even further from the original intentions of psychoanalysis. There is no doubt that the analyst should be receptive and responsive to everything the patient does or says, and he may be engaged with his whole body and person in this reception. But to make it the manifest occupation and topic of the ongoing analysis is another matter. We have gone too far from the original relative anonymity of the analyst. In groups we have a similar proposition, namely, that a number of neurotics battle with their problems together, but the situation is different and has a balancing effect also on the conductor, who can be freer to show his engagement and more ready to do so than in the individual situation. Nevertheless, he has to discriminate how far to go at each particular moment.

(7) Transference is the motor force in psychotherapy. It has an almost magical quality, as if it was more intense than any other relationship. I am not sure that we really understand it fully. It varies not only according to the method used but also the person of the analyst. At the end of the session I gave one of my patients a letter and asked her to be kind enough to put it in a letter box for me. Next session she told me how

surprised she was, especially also that she had carried this out in a quite natural spirit. It turned out that her former analyst had once made a quite similar request of her, whereupon she had promptly fainted. Insofar as transference is a revival of an infantile relationship, it can only be understood as the repetition of the earliest mother/child relationship which we produce in psychoanalysis. From that point of view we *start* with the deepest level of regression, and from the beginning our treatment is also a form of weaning. This elementary vital relationship is the strongest force in our whole procedure. When we make the decisive step from this completely individual-centred, even symbolic, situation to the group, say the family group, we are forced to change the frame of reference of our method and our concepts fundamentally.

(8) There is much lip-service and dishonesty about countertransference. Psychoanalysts wonder far too little about the fact that, by and large, a great majority of them become essentially like their training analysts and share their ideas. This is quite different between parents and children. Like other people, analysts also arrive at their various philosophies in order to suit their interests, be they material, their career or their particular situation, and, like other people, they are often quite unaware of this.

(9) Why do we fail? The strongest factors are two. One is the enormous resistance in people to change, to learn or to unlearn. The other factor is the need for self-damage, self-destruction. This is also universal, and one could say that it is the amount and nature of unnecessary suffering that people add to that inevitable suffering which is part of human life. It may help if we conduct our analyses with the conviction that life contains great and deep pleasure and satisfaction, but inevitably is weighted on the side of suffering. The aim of a true therapy should be for the patient to be better able to avoid unnecessary suffering, to avoid creating more suffering, adding his own self-torture to his misfortunes, and not merely to liberate the capacity for sexual satisfaction—though the importance of that need not be stressed.

(10) When we look seriously at the group as the essential frame of our reference in psychology, we understand that the individual is inevitably a fragment shaped dynamically by the group in which he first grew up. The best way I can think of illustrating my image of the individual in this respect is that of a piece of a jigsaw puzzle in isolation. Imagine this to be three-dimensional as well as in constant interaction with the other pieces. When you take this individual fragment

out of its context, it is shaped and formed, or deformed, according to the place it had and the experiences it received in this group. The first group is normally the family. This family, willy-nilly, reflects the culture to which it belongs and in turn transmits the cultural norms and values. The individual's development is a continuous story starting from before birth. Libidinal development, its culmination in the infantile Oedipus complex in the classical sense, the various defence mechanisms which fit in with various phases—all this remains undisputed, though I think that even the libidinal phases and reactions to bodily functions are culturally conditioned. In this continuous story, therefore, the superego and the ego develop *pari passu* with the id inside the family context. I believe that the early development produces many of the phenomena that are stressed by Melanie Klein, but I see this development as being brought about by the interaction of the whole family on these primitive levels.

The basic human problems with which psychoanalysis is so much concerned I therefore see as being more transmitted than inherited, although the two are never watertight and apart. Complicated emotions can be felt even by the small child as they are actually represented and transmitted, however unconsciously, by the parents, brothers, sisters and so on. These norms and values are engraved in the individual; they form his ego and his superego from the beginning and are of incredible strength. I believe that psychotic mechanisms are operating in all of us, and that psychosis-like mechanisms and defences are produced very early. This does not mean, however, that later psychotic illness, later psychotic disturbance, is a regression to these early stages, as one might say that neuroses or neurotic reactions are.

In my presence, and under pressure from my late friend Robert Walder who was then in London for a discussion, Mrs Klein retracted the idea often ascribed to her that psychoses are regressions to these early stages. As far as primitive functioning of the ego or of language comes in, this has of course some similarities, perhaps even some relationship to a falling-back to early defective thinking. Undoubtedly the person who later develops a psychosis is also conditioned by his early group, and vice versa. In a certain sense one might say that the norm is in itself a psychosis. By that I do not mean that we live in a mad world, which, though true enough, is not a very meaningful statement. I mean rather that we share with our culture some totally mad assumptions that pass as normal. As in psychosis, the ego takes the side of these beliefs and habits. We must on no account make the mistake of explaining group phenomena with concepts taken from individual observation.

In the light of what has been said, it makes more sense to ask in what way the patient who comes for treatment differs from the one who does not come. This complicated question can only be answered in the context of the network in which he lives. If an adult, this will be his own family, his friends, the various close and intimate networks in which he works and in which his needs for love and recognition are met, and where motives of rivalry, competition and hatred are playing.

Where possible, the examination of the most relevant persons involved in a certain conflict together is a valuable and time-saving diagnostic step, even if it is then decided to treat the individuals by themselves or in an analytic group. Family therapy as such has great possibilities. I have often found that the inner conditions between the members do not allow a frank and thorough, deep-going and uncovering approach that applies to them all. I am more impressed by the diagnostic value of seeing families together and prefer the situation of the group-analytic group for actual treatment.

In the group-analytic group, the original family is represented by transference, the cultural group by the matrix insofar as it is shared and has to be shared to start with, the "foundation matrix." The operative network is the treatment group itself. The "dynamic matrix" develops with the progress of treatment.

When we take the step from the traditional psychoanalytic situation—therapist and patient—to the group, we step out of one of the necessary pre-conditions of psychoanalytic technique, that is, the complete isolation of the patient himself, so that we analyse this patient only in relation to us. When we make this step to the group, the simplest scheme is the family, because of its intimate connection with the conflicts of the central patient. In this case, of course, the members of the group have contact with each other. When we move from this to the equivalent of the psychoanalytic situation, but in a group—that is to say, the group-analytic situation—everything in this group belongs only to the group, and members should have no outside contacts or mean anything to each other in life.

(11) In treating man as a social being in a social context, we are forced to review far-reaching concepts—such as, what is an individual, what is mind?

What is mind? It will have become clear that I do not think that the mind is basically inside the person as an individual. I think our type of group clearly shows that. The mind that is usually called intrapsychic is a property of the group, and the processes that take place are due to the dynamic interactions in this communicational matrix. Correspondingly, we cannot make the conventional sharp differentiation between inside and outside, or between phantasy and reality. What is inside is always also outside, what is outside is inside as well. Although, for special reasons, groups or some individuals occasionally make strong use of such differences, this is motivated behaviour and not philosophically correct.

I think that the real nature of mind lies in each individual's need for communication and reception, in every sense of the term. We need only think of language itself, which is indispensable if complete communication on the human level is to proceed. Language could not be acquired by any individual without his capacity to acquire it in his brain. Insofar as it is his own thinking, it is what goes on in his "own" mind, but at the same time it is a shared property of the group, and the individual is forced into it from the beginning by the surrounding culture. Language is one of the main and most significant mental phenomena and can only be maintained and be meaningful as a group phenomenon. Individuals do not continuously communicate as a whole with each other, which is the most normal way of doing it, but they also communicate without knowing it, so that one could say that it is in the first place these unconscious processes that go on between them which permeate each individual. I speak therefore of transpersonal processes.

When we look at or listen to another person, our experience is that we know what he says, what he feels, how he feels towards us, whether he is being frank or not; we can tell immediately if he is angry. I should start from there. No doubt it is a highly complicated process physiologically, but so is recognizing an apple tree. Yet when I see an apple tree I know that I have seen an apple tree; this is an elementary fact. Psychologically we are not concerned with all the processes that operate in order for this to come about. I must have learned to differentiate this object from another, this tree from another, and that this is called an apple tree. The object, however, contains me, it incorporates my potential actions.

The same is true for our experience of other people. True enough, one can be mistaken, but there will be special reasons why a mistake has been made, why we interpreted an expression or an utterance in a certain way. We can therefore never be completely mistaken—except in the "location" of our experience. This is where observations such as "projection," identification and projective identification come in. This short comment must suffice to give at least some idea of a highly complex yet basic matter.

(12) I am often impressed by human beings behaving like drilled circus animals. When you listen to footballers being interviewed on television, for example, you find that they live in a world of their own, with a language of their own, while they are at the same time good or bad husbands, billiard players, friends. The same is true of dancers, horse riders, bankers, industrialists, teachers or doctors. We cannot help sharing a way of thinking with our colleagues.

There is something sad about the fact that the human person, with all his potential capacities, is in many ways so restricted to a special field in which his own world reflects. I have been much impressed by the fact that we live and have the disturbances that correspond to animals in a zoo, not to animals in their original free state (Morris, 1969). Our own zoo is, up to a point, self-inflicted; on the other hand, it is like anything else—we develop in a certain way because we cannot do otherwise under the practical pressures of our vital needs and the conditions in which we have to satisfy them. If one is aware how deep-going and decisive is the influence of the particular culture, and more particularly the family culture, on our total structure, this is less surprising. Just as a mind is shared, so is what is social, not outside but deep inside the person, as well.

The true therapist has, I believe, a creative function—in a way like an artist, in a way like a scientist, in a way like an educator. If he can avoid wanting to educate people in his own image, he will be able to help them creatively to become themselves, to lead a fuller life, to make use of happiness and to avoid adding too much further suffering to their miseries. There is great satisfaction in this creative part of our function. I have sometimes compared this function to that of a poet, especially in conducting a group. By this I mean the therapist's receptiveness, his *ability to see* a bit better, a bit deeper, a bit sooner than others what his patients are really saying, wanting or fearing; to help them to express this and sometimes, though rarely, to express it for them.

The allusion to a musical conductor is not incidental: it is meant to differentiate our function from that of a leader. A therapist with a sense for depth may agree that, in the general run of our profession, there is a false idea of depth and surface. Depth is always there: it is always possible to get hold of it on the surface, it is there all through, visible and tangible. It depends on who is looking, who is listening; one need not jump from what is going on to what is behind it. This also has a bearing on a partially mistaken idea of interpretation.

(13) Undoubtedly we need to have the capacity for empathy with our fellow humans. We are involved far more than we usually know; too much so, perhaps. The ideal of this empathy comes from a certain philosophical attitude, by seeing things in proportion, as part of the human problem in which we are all continuously involved. With that capacity and with maturity we can retain a certain necessary detachment, despite all empathy; these do not need to be in opposition to each other. The good therapist should, at the same time, be above the situation. Such an attitude will make it easier to see both the tragedy and the comedy of human existence, see the absurdity in certain respects. It allows a feeling for a sense of humour; if we have that, we are not merely better off ourselves but also in our function as therapists. In this way our work becomes more interesting, more satisfactory and more effective for our patients.

References

Bird, B. (1972). Notes on transference: Universal phenomenon and hardest part of analysis. *Journal of the American Psychoanalytic Association, 20*: 267–301.

Morris, D. (1969). *The Human Zoo.* Jonathan Cape: New York.

CHAPTER SEVEN

Group-analysis: taking the non-problem seriously*

Caroline Garland

There is a sense in which, at the moment, group-analysts are in a position comparable to that of biologists in the early nineteenth century. Erasmus, Darwin, Lamarck, Buffon and Chambers—these men were sure that evolution occurred, in spite of public ridicule and professional opposition, but they were unable to do much more than retain the notion of evolution as a private conviction, discussed among small groups of like-minded individuals. Their reticence was enforced by the need to find an adequate causal mechanism. They were sure evolution occurred, but they could *not* see how; and if one is going to be taken seriously by fellow-professionals, let alone the general public, they—and we—know that one must base one's convictions on more than an act of faith.

As group-analysts, we know that groups "work"—that is to say, we are confident that the majority of people who enter a group-analytic group, at the very least, express themselves better off for having had the experience. However, we are to some extent still in the dark about just why that should be so; about the fundamental nature of the mechanisms

---

*This chapter was previously published as: Garland, C. (1982). Group-analysis: Taking the non-problem seriously. *Group Analysis, 15*: 4–14.

enabling change and growth in the analytic group. One reason for saying this is that we have such a very wide range of potential answers, or mechanisms, on offer, ranging from the systems point-of-view to the psychoanalytic ... from, one might say, the *group* theorists on the one hand to the *analytically* inclined on the other. But as for *group-analysis*, the combination of the two, we are, I suggest, still in search of an underlying mechanism that will have the simplicity, clarity and above all, the satisfactorily obvious quality that graced natural selection as the fundamental mechanism of evolutionary change.

Let me say at once that I do not have the answer and simultaneously that I think we all already have partial answers to the question, in that each of us conducts our groups within the framework of, at the very least, a working hypothesis as to why the experience we offer should be beneficial to our group members. But what we do not have is a consensus, beyond the knowledge that if we conduct our groups in the Foulkesian tradition, we can feel reasonably confident that they will do some good. But why? And how? How is it that individuals who differ so fundamentally from each other in age, sex, nationality and temperament can be permitted, indeed encouraged within the group-analytic model, to make use of their very uniqueness as part of their therapeutic armoury and yet still be regarded as part of the single tradition that is group-analysis? What kind of underlying therapeutic mechanism could be sufficiently powerful to underpin us all in our variety?

In this paper, I want to try to clarify some of the issues that are important in trying to answer such questions.

The fundamental question is therefore "what is the nature of the therapeutic process within the group-analytic group?" Although we tend to ask it as one, this question is in fact composed of two separate questions which are logically distinct in that one is superordinate to, or inclusive of, the other. (By that I mean that the question "What shall I have for breakfast today?" occupies a subordinate position in any possible hierarchy of personal reflections to the question "Is there any food in the house?", in that the answer to the second must be known before the first can become meaningful.)

The way in which I would like to rephrase the original question about the nature of the therapeutic process is as follows:

a) what causes change?
b) what makes the change therapeutic?

Here, *what causes change*, is the superordinate question, since there is no therapy without change, but not all change is of necessity therapeutic. One can change for the worse, or indeed change without things improving very much at all. However simple such a distinction between these two questions may sound, I suggest that it has far-reaching consequences for our thinking on the subject.

We are used, at an implicit level, to thinking of the therapeutic process as the factor that produces, or initiates, the change in the individual. The consequence of this rephrasing of our original question is to reverse the direction of the underlying assumption. I would like to put it this way: the therapy is *not* what is responsible for initiating change in the individual, although it *is* certainly what makes any change there may be a change for the better. The change-producing factor co-exists with what is therapeutic in the analytic group, but is distinct from it. We must all have had patients in whom therapeutic insight grew apace without producing any effective change at all. Conversely there are individuals for whom a group experience that has included relatively little analytic interpretation has produced marked change and growth. A real distinction exists therefore between insight and change, certainly at the practical level; and this distinction must be reflected at the theoretical level if we are to understand and make use of its implications. Hence my separation of these two distinct elements as sub-sets within the inclusive question about the nature of the therapeutic process. The suggestion is therefore that change is a necessary pre-condition for therapy, rather than that therapy is a necessary pre-condition for change. Change is the agar jelly in which therapy can, if you like, be cultured.

What is it, then, that produces the change? This question forms the focus of this paper, since we already know a great deal from many major theoretical sources about the second, the nature of the processes, or part-processes, that enable the change to become therapeutic. I think we know less about change itself. To try to take this quest a little further, let us attempt to see how a group works. By a group I mean a self-contained social system that, as Palazzoli and her colleagues (*1978*) in their remarkable work on *Paradox and Counter-Paradox* have put it, has come to exist over

a period of time through a series of transactions and corrective feedbacks. These assay what is permitted and what is not permitted in the relationship until the natural group becomes a systemic

unit held together by the rules peculiar to it alone ... transactions
which have the quality of communication, whether on the verbal or
non-verbal level.

Palazzoli is of course describing a system, in her case the system that
is the family but it applies with equal validity to the system that is the
group. Now, in work with families one is permitted to enter the very
system that is, at the very least, maintaining the pathology manifested
in the individual and attempt to "change the rules" that govern it in an
active and imaginative way. In group-analysis that is not of course possible, and many of us would go further and say neither is it desirable.
We prefer the impetus for, and source of, the change to be located in
the individual patient rather than in the therapist, however ingeniously
and gracefully the therapist is later able to disengage himself from the
system he has entered.

Yet we are without immediate access to the family systems of our
group members, having instead only a collection of simple representatives from each family firm. Nevertheless we are obliged to work with
what we are offered. The proponents of General Systems Theory speak
of Ps, or

> the point of a system at which the maximum number of functions
> essential to its existence converge, and which, if modified, effects
> the maximum change with a minimal expense of energy.

As group-analysts, we really have no choice other than to accept the
individual who presents himself to us as the focal or nodal point of
the pathological system in which the functions essential to his existence
converge. He is the only point of leverage within his own system that
is available to us.

If we now move from theory to practice we can attempt to trace the
natural history of an individual's involvement with a group a little further. A patient comes to a therapist with a problem of an intractable
nature: he is stuck, with an unhappy marriage, a failure to progress in
his work, a terror of enclosed spaces, whatever it might be. He says in
effect to the therapist: I can't solve my problem; help me. The therapist
replies: Join this group; it may help.

What does this actually involve? The new member expects to present his problem to the group at large, and to have the benefit of not one,

but a number of sources of advice, encouragement and support. Indeed he is obliged to talk about his problem, however reluctant he may be at first, because this is his *entree*, his right to a place in the group. If he says nothing, he will eventually be asked, "Why are you here?", and for the group's attention to be engaged sympathetically, the answer must consist at least in part of the presentation of the problem. It is a necessary part of the initiation process that there is a confessional stage, in which credentials are presented. It serves several short-lived functions: principally, it is that the new entrant presents himself as a supplicant, not as a challenger.

Next, depending on the stage of development and maturity of the existing group, there is a period in which the individual's presenting problem (which I will now call the Problem) is accepted by the group, who indicate their acceptance by expressions of sympathy, advice and a certain amount of comparing and contrasting with their own Problems. However, after a while, mysteriously the presenting Problem is dropped. There is a limit to the amount of time the group is prepared to give it, and perhaps the new member senses that "just going on talking about it" isn't making any difference. Sometimes both these feelings are expressed quite explicitly. At any rate, it is seen to take a back seat in favour of something that is clearly *not* the Problem, *not* what the individual patient believed he joined a group to involve himself with—it is dropped in favour of the passionate discussion of and involvement with the shifting roles, relationships and behavioural communications that make up the system of the group itself. Our individual with a Problem, therefore, representing the nodal point of the system within which his pathology or Problem exists, comes to find himself increasingly concerned with what is *not* his problem—or the Non-Problem.

This is the foundation stone upon which change in the individual is constructed.

The more discussion of and involvement with the Non-Problem, the here-and-now of the group itself, is enacted within the set of rules "peculiar to it alone," the more firmly established does this alternative system, and the new member's involvement with it, becomes. It is precisely through attending to the Non-Problem that the individual becomes a member of an alternative system to the one in which his symptom, as an expression of its pathology, was generated and maintained—and this process alone, this becoming part of the group (as opposed to attending it) is sufficient to effect change.

The Palazzoli group, in their brilliant work with the families with a member suffering from schizophrenia, express it thus:

> Since the symptomatic behaviour is part of the transactional pattern peculiar to the system in which it occurs, the way to eliminate the symptom is to change the rules.

In a group, of course, the difference is that we cannot change directly the rules governing the individual's pathological transactions within his own system, but we *can* bring about change in the individual by making him part of a powerful alternative system, in which a different set of rules is operating.

If this is true, we may see every attempt to escape from the here-and-now of the group back to the familiar terrain of the Problem as an attempt to cling to the transactional patterns, and hence rules, peculiar to the system from which the patient originated, and which delineated and maintained his symptom; and conversely we may see every expression of interest and concern manifested in group matters as a step towards an involvement in the alternative system offered by the group, in which the rules, simply by being different, no longer serve to sustain the *status quo*.

If this formulation of the fundamental mechanism underlying change, the necessary condition for therapy, has any validity, it must begin to affect our notion of what constitutes a major form of resistance in a group. Indeed, it now places it at the opposite end of the spectrum from the kind of behaviour we are used to thinking of as resistance in the individual setting. In individual work, by and large we tend to focus upon the Problem, although by stripping it of layer after layer of the accretions and debris of a lifetime, we tend to redefine it in terms of its most fundamental and original point of existence. Resistance on our patient's part is his evasion of this task, and his unwillingness to accede to our analysis of its various vicissitudes and transformations. In a group we do something rather different. Our first task as conductor is to enable the group to abandon the Problems in favour of the Non-Problem. We may consider therefore harking *back* to the Problems as a form of resistance to the therapeutic task, which is to say the creation of a system with its own rules and traditions of behaviour-communications, which will come to function as an alternative to the system from which each individual has emerged.

Here, the significance of boundaries must be emphasised. In order truly to be an alternative system, the group must have no actual connection with the individual's "normal" world other than through the existence of the individual himself in both settings. The more precisely defined are the border limits of each territory, the greater the change that is effected in each individual as he becomes incorporated into the new system, and the greater is the consequential "lack of fit" in the nature of his interaction with the old.

We must ask whether every individual is capable of becoming part of the new system that is the group. We already know the answer to this question, although this hypothesis may provide us with a clearer rationale as to just why the answer should be no. There are individuals who come from systems, both public and private, that may explicitly or implicitly forbid, or otherwise render impossible, change of a particular kind or in a particular direction. Fervent Marxism might be an example of one such public system, and well-established paranoia an example of a private system; neither dedicated Marxists nor paranoiacs make good group members precisely because of the powerful and rigid nature of their system of origin (or primary system) which renders it subordinate to that of the group's system of creation (or secondary system).

It makes the initial question on which one bases the selection of patients for a group relatively straightforward: is this person already part of a system that is more powerful than, or even as powerful as, the one a group-analytic group can create? Fortunately for our patients, the answer is only relatively rarely yes.

We can now also clarify the rationale for mixing symptomatology within a group, or at least types of pathology: two or three patients with shared pathology or symptomatology can unite to delay or damage the development of the secondary system necessary to effect change in each of them. Cumulatively, even though it may be unconscious, their systemic "pull" may be greater than that the group can exert and sustain.

There are thus two aspects to the group experience. Firstly, there is the process of change itself, originating in the patient's becoming part of a system that is other than the one from which he originated. Secondly, there is the therapeutic transmutation of this change into change-for-the-better. Within a therapeutic group, therefore, change can become growth.

If we accept this hypothesis, we may see it as our initial task to create and sustain a setting in which the substitution of the Non-Problem for the Problem may happen. During this substitution, two things are happening simultaneously. Firstly, a process of change is initiated as the individual becomes incorporated into the secondary system that is the group. Secondly of course, the Problem is still present, but is now being dealt with at the level of metaphor, a theme I will return to later. Each individual's Problem is, in the Foulkesian sense, his "Group Problem" and is present through the patient's importing it in encapsulated form into the group. Thus as conductors we cannot help but gain some notion of the transactional patterns, and hence rules, governing the individual's primary system, since through the multiple transferences that are possible within the group, the patient will try his hardest to recreate his "Group Problem" once more. Partly he cannot help himself: he behaves according to the systemic rules that have long determined his expectations and behaviour, and with which, however unhappy, he is at least entirely at home and therefore safe. Partly too, there is the implicit message to the conductor that the patient's assessment is correct, in that he is seen to be helpless as events take on a shape and form he has long been familiar with, so that he can demonstrate his absolute blamelessness in the face of a malevolent world.

It is, of course, inevitable that to the extent to which the individual is responsible for his own Problem (that is to say the extent to which it exists within the damaged, distorted or fossilised parts of the psyche), it will come to be manifested within the behaviour-transactions and communications that he engages in within the group. Is there then a contradiction inherent in the need to work on the individual's own neurotic Problem (in whatever guise) without actually working against the creation of the alternative system that it is the conductor's task to foster and maintain? I should like to offer a gardening analogy. Faced with a chaotic and abandoned flowerbed, the gardener may either spend his time pursuing the root-systems of the weeds that infest his chosen patch, or, adopting an alternative strategy altogether, he may plant ground-cover between the plants he wishes to preserve, and allow the new and healthy growth to encroach upon the territory originally occupied by the weeds. Both approaches concur in agreeing that the weeds are unwanted, but the approach to eradicating the problem is radically different: one involves direct assault, the other the nurturing of alternative elements of healthy growth that simply begin to occupy enemy territory. Within this analogy, groups, in involving the substitution of the Non-Problem for the Problem, employ a ground-cover rather than a direct weeding strategy.

There are processes within the group itself that will work for the exchange of the Problem for the Non-Problem. One of course is that competing individual claims for time and attention will push the group towards a focus on a concern that is of equal valency for all, rather than the property of a single individual. Another Solution to the problems of rivalry is time-sharing—*it's your turn to be the patient*, i.e. to talk about the Problem, and it is one that may well be adopted by a group that is operating below optimal strength in terms either of numbers or in the level of group arousal (the "emotional temperature" of the group). It is a positive function of having seven or eight in a group that it lowers the chances of time-sharing being adopted as a way to negotiate rivalries, since although it is a possible solution, it is infinitely less powerful than one which adopts the communal Non-Problem as its focus.

However, in time-sharing one may observe a paradoxical effect: traditionally it is this week's "patient" that is felt to benefit from being the focus of the group's sympathetic and empathic attention, and there is often overt envy for those in this favoured position. Yet however restored the recipient may feel, it is my contention that it is those who are actively applying themselves to the understanding and clarification of their colleague's Problem who are benefiting most from the transaction. It is in them, if you like, that ground-cover has taken most active root and is spreading—in them that their original focus is being most visibly exchanged for the alternative attitudes and approaches that form the group's system.

In calling the *group's* concerns the Non-Problem, I am not implying that the issues, passions and concerns that emerge within and as a function of a group's activity, are any less significant or problematical than those which brought each individual into the group in the first place. If anything they are more so, since they inevitably contain within them at one level the metaphorical, or transferential, restatement of the seven or eight original Problems in a group form. What I am saying however, is that the focus of concern in an optimally functioning group will be of common and relatively equal valency for all members, rather than of particular concern to one individual alone. The group's Problem, to reverse the direction of gaze, is the individual's Non-Problem or certainly what he would have perceived as a Non-Problem on entry.

In summary, therefore, the therapist's task is to enable every member of his group to become part of the alternative system that is the group's own. However, the very act of encouraging an individual to join a group may be seen as paradoxical in that one knows that his problem is going to be the one thing that a powerful group will not encourage him to talk about at any length, certainly not once he has been incorporated as a group-member. Thus the message is: take your problem seriously—it is worth joining a therapeutic group in order to do so. But the result of joining a group is that the presenting symptom is what will receive the least of the group's attention, and that the substitution of the group's concerns for the individual's will itself be what initiates change in the novitiate.

There is of course a tremendous tension created in the individual by this apparently incomprehensible separation of him from the centre, the pivotal element in his life, his Problem. At times he will burst out in frustration about how no one cares about his Problem, about how this group is all very well, but it isn't making any difference to how awful his life is. Yet groups "know" at one level that direct assaults upon the Problem are ineffectual, and tolerate and absorb such assaults as part of the process each and every member is engaged in.[1] It is another of the paradoxical strengths of the group that while it is in itself a place of comfort, or at least containment, at the same time the *fons et origo* of that support is invisible, intangible and ultimately unattainable. The individual members attempt to locate it variously in each other, primarily of course in the conductor, but attempts to merge with one or another of these imagined sources of comfort and joy are invariably disappointing; the true source is the group itself and no single member of it, even the conductor, *is* the group. Such a state of tension, the permanent sensation of "so near and yet so far" is, I suggest, an extremely potent force obliging the individual to search actively for other ways to achieve his goal of merging with this ultimate source of power and love—variously mother, father, transitional object, and all the multitude of other things the group comes to represent. The creative tension that this sustains in the individual may maintain the process of change set in motion by the act of joining a group, this time voluntarily rather than involuntarily, as the individual searches for ways to achieve the state of merging, or total intimacy, from which he emerged in the beginning and to which he can return ultimately and permanently only in death.

I want to turn now to a consideration of the nature of *playing*, and what we might mean by it. I hope that what may at first appear to be a digression from my main theme will eventually serve to strengthen it.

Play is easy to recognise, hard to define. However, we must distinguish between play as an index of health, and play as a cause of health (something I have discussed in more detail elsewhere), since in whatever way one looks at a great deal of absorbing writing on the subject of play by therapists of various theoretical persuasions, one is left with an unresolved problem: one connected with a persistent confusion between the nature and the functions of play. There must be about playing some unique feature that makes it conducive to health without just being another way of describing health; moreover some unique feature that has particular relevance for us as therapists, as Winnicott has expressed most clearly:

> Psychotherapy takes place in the overlap of two areas of playing, that of the patient and that of the therapist. Psychotherapy has to do with two people playing together. The corollary of this is that where playing is not possible then the work done by the therapist is directed towards bringing to the patient from a state of not being able to play into a state of being able to play.

To identify what it is about the nature (as opposed to the function) of play that is significant for the group experience, I suggest we must turn for help to the work of those in other fields—ethologists, sociologists and anthropologists—bearing in mind the distinction made by Freud: The opposite of play is not serious occupation but—reality.

How does one tell whether behaviour is "real" or playful? There seem to be two main sources of information within which many complex and subtle variations are possible: the first is the absence of signals specifically associated with the non-play context in which the behaviour occurs (the absence of, say, change of skin colour, or persistent eye contact); and the second is the presence of signals that are specific to the play context. In our case, perhaps the widened eyes and raised eyebrows that are accompanied by the smile. These highly ritualised forms of communication, social signals, are signals about the nature of the communication that is about to follow. That is, they are signals about signals, or what Bateson and others call *meta-communication*. Bateson puts it in detail in this way:

> Expanded, the statement "this is play" looks something like this: "These actions in which we now engage do not denote what those actions for which they stand would denote."

Goffman has a similar view. He includes playful behaviour in his detailed discussion of "primary frameworks"—the perceptual set implicitly adopted by an individual that enables him to make sense of what is going on around him. One of the central concepts in his analysis of framing is that of *the key*:

> ... the set of conventions by which a given activity, one already meaningful in terms of some primary framework, is transformed into something patterned on this activity but seen by the participants to be something else.
>
> The systematic transformations that a particular keying introduces may alter only slightly the activity thus transformed, but it utterly changed what it is a participant would say was going on.

Perhaps the relevance of this for the therapeutic group is already apparent, but for the moment I shall continue with the argument. The "key" for a play-fight in, for example, chimpanzees, is the refined and highly ritualised facial expression that announces "this is play." It utterly changes what it is the recipient would say was going on. In chimpanzees, fighting results in dispersal and separation of the contestants; however, the end-point of a bout of play-fighting results, in a significant proportion of instances, in the participants sitting closer to each other than they were at the beginning of the interaction. It is behaviour that in a rather literal and measurable way produces what we most desire in our analytic groups, the mysterious social glue of cohesiveness.

It is precisely this doubling up of behaviour patterns that allows us to have a category *play* in the first place. It is the very contrast between the consequences of the same behaviours as they occur in the two contexts that allows us to identify behaviour with any certainty as playful. Perhaps we are now able to get back to Freud's original distinction between playing and reality. The fighting chimpanzees finish up in great good humour sharing a bit of fruit, and the observer concludes their fight cannot have been real. "They were only playing."

How does this apply to group-analysis and our interest in the origins of change? These observations of the paradoxical nature of play behaviour can be looked at from the point of view of the systems analyst. This is how Reynolds, a psychologist interested in the evolution of language has put it—and here I feel we get a statement about the nature of play which we can use to clarify its role as a powerful mechanism within' the therapeutic group.

If we think of a system as operating in conjunction with other systems, so that its output serves as inputs to the others, then a system whose output is temporarily uncoupled from its normal input relations to other systems will be said to be functioning in the simulative mode. It can in fact be shown that play involves the simulative execution of systems at several levels of biological organisation ... the function of play must be understood in the light of the function of simulation in general.

Next comes the crucial bit for psychotherapy:

The essential feature of the simulative mode is that the system, *while functioning normally is uncoupled from its normal consequences* vis-a-vis *other systems*. However, the feedback consequences within the acting system are unimpaired ... the simulative mode of action is paradoxical; the system's operations should have their normal consequences, *yet those consequences must at the same time be rendered inconsequential.* (italics by CG)

It seems clear that it is possible to think of the therapeutic group as, in a rather special way, a social system operating in the simulative mode in precisely the sense in which Reynolds uses the term. The interactions that take place within the group are of the same kind, and are enacted to the same degree, as those that take place outside the group, although the situations that elicit them will be a function of the group itself. However, the *consequences of these* interactions, generated within the group, are temporarily uncoupled from their normal input relations to other systems (or "reality"), while at the same time "the feedback consequences within the acting system are unimpaired." In other words, what takes place within the individual member as he, for instance, experiences pain, anger or joy, is unimpaired by his doing so within the group; however, the consequences of his having and expressing these feelings are temporarily disconnected from "reality" precisely because of their occurrence within the group's setting.

Moreover, and clearly here we are already moving into a discussion of what is therapeutic about the group experience, as opposed to what is productive of change, there is the opportunity for second-order uncoupling; a chance to examine the connections and couplings between cause and effect that occur within the group system itself, so that insight (both historical and contemporary) may accompany and illuminate experience. Insight may have a significant part to play in "fixing" change; that is to say in rendering permanent the freshly developed image of the individual.

A group is in fact, most seriously and dedicatedly at play. Its members are liberated from the need to meta-communicate, to signal to each other on each occasion "these actions in which we now engage do not denote what those actions for which they stand would denote ..." because *the key* to the primary framework already exists, connoted by their status as "members of a therapeutic group." This primary framework is provided and maintained by us, the conductors, although we tend to refer to it in the plural as "the boundaries." With this in mind, the importance of maintaining the relationships between group members exclusively within the boundaries of the group is made quite clear, since it is only when such relationships are truly uncoupled, totally disconnected from their normal consequences that it is safe to explore them.

It is of course part of the conductor's task to make plain the simulative nature of the experience the group is engaged in. Here the interpretation of the transference is central. Although the conductor points the way, equally important are the other members. In negotiating the distribution of the multiple transferences inherited from significant figures in the past, there is also a sense in which each member of a group acts as a naturally occurring restraint upon the development of an extreme transference in any other member. Conflicting needs—X's loving mother may also be Y's envious sibling—clarify the simulative nature of the enterprise, and maintain the as if status of the interactions.

This in itself, it is perhaps worth mentioning, this learning to interact in a simulative mode, has important therapeutic consequences, important ramifications for adaptive individual behaviour, whether it is learned spontaneously through play in childhood (in which the learning proceeds from actions to language), or later on during the special sort of playing that characterises the therapeutic group (in which the process is reversed and learning moves from language to action). As Bateson points out, schizophrenic behaviour

> can be described in terms of the patient's failure to recognise the metaphoric nature of his fantasies ... the frame-setting message (e.g. the phrase "as if") is omitted and the metaphor or fantasy is narrated and acted upon in a manner which would be appropriate if the fantasy were a message of the more direct kind.

The capacity to shift primary frameworks, to adapt one's behaviour according to the prevailing contextual conventions, so markedly lacking in the psychotic, may be regarded as a prime element in mental health. The capacity that young children have in abundance to exploit the possibilities of the "as if," to harness and to enjoy the kaleidoscopic nature of words and actions are part of a crucial ability to look at things in a number of ways; crucial that is for a species that relies so heavily upon learning for its individual and biological success. In a group one is free to make errors of contextual judgement in comparative safety, over and over and over again, until finally through repeated engagement in that "serious occupation" that is not yet "reality" one grows aware of the multiplicity of relevant cues that are necessary for the sensitive and successful regulation of behaviour.

There is, one might reasonably feel, some important element lacking in this discussion of play; it does not sound, from the way in which I have been talking about it, as though it is much fun—and surely having fun is a crucial element in play. Or is it? It is all too easy to assume that the burst of shared laughter must mean that good things are happening, and they often are; it represents a shared acknowledgement of a situation that has momentarily appeared in the same light to everyone present, and therefore is both a cause and an effect of group cohesiveness—but, I suggest, not necessarily either more or less than shared tears. Play is passionate, but not always euphoric. Having fun overlaps with playing, but not all play is fun, any more than all fun is playing. If our working definition of play is that of engaging in a simulative system, then merriment or gaiety may accompany it, but with no more or less likelihood than merriment or gaiety may accompany not playing, but reality.

Having fun, it should also be noted, can be defensive. A manic merriment may serve to obscure the anxiety of a beginning or the pain of an ending. Perhaps it is worth remembering in this context that the older meaning of "fun" is that of a hoax or trick, something intended to cheat or deceive, even to cajole-something perpetrated in the service of getting one's own way. We should not let ourselves be taken in by the sheer fun of fun into thinking that all is well. Playing, or getting on with the therapeutic work, is hard work, and is often not fun at all.

In summary then, this paper has attempted to tease out and elaborate upon the change-producing or *transformative* properties of the group-analytic experience as opposed to those that determine the direction of change, or its *therapeutic* properties. I have attempted to show that the transformative element is inherent in the process of becoming a member of a therapeutic group. The therapeutic group:

a) forms a system that is other than the ones from which the individual members originated.
b) It does this initially and most powerfully by its substitution of the Non-Problem for the Problem.
c) It is a particularly powerful alternative system in that it functions within the primary framework of a simulative system, enabling its members to retain the knowledge that although what takes place within the group is serious, it is yet not reality.
d) To this extent, the analytic group is in a category of behaviour that also includes play.
e) We may thus describe the kind of playing that takes place within the group-analytic group as *taking Non-Problems seriously*; like the best of play it is both passionate and productive, permitting the individual to negotiate and renegotiate change—as well as ex-change—between the inner world and outer realities, within himself, between himself and the group, and between the group and the outside world.

These then are the transformative factors that enable the powerful and beneficent forces of psychoanalysis to gain a therapeutic foothold, combined within the unique system for which we are indebted to Michael Foulkes—group-analysis.

Note

1. Who knows? Possibly the conductor, though there are many good conductors who do not "know" it in quite that way; possibly, too, it is dimly perceived by individual members. But the group itself behaves as though it "knew" it quite explicitly. Since one function of the group is "knowing" it is perhaps relevant to quote this passage from Sherrington, on the brain. If Foulkes was not already aware of it, he would surely have been delighted by so elegant an account of the group Matrix:

    "A scheme of lines and nodal points, gathered together at one end into a great ravelled knot, the brain … Imagine activity shown in this shown by little points of light. Of these some stationary flash rhythmically, faster or slower. Others are travelling points streaming in serial lines at various speeds. The rhythmic stationary lights lie at the nodes. The nodes are both goals whither converge, and junctions whence diverge, the lines of travelling lights."

The passage goes on to describe the brain waking after sleep.

"The great topmost sheet of the mass, where hardly a light had twinkled or moved becomes now a sparkling field of rhythmic flashing points with trains of travelling sparks hurrying hither and thither. It is as if the milky way entered upon some cosmic dance. Swiftly the head mass becomes an enchanted loom where millions of flashing shuttles weave a dissolving pattern, always a meaningful pattern though never an abiding one. The brain is waking and with it the mind is returning."

References

Bateson, G. (1972). *Steps to an Ecology of Mind.* Paladin, London.
Foulkes, S. H. (1964). *Therapeutic Group Analysis.* George, Allen & Unwin London.
Freud, S. (1908). The Relation of the Poet to Day—Dreaming. Standard Edition, Vol. IX.
Goffman, E. (1975). *Frame Analysis.* Penguin, London.
Palazzoli, M. et al. (1978). *Paradox and Counterparadox.* Aronson, New York.
Reynolds, P. (1972). Play, language and human evolution. In *Play: Its Role in Development and Evolution.* (Ed, Bonner), Penguin, London.
Winnicott, Donald (1971). *Playing and Reality.* Penguin, London.

CHAPTER EIGHT

Destructive phases in groups*

Jeff Roberts

Did he live his life again in every detail of desire, temptation and surrender during that supreme moment of complete knowledge? He cried in a whisper at some image, at some vision—he cried out twice, a cry that was no more than a breath—"The horror! The horror!"

(Conrad, 1902)

The offing was barred by a black bank of clouds, and the tranquil waterway leading to the uttermost ends of the earth flowed sombre under an overcast sky—seemed to lead into the heart of an immense darkness.

(Conrad, 1902)[1]

Kurtz, the speaker of the first quotation above and mysterious anti-hero of Joseph Conrad's (1902) novelette *Heart of Darkness*, was claimed by T. S. Eliot as "standing for the dark heart of the twentieth century."

*This chapter was previously published as: Roberts, J. P. (1991). Destructive Phases in Groups. In: *The Practice of Group Analysis*, (ed. J. P. Roberts and Malcom Pines), pp. 128–135. Routledge: London.

Sigmund Freud also explored the dark heart of the twentieth century. One of his deepest and most fundamental works is *Beyond the Pleasure Principle*. The core hypothesis of this book is that the human being has internal drives towards both creation and destruction. The language Freud chose to use to describe these motivational sets was that of "instinctual drives." This was compatible with the main body of his theoretical work and the state of biological science at the time of writing the book. He hypothesized the existence of a "life instinct" and a "death instinct," which he named Eros and Thanatos. At the core of his argument was a quasi thermodynamic point of view, which in effect points out that human consciousness is a pinnacle of achievement from which descent is inevitable. In other words, implicit in the development of a conscious self is a tendency to disintegrate either wilfully or by default.

The psychoanalytic school which picked up on these difficult notions was founded by Melanie Klein. The work of the "Kleinians" takes us to the very heart of human destructiveness and appears to many to insist arbitrarily that although a proportion may be reactive, much that is nasty about the human being is innate and must be confronted in the interest of the health and maturity of the individual. Moreover, the Kleinians insist that this innate destructiveness becomes active in very early infancy. The work of the Kleinians is marred by dogmatic presentation, a lack of willingness to engage in research and discussion and a tendency towards a somewhat rigid therapeutic technique. None the less, the Kleinian group's work on primitive defensive manoeuvres and the human being's relationship with his or her destructive drives and impulses is seminal.

The fact that destructive processes in group settings can be long-term and destructive to the members of the group that has been brought into focus over the past 15 years. Prior to this, pointers to these phenomena were given by W.R. Bion (Bion, 1959). Bion reported in his *Experiences in Groups* how primitive and destructive modes of functioning emerged in groups whose attempts at developing defensive or co-operative solutions to the problems of being in a taskless group were relentlessly undermined by their conductor. These destructive modes of functioning he termed "basic assumptions." Bion had no intention that his groups would be therapeutic, and this appears to have been the experience of most of their members. However, groups which are conducted in a more nurturing and less anxiety-provoking manner than Bion's have repeatedly proved to be able to transcend the destructive forces within them and produce good outcomes for most committed and well-motivated patients. The group-analytic technique is one such method, which on the whole, we confidently expect to facilitate the creative management of destructive trends in our groups in the [Group-Analytic] Practice.

Two important works have been produced by group analysts. The first, by Zinkin (Zinkin, 1983), identifies a phenomenon which he names "malignant mirroring." The second, by Nitsun (Nitsun, 1991), invokes the "anti-group," and is a scholarly review of the processes whereby groups set up with therapeutic intent enter phases in which darker motivations emerge.

Malignant mirroring

The group-analytic therapy group has been poetically compared to a hall of mirrors (Foulkes & Anthony, 1957). In most writings on mirroring the assumption is made that the effect of finding oneself in such a hall of mirrors is beneficial to the individual and contributes to the positive development of the group. That this is not always the case was pointed out by Zinkin (1983) in his article on malignant mirroring. He makes the point that the view of oneself gained in the "hall of mirrors" can be experienced as intensely persecuting. The results of this opportunity for outsight to become insight can be joy, transformation and growth; it can also be rage, panic, denial and flight. As Zinkin suggests, the sight of oneself in a mirror can be an intrinsically alienating, rather than affirming experience. As indicated in his article, peculiar and terrifying phenomena can be associated with this quasi-magical reflector of images. However, mirrors also display the truth (Garland, 1982 and page 53 of this volume). The ultimate horror for some may not be contained in the mirroring process itself nor yet in the distortions which may be present in the image. The hated and truly dreadful experience, often repudiated with amazing violence, is almost certainly an experience of the difference between what is perceived in the mirror and the individual's expectation of what he or she will see. A patient in a group of mine is, in effect, transfixed, for much of the time (as was Narcissus) in front of a mirror he holds up to his life and self. He is transfixed however, not by the beauty of what he sees, but as was Kurtz, by "the horror, the horror."

The psychoanalyst and group analyst are, I believe, engaged in a quest for the truth, with the expectation that an uncovering of the truth will facilitate healthy growth and development in the individual and the group. Some people, however, are not ready to face the truth about themselves, when it arrives, and indeed may never be ready to encounter their truths. These people are likely to react catastrophically if the truth arrives, too soon, too explicitly or in too large a quantity. The likelihood of a catastrophic reaction to experiencing this truth will also vary according to the mode of its delivery and the context in which it arrives. A tactless confrontation in a new group is entirely different from the slow emergence of truths in an established and caring matrix. The effect on a group of the catastrophic reaction to self-discovery through mirroring is likely to be the initiation of a destructive phase or the amplification of destructive processes already in train. One such destructive phase is vividly described by Zinkin in his article.

Awareness of these issues has important implications for the selection and composition of groups and also for the timing of interventions in the group process. It also gives food for thought about those patients who suddenly leave groups, whatever the manifest reason for this. It is likely that such patients are having problems facing truths about themselves, which are being exposed in the group. The more energetic the departure the more likely it is that the truth will never be faced. After all, Kurtz's confrontation with his truths was on his death-bed.

The anti-group

Nitsun (Nitsun, 1989) points out that the belief that the group is intrinsically creative and hence therapeutic can only be the consequence of a blinkered idealism. In his experience, particularly in a new group, and particularly if errors in selection have been made, an anti-group will develop whose "aim" is to fragment and undermine the group, thereby defeating its integrative and therapeutic potential. He also makes the crucial point that balance between group and anti-group is far more precarious than we would wish to believe. Indeed I suspect that a feather might tip it either way. I would like to think that Foulkes would agree with me that at the right moment the feather is in fact the intervention of the conductor, which gently tilts the process in favour of group rather than anti-group.

The central thesis of this chapter is that there are groups in which for significant periods of time the death instinct gains the upper hand and that in most groups there will be transient destructive phases. The problems in such groups may appear to be located in one destructive individual or be manifest in the group as a whole.

In the following section of this chapter a number of anecdotes from group analysts working in the [Group-Analytic] Practice will be presented as examples of the type of destructive phases we encounter in our practice groups. In each, the conductor will present his or her moving from hope to despair and back to hope again, as the destructive phase develops and is resolved. The conductor will outline the problem he or she experienced and then talk of the way he or she intervened to facilitate a resolution or maybe observed as his or her group found its own resolution. Each of the anecdotes is presented below in the conductor's own words. It is necessary in the interests of confidentiality that the conductors are anonymous.

1. The group conductor of a group-analytic group would view one of the markers of a healthy group to be a capacity to engage in a free-floating conversation. Moreover, this conversation would tend to resemble creative human thought, as if in some way the group were an organism manifesting a mind of its own. This phenomenon is a significant contributor to the group's potential as a therapeutic instrument. The "group mind" is, according to Foulkes (Foulkes, 1973) embedded in the network of communication or "matrix," established by the interaction of the members. Some groups appear to resist with remarkable tenacity the development of a free-floating conversation. I have an experience with a once-weekly group which consistently behaves in this way. The group was originally started 25 years ago. It has established a way of working which is normally seen in the early months of a group's life. Each member takes it in turn to present a problem, which the others then compulsively and attentively work on. In the course of two recent meetings, attention was given to the transfer of money from one country to another, how x might arrange the sale of her house, how y was having legal difficulties with an inheritance, how z was losing money through others taking advantage of his lack of business sense. Each of these issues was discussed in turn at some length, in an entirely concrete way with a conscientious attention to the niceties of points of law, and principles of banking and accountancy, as misunderstood by successive contributors. There was a complete avoidance of attention to emotional implications, little personal interaction and no attempt to

consider any latent meaning in communication. The conductor felt unable to intervene in any way to promote a more healthy process. The group tends for the majority of its life to be fixed in this type of interaction. The group is a Tower of Babel in which eight individuals apply themselves diligently to solving problems, while retaining their individuality and hence resisting the development of an integrated group. This group is dysfunctional.

2. The events to be described occurred in a once-weekly group, which was tending to be supportive rather than analytic. The group comprised a number of youngish, quite damaged individuals. Over a period of a year, there developed more and more contact outside the group, even though the members knew that this was not encouraged. People started meeting in a planned way, until eventually one of the members had a birthday party and decided to ask the other members of the group and their spouses or partners to it. This was not reported until after the event, and I was faced with a fait accompli. I had tried previously to deal with things in an interpretative way, looking at the sense of deprivation and frustration within the group which was being more practically satisfied through contact outside the group. Clearly this intervention had failed. I felt that I had to make a decision on the spot and came down heavily on the side of confrontation and authoritarian prohibition. I said that this could not continue, that they had to choose whether they wanted friendship with continuing contact between them all and their partners outside the group, or group psychotherapy. If they desired the latter, I said, they had to agree to make a commitment to cease meeting outside the group, and particularly to avoid involving their partners. This was accepted, the acting-out ceased and the group continued thereafter in a more conventional style.

I was conducting a training group in which two members, male and female, started meeting outside the group. They began to consider whether to develop a full relationship and become sexually involved. This was brought up on several consecutive meetings of the group and it seemed as if they were moving inevitably towards the reality of accepting their mutual attraction and the gratification which could be achieved through an intimate relationship. I felt that this would happen if I did not intervene. I decided again [the same conductor as in anecdote 2] to confront the situation, and said that the contact outside the group must cease, but if they felt they could not continue in the required state of abstinence, they would both have to leave the group. This was accepted, they remained in the group and things went well thereafter.

3. A slow-moving, once-weekly group containing a man and a woman who had been members for more than ten years, found it difficult to move from "fire-fighting" and concentration on one member at a time, especially following the summer break, when I returned with a physical complaint which necessitated my missing several group sessions. This restriction of group functioning seemed to be an attempt to satisfy deeper longings for individual attention, which at the same time was feared, especially by the women. All of them had conflictual and disappointing relationships with their fathers, one of whom had abandoned her at birth and another abused her sexually. When I came back to more reliable attendance, there was a period of repeated intense attacks on me by the women; firstly, for favouring the two long-term members, and secondly, for sexism. So fraught did the group become that fears were expressed that it could not continue. Not only was I so unfair and discriminatory, but the violence in the group made it too uncomfortable for people to feel they could continue in it.

My destructiveness was seen as obvious by the women, while the more diffident men on the whole seemed at times to collude with this belief and its exploration in terms of unconscious conflicts, and transference was resisted.

The situation only changed when, staying firm and flexible, I put it to them that they consider what was happening in transference terms. At the same time I showed a preparedness to think how I had contributed to the situation through countertransference problems. I also indicated my belief that they all needed parental reassurance and comforting, a need which had been exaggerated during my period of illness. Subsequent concern about my health had promoted jealousy of me and denial of their own needs. This enabled one woman to turn from her "spiky aggressiveness" to grief at the loss of an important mother-figure (she had been abandoned by both her parents at birth), and another (the one who had been sexually abused by her father) to share a dream in which I had sexually exploited her. The group began then to work more as a group again. In the session before the next break, one woman gave me a card in which she had written, "It is only after we have accepted our rage that we can CHOOSE to love.

It is only after we have accepted our rage that we can CHOOSE to be more understanding. Otherwise we are just pretending to be nice."

5. For over two years I had a female patient in a group whose diagnosis was that of a borderline character. She was a very intelligent woman with university education, but whose personal and professional life had deteriorated considerably. Within the group she became increasingly bitter and destructive towards most other members, but particularly towards, men upon whom her attacks became overtly castrating. Although she was responded to with considerable warmth and understanding in an attempt to get behind her destructive envy, she continued to escalate her attacks. At times this led to violent confrontations. On one occasion she added some strong racial comments, to which a sensitive member responded with such anger that he could scarcely contain a physical attack. Though temporarily contrite, the offending patient was not able to make reparation or to take adequate responsibility for her provocative stance. As therapist I eventually asked her to leave the group. This is the only time I have ever done this and it was a great relief for both the patient and the group that I finally took this action. She left owing a considerable amount of money, which she promised to pay, but never did. I did, however, hear from her some months later, when she had left London and was setting up in a handcraft industry in the country. Her letter was reasonably balanced and appreciative of the care she had received.

6. Another very destructive patient was a woman whose aggressive behaviour increased to such a point that she was marching out of the group in mid-session and locking herself in the lavatory. Sometimes she would refuse to open the door at the end of the session and disturbed everyone by very loud, agitated sobbing. I attempted to deal with this by offering individual sessions, which was clearly a mistake, since her behaviour became even more regressed during these sessions. She eventually decided to leave the group and go into individual therapy.

Conclusions

The examples above give some valuable insights into the group-analytic process as it is influenced by a variety of destructive processes. These may be grouped as follows.

1. Collusive activity in the group, whose goal appears to be to prevent the development of a group (or group matrix). This collective resistance can be assumed to be a manifestation of the "anti-group." The anti-group is determined to maintain neurotic and psychotic defences and is an enemy of the truth.
2. Energetic and usually destructive responses to the emergence of more truth than can be borne.

Various phenomena may be identified which played an important part in the events described.

splitting	fragmentation
projection	shortsightedness
projective identification	bad faith
callousness	ill will
narcissism	meanness
lack of empathy	murderousness
lack of cohesiveness	perversity
	collusion

These little dramas, as one might expect, manifest all the usual components of humans' nasty and tragic behaviour. The truth of the matter is that human beings are both destructive and creative. Not entirely surprisingly, the extent of human destructiveness is not generally accepted and our groups are no exception to this. Members of the groups individually and collectively avoid confrontation and exposure of destructive motivation and often choose destructive modes of behaviour to achieve this. In destructive phases in the group, then, it often appears that the group is delicately poised between collusive avoidance of the nasty truth and a traumatic individual experience of it.

The role of the conductor in these destructive phases of the group's life is, on the one hand to encourage the group to continue its voyage of discovery, while on the other help it to live with what it finds—With "live" here meaning, among other things, that the group retains its integrity.

In the examples above it is possible to identify various ways in which the conductors succeeded and failed in their task. The techniques adopted include: *confrontation* (examples: 2 and 3); *holding* (example 1); *letting go* (examples 5 and 6). Foulkes's notion about destructiveness in the group was that the members of the group would apply their aggression to attacking one another's neuroses, rather than one another. With this in mind he could afford to sit back and allow the group process to continue in a self-analytic fashion. Group analysis is, according to Foulkes, "analysis of the group, by the group, including the conductor." When a group enters a destructive phase this I believe no longer holds true. What one may then see is "destruction of the group, by the group, including the conductor." We are increasingly aware of this and are now prepared to be as active as is necessary to maintain optimally safe and creative groups. None the less the most difficult task for the conductor is actually to face the truth about the destructiveness of his group when it emerges.

Note

1. This is the final paragraph of Conrad's novelette *Heart of Darkness*.

References

Bion, W. R. (1959). *Experiences in groups*. Tavistock: London.

Foulkes, S. H. (1973). The Group as matrix of the individual's mental life in group therapy. In Group-Therapy: An overview. ed. L. R. Swartz & E. K. Wolberg, Stratton: New York.

Foulkes, S. H. & Anthony, E. J. (1957). *Group psychotherapy: The psychoanalytical approach*. Penguin Books: Harmondsworth.

Garland, C. (1982). Group analysis: Taking the non-problem seriously. *Group Analysis, 15*: 4–14.

Nitsun, M. (1989). Early development: Linking the Individual and the group. *Group Analysis, 22*: 249–260.

Nitsun, M. (1991). The anti-group: Destructive forces in the group and their therapeutic potential. *Group Analysis, 24*: 7–20.

Zinkin, L. M. (1983). Malignant mirroring. *Group Analysis, 16*: 113–126.

PART III

PSYCHO-ANALYSIS
AND GROUP-ANALYSIS

PART III

CHAPTER NINE

Psycho-analysis and group analysis*

Malcolm Pines

Introduction

I preface this article with an attempt which is approximate and tentative to define the conceptual boundaries of psychoanalysis and group analysis. In their present state they are provisional and I hope to amplify them in later, more formal articles.

Psychoanalysis as a system

Within this system there are definite notions of time, space and causality which were created in response to the interpersonal field, the meeting place, of Freud and his patients and which represent his creative response to the discovery and exploration of the psychoanalytic situation. This situation can be used by two persons who are aware of their separateness and who are able under the conditions of psychoanalysis to maintain their autonomy, their boundaries, under the conditions that stimulate strongimpulses to pairing. The underlying ideological model

---

*This chapter was previously published as: Pines, M. (1978). Psycho-analysis and group analysis. *Group Analysis, XI*: 8–20.

is that of the observer and the observed, a reductive analysis of the phenomena stimulated by the clinical situation. The technique of free association offers a stream of consciousness from the mind in action with the body restrained and is conceptualised as the product of forces acting upon the mental apparatus, the instincts. The psychoanalyst offers his understanding to his patient, which is based on the psychoanalytical ordering of psychological data, through his interpretations and, hopefully, helps his patient to bring about a fundamental re-structuring of his psychology.

The boundaries of this system are fairly clear. There is a defined situation in time and in space; the theory of causality is that of psychoanalysis ; the physical boundary between patient and analyst is usually indicated by preserving an uncrossed spatial area with no physical contact between the pair; the information levels are the patient's verbalised free associations, on the whole at a lower level of organisation than those of the analyst; the personal revelations and flow of affect are from the patient to the analyst; the analyst's experience of his own fantasy and affect, his countertransference is organised by him on behalf of his understanding of the analytic situation particularly of his patient's inner life and projections. The psychosocial boundary has a particular type of selective permeability based on the above considerations. The data of the systems are organised on the basis of these considerations.

Group analysis as a system

Group analytic theory has definite notions of time space and causality. These were devised by Trigant Burrow, Moreno and Foulkes as therapists, as ideological models which differ from that of psychoanalysis. The system differs from that of psychoanalysis because the data are derived from persons in active interaction. In the group analytic model of Foulkes, persons are in face-to-face verbal communication without being in dramatic action. The therapist conductor, though he does not participate as fully as the patients in his own person, is nevertheless a member of the group in-the same face-to-face position as the patient. The conductor's communications and responses are dictated by his theories. He recognises two basic levels of action, those of communication and of change. Persons communicate and both understand and misunderstand each other. Individual reactions and counter reactions occur and can be understood in terms of their individual characteristics;

underlying phenomena which can be understood as arising from a distant level, from the group as a unit and not solely understandable in terms of individual interactions are also recognised. The underlying ideological model is that the person's sense of self, of individuality, is the result of extremely powerful social forces. A person is part of a social field and has made significant inputs into the social field; the social field itself develops as the interaction of the input of the individuals who comprise it; the nature of the field and the changes which arise in it can be analysed in terms of the meaning of the communications and of their inter-relationships.

The role of the conductor

Through his understanding, based upon a psychoanalytic ordering of the psychological data and a group analytical ordering of the social data, he offers this to the group with the aim of enabling the members of the group to obtain a different understanding of the processes occurring in themselves and within the group as a whole or in order to be able to move the interaction patterns and communications to a different level from that prevailing. The analyst's activity, based upon his understanding on the levels both of group analysis and psychoanalysis, is aimed at helping the patients to bring about a fundamental re-structuring of individual psychology.

The boundaries of the system are fairly clear. There is defined situation in time and space for the group analytic situation. The theory of causality is that of psychoanalysis and of group analysis. That of group analysis is based upon communication being a meaningful information that forms links between human beings. The physical boundaries between the members of the group are usually indicated by preserving uncrossed spatial areas between the individuals and an uncrossed central area of space at the centre of the group. The informational levels are the members' verbalised free communication, group association. The level or organisations of these communications varies very considerably and can be at one time at a relatively low level of organisation and at other times at very high levels. The level of communication of the conductor is also variable although they tends to remain at a high level of organisation. Personal revelations and flow of affect are from member to member and from member to conductor. The conductor's experience of his own fantasy and affect, his counter-transference, is organised by him on behalf of his understanding of the individuals and of the group situation as a whole and may be shared with the group and seen as a significant input to the informational data. The psycho-social boundaries between the members of the group have a particular form of selective permeability with the facilitation of psychological intimacy and free informational change across individual boundaries.

Preface

This paper was given to the Danish Psychoanalytic Society in 1977. I have not yet revised it but am preparing an amplified version for my contribution to the forthcoming volume "The Evolution of Group Analysis" (International Library of Group Psychotherapy and Group Process). The paper was designed for a psychoanalytically sophisticated audience but had to cover the history of the development of group analysis from psychoanalysis as well as trying to deal with more recent developments. In that sense I feel it is a not very satisfactory compromise as a written paper.

Freud in his group psychology wrote "the psychology of groups is the oldest human psychology." He also acknowledged that "all the relations that have hitherto been the chief subjects of psychoanalytic research can be considered as social phenomena." Yet he had no interest in the psychotherapeutic use of groups though again he noted that, "Neurosis may diminish and temporarily disappear when a powerful impetus has been given to group formation. Justifiable attempts have been made to turn this antagonism to therapeutic account." Freud's observations on groups related to large organised groups such as the Church and Army or else to mass phenomena as exhibited by mobs and crowds. In the crowd regressive characteristics appear such as impulsivity, omnipotence, the increase of a contagion of affect, though he acknowledged that the crowd is also capable of high ideals devotion, unselfishness, and abnegation. Social psychologists of Freud's generation were still very much under the influence of the lessons of history of the French Revolution and of the revolutionary movements of nineteenth Century Europe. In his study of artificial groups such as the Church and the Army, he pointed out that members of both these organisations share the illusion that there is a head, a substitute for father, who by his very presence creates feelings of comradeship amongst the members. The idealised over-valued love object serves as a substitute for some unattained ego ideal of one's own. The object which has been put in a place of the ego ideal, when shared by a number of individuals who have put one and the same object in the place of the ego ideal, form a group through identification with each other in their egos. The love shared between the group is accompanied by hard and unloving feelings to those outside the group. Freud considered that the narcissistic barrier of self-love produces aversion to other people and wrote that "Love for oneself knows only one barrier, love for others, love for objects." The background for Freud's thinking is an attempt to see how the instinctual drives manifest themselves in the social life. He saw the forces of identification and of sublimated homosexual libido in the relationships of persons to each other in large groups and to a leader.

Freud had the merit of showing how unconscious forces in the individual can be rediscovered, in group formation, but as his ideas only related to very large groups and masses, they shed little light on the psychology of small groups. Freud certainly was not interested in the ideas or the development of a group therapy arising out of psychoanalytic concepts and he was hostile to the first analyst who tried to interest him in group therapy. This was Trigant Burrow who was an analysand of Jung and rose to the eminence of being President of the American Psychoanalytic Association in the early 1920s.

Burrow, little known now among psychoanalysts, is a figure of much interest. While still practising as a psychoanalyst he wrote an interesting paper on Primary Identification emphasising the importance of the child's tie to the mother and its identification with the mother. In this he showed an early and sophisticated interest in object relationships at a time when psychoanalysis was mainly instinctually based. His interest in groups was aroused in a dramatic way. A patient of his, Clarence Shields, challenged the very basis of some of Burrow's interpretations particularly of the Transference, and suggested to Burrows that the phenomena that he was analysing did not arise solely from the patient's own individual past and psychopathology, but that they were, to some extent, a reflection of the forces operating in the psychoanalytic situation itself. The different roles of patient and analyst in the social situation and setting of psychoanalysis played an important and ignored part in the transference situation and Shield asserted that the same social forces would manifest themselves if patient and analyst reversed roles. The former analyst would find himself equally at the mercy of these powerful forces despite his previous analysis. Burrow accepted this unusual challenge, reversed roles with his patient—and was convinced! He began to explore the group relations and group phenomena and pioneered the movement that has led to so many experiences and experiments in group relation programmes, in group living and in the therapeutic community (Burrow, 1927, 1928).

Burrow was deeply saddened by Freud's rejection of his work and by his eventual expulsion from the International Psychoanalytic Association. Burrow's work interested Foulkes and influenced to some extent his turning towards the study of group analysis. The next analyst of note to interest himself in the possibilities of group psychotherapy was Paul Schilder (Schilder, 1951). In the thirties he began to experiment with treating small groups of patients segregated by sex, who continued in individual psychotherapy at the same time. Though he treated them more or less individually in the group setting, he was impressed by the efficacy of the group situation and method of treatment. He noted that it worked through overcoming isolation, that patients could learn through their identification with others in the group and that transference problems appear in groups and can be worked with. The group situation seemed to reduce resistance to the bringing up of repressed material and added force and reality to the explorations of problems concerned with money, with occupation, with sex, as these are all issues that are meaningful only in social relationships and social situations. His early death prevented him from going further.

A major step forward in theory was contributed in 1939 by Fritz Redl in his paper Group Emotions and Leadership (Redl, 1942). From his work with children at school and therapeutic environments Redl recognised Freud's model of the relationship of the group to its leader needed to be made more flexible and related to actual observations. He observed that the relationships with children in a class to their teacher and to each other differed greatly according to the personality and manner of the teacher, i.e. the style of leadership. For instance, the revered elderly teacher, respected for his ability, his personality and his qualities of justice and fairness produced a group atmosphere in which respect and obedience of the class to the teacher and for each other were evident, but which could be seen partly to be based upon the fear of loss of love by this highly respected teacher. Group loyalty was high and impulsivity kept under strict control. By contrast the children in the class of the teacher who tyrannised them through harsh discipline and the evocation of fear were subdued, angry, hostile to each other and to any individual who threatened by rebelliousness to evoke the teacher's punishment. Again, by contrast, the atmosphere in a class where the teacher was young, had close relationships with the individuals and was an object of libidinal interest, was very different. Redl showed that Freud's model of relationship to a group and to its leader based on identification could be used much more clinically and flexibly, though not yet therapeutically.

Independent of each other in the 1930s a number of psychoanalysts began to think about and to experiment with putting their individual patients together in a group. In America Alexander Wolff, like Schilder, was impressed by the fact that psycho-pathology emerges in the transactions in a group between the individual patients and the therapist and that the tools of interpretation of transference, of defence of unconscious processes and of genetic reconstructions maintained their effectiveness. He influenced the development of group psychotherapy in America very considerably, together with the later work of Slavson (Slavson, 1943), and in America there grew up the school of Group Psychotherapy which could be called "Psychoanalysis in the Group." Here one can imagine a star-shaped configuration with a therapist at the centre of the group, dealing with a number of patients almost as it were individually in the group and using as the material for therapy the phenomena in the group, particularly as they pointed up such situations as sibling rivalry, dependency, aggression and the oedipal configurations. In this, they differed markedly from the approach of Foulkes who around about the same time began to work with individual patients whom he had had in analysis meeting together in a group situation. Foulkes' approach, to which I will pay more attention soon, was based not simply upon a curiosity as to how individual patients would manifest their behaviour in the group but much more upon an interest and a belief that patients in a group situation would be likely to show a very considerable understanding of each other and would thereby be able to contribute to their therapies. By readily invoking the patients as instruments of their own and of each other's therapy, he pioneered the approach that we would call psychoanalysis by the group.

The third main approach that is psychoanalytically influenced in group psychotherapy is that which can be called "Psychoanalysis of the Group" and which is associated principally with the work of Bion and Ezriel. Here essentially the therapist conceptualises the phenomenon of the group as being the manifestation of that group of individuals who in some way combine their psychic lives in the formation of a group, which then reacts to the therapist, more or less as an individual entity. The group in relationship to the therapist acts more or less like an individual. The psychopathology of all the patients combine together in the phenomenon of a group, and from this view point the therapist can legitimately restrict his interventions and his understanding to the transference meanings of the group as a whole. The work of this school is very influenced by the object relationship emphasis of the Kleinian and to some extent of the Fairbairnian Schools, and accordingly pays much attention to primitive mechanisms of early psychic life. In retrospect we can see how the interest in group phenomena by psychoanalysts reflects the shift in psychoanalytic theory from an instinctually based model of the mind to one in which object relationships takes predominance over the instinctual life. The gradual emphasis on the importance of transference and counter-transference in the individual psychoanalytic situation shows up the importance of the frame work, the setting, and basically of the interpersonal relationship of patient and therapist rather than it being a situation in which the unconscious life of the isolated individual, the patient, manifests itself in the neutral situation with the non-participative therapist.

Let us look at what Masud Kahn (Kahn) has to say about this. "There are rules and procedures of conduct in the analytic situation which we inherited from Freud, such as placing the patient on the couch, more often than not sitting behind the patient regulating the length and frequency of the sessions, etc., and inviting the patient to use verbal behaviour as a preferential vehicle for expressing his problems and inner conflicts." However, in Freud's own writings there is very little discussion of what one might call a metapsychology of the treatment frame. Kahn, using an anthropological view point, shows how Freud isolated the patient from his social frame—that is, from a position in a given society where there are inherent and culturally determined beliefs as to the meaning of illness and of the relationship of the patient to his illness and of the doctor to the illness, and placed him in a therapeutic frame—that is, the analytic situation. By being open minded and by listening to the patient, Freud created a new therapeutic frame where there was no tradition between the patient and the therapist of a shared belief in the aetiology of the ailment or indeed of a shared agreement about the potential therapeutic efficacy of the frame and the psychological processes entailed. "At a very fateful and historical moment Freud arrived and had the genius to evaluate the situation and to give it a new frame in which the alienated individual could find his symbolic, therapeutic, speech and expression." "Toward the tail end of the 19th century when Freud arrived on the psychiatric scene he found the psychiatric patient being treated as a bizarre social fetish or endured as a familial nuisance. When he isolated this potential patient into a therapeutic frame what emerged was a therapeutic situation unique in the history of human experience." "Within the frame of the analytic situation the analyst and the patient were phenomena unknown to each other with no tradition of reliable shared symbols that could help them negotiate with each other and Freud had the integrity and the acumen to respect this paradox."

By isolating the potential psychiatric patient in the therapeutic frame Freud had achieved three things. One, he accepted the identity of the patient as ill, in a way that was valid for the patient even though incomprehensible to everybody else. Instead of treating the patient as a person who had to be treated for an illness, based upon a germ theory in which the illness is an irritating foreign body that has to be got rid of, he created a situation in which both patient and analyst work towards an understanding of the illness which leads to its integration and assimilation into the patient's total personality functions. What group analysis has done, particularly in the work of Foulkes, is to enlarge the therapeutic frame from the individual patient and his analyst, to a group of patients who make up a therapeutic social frame in which not only individual processes but group i.e. social processes can occur, be observed and be understood. In such a situation, increased emphasis has to be given to plurality, to the many voices that can be heard. What we observe, and what we try to understand are processes of communication, of the ways in which persons manifest their personalities in their engagement with each other and within the situation of the group. Now if we return to the study of what Freud called the Older Psychology, of social relations, as John Rickman pointed out (Rickman, 1957), there are basically three types of language, three types of theory in psychology which can be related to the framework of numbers. We can have a one body psychology where the isolated individual is studied. Here is the model of the instinctual drive and the impact upon the mental apparatus. Freud's instinct based model is the most striking example here. If we move on to a two body psychology we have the beginning of the study of object relationships and the study of the two person relationship with the forces of transference and countertransference.

Naturally, the study of the mother-child relationship comes in here and the three body psychology situation leads naturally to the oedipal relationship and to the family situation. It is evident, however, that though we started in psychoanalysis from the one body psychology situation, the natural point to begin is that of the three body situation. No child survives unless it is born into a situation where survival is assured by the presence of a social unit. The clearest exponent in psychoanalysis of this point of view is Erik Erikson (Erikson, 1950). His re-elaboration of the stages of psycho-sexual development and the stages of psycho-social development brought together in one frame of reference the study of individual unconscious and of the enormously powerful, social and cultural forces.

The shift of emphasis in psychoanalysis from drive theory to object relation theory is exemplified in the work of Fairbairn, Winnicott, Balint and even that of Klein though on the surface she presents a reinforced view of the basic importance of the instinctual drive. However her emphasis on the importance of object relationships is part of this general shift. Fairbairn in his revised psycho-pathology of neuroses firmly presents the infant as object seeking from the start. His theory of emotional development replaces libidinal stages by the move from immature dependency on' objects to mature dependency, that is the capacity for full and equal adult relationships.

For Donald Winnicott paediatrician and psychoanalyst the human environment is of primary importance. As shown in the title of his book The Maturational Process and the Facilitating Environment (Winnicott, 1950), the primary relationship to mother is to mother as object with which go all the problems of the establishment of a basically good relationship that will help the infant to grow, to survive its omnipotent destructiveness and to affirm its capacity for love for an object and for itself as object and as container of internal objects.

As well as mother as object, there is also mother as environment, as the setting, the space in which one becomes oneself and where the developing infant can develop a crucial capacity for being alone, for accepting in safety the experience of self that comes about through the security of being alone in the presence of another. This he called basic ego-relatedness. This is something which emerges in psychoanalysis in the capacity of the patient to experience a particular type of silence, both of his own and of the analyst. Winnicott showed us the vital importance of the function of play, of creativity as an area for emerging infantile omnipotence and which enables it to come to terms with the reality of a world of dependency and shared relationship as the child moves through a transitional space, from symbiosis to dependency, and then to sharing in a world of other human relationships.

The notion of environment of space and of play illuminate the meaning of the psychoanalytical environment and even more so that of the group situation where a space created primarily by the therapist who conceives of it and then who manages the group as a special place where people meet. People are available to each other as persons and objects with whom to relate and together they explore their inner selves. The situation can function as a transitional space, the group as a transitional object.

As Guntrip (Guntrip, 1968) puts it "The part of the human environment that is most significant is the society of his human fellow being." "Personal object relations are essentially two sided, mutual by reason of being personal and not a matter of mutual adaptation but of mutual appreciation, communication, sharing and each living for the other."

As the interaction in the therapeutic group develops over time this is what we see happening. Relationships are built, though for a long time we see fear of intimacy, of self revelation and of self exploration. This long slow phase cannot be forced or hurried artificially as it is done in some forms of group technique, if it is hurried it cannot be authentic. It seems to represent the achievement in the group of the equivalent of Erikson's stage of basic trust, that earliest social relationship which is achieved in the oral phase. The achievement of this in the group is facilitated by the therapist's attitude and technique while accepts all communications and which gradually encourages and allows these communications to be understood at a deeper level, to be reacted to more meaningfully. The insertion of meaning into all communications is what Leowald points to as the basis for the psychoanalytic technique. This deepening comes from the introduction of the interpretative mode, that all communications have a deeper meaning which is elucidated and arrived at through the full interaction of the participants who combine both their emotional responsiveness and their cognitive awareness. The best interpretations, by which I mean those that can be accepted by the individual member of the group, are those that come from the other group members based upon their actual concrete experience of what it has felt like to be in a relationship with the other member or members of the group including the therapist. On this peer level the patient seems to feel safer and freer both to project and to internalise. To say to another patient "I know now that you look and feel to me like my mother in the way that you are disapproving of me now because I seem to have managed to get my father to pay attention to me" and for the other person to reply "No for me it is not like that—it is as if you were my successful older sister who is now married and has children" (even though the person to whom she is talking has just broken up her marriage and has no children and is frigid), reveals clearly how each member of that dyad his experienced a transference relationship, has become aware of the important motivational pattern involving guilt, jealousy and fear and so on and is now more in possession of themselves. This communication is not only shared by the immediate speakers but by all the members of the group who thus gain access to related areas of their own experience.

What we see in the group analytic group is the emergence of a shared experience of the enormous power of anxiety to restrict awareness and communication both with oneself and with others. The group members become aware of the role that both they and the others are forced to play in order to maintain their precarious sense of security and at the same time to become much more conscious of how limited, how neurotic such a position is. The central, overwhelming importance of anxiety and the defence against it was emphasised by Sullivan in his interpersonal scheme of psychic development.

The anxiety laden attempts to change are often very poignant to observe and it seems to be very important that groups do offer so much understanding and support to persons who are beginning to try to change their individual modes of reaction. The shift from ego syntonicity to dystonicity of character traits is indeed painful.

The essential features of group situation are those that it is a small group, a small face-to-face group with no other occupation, no other goal than that of psychotherapy. The therapist by now accepting the leader role that the group naturally invests in him, withdraws from the psychological centre of the group leading members to the task of beginning to relate to each other. It is inevitable, as repeated experience shows, that the therapist is invested with all sorts of feared and desired qualities of omnipotence, of omniscience, of heartless withdrawal, of primitive parental superego attributes and much of the working through that takes place in a group is that of replacing, through the growth of self-reliance in the individual and the whole group, those missing parts of the self projected on to the leader. Psychoanalytic theory and experience increasingly show us that the difference between the more healthy and the more neurotic person lies in the capacity of the healthy child, to move from more primitive to higher forms of self-integration and autonomy through the internalisation of parental imagos. This internalisation allows for the creation of basic structures of ego and superego which represent higher-order structures that regulate and order the primitive strata of the mind. Writers such as Jacobson, Kohut, Kernberg and others describe the process in such terms as "Mutative Internalisation" and "metabolism" of internal objects. A common idea is that functions and fantasies originally connected with the adult world are progressively internalised, the organising functions and capacities are gradually taken over by the developing person who creates through this process his own capacity. I. Feeding, caring, tension regulating and tension reducing functions of the mother in the first place, are taken over by the infant so that the child progressively becomes "he who can take care of himself," not any longer as being mother to himself but because these functions have become depersonified and autonomous, distributed between ego and superego areas of the mind. By contrast, archaic and unintegrated parental introjects are easily mobilised and projected as persecutory objects revealing the original conflicts and tensions in the infantile object relationships. The central ego or self is weakened by these splits and dissociations and is strengthened by the discovery that one can grow in the group setting in one's capacity to understand, to satisfy inner needs through the work of the group. The fantasy space originally occupied by the conductor into whom these unintegrated superego aspects were projected and from whom was so urgently demanded satisfaction of dependent needs is replaced by an increasingly powerful group, matrix—the growing capacity of the group as symbol and as entity to contain, cope and to respond to the individual's need for relationship and for understanding. This group atmosphere, culture and style of relating is what is internalised and it is that which can bring about profound changes in basic personality structure.

It is in this sense that the group can represent what Grotjahn (Grotjahn) called a Corrective Emotional Family Experience that is, the group as a family that creates its own history and can replace some of the earliest learning, experiences of childhood. The personal experience of the patient is what S. H. Foulkes (Foulkes) called "ego training in action," dealing actively with a constant variety of adaptational tasks. How early are these learning experiences of childhood and how deep does the social experience reach into the basic structure of personality?

In psychoanalysis this is classically the area of the superego through B internalisation of culture, of parental relationships through whom the child I becomes a member of the community of which the parents are representatives.

Father principally represents the world beyond the family and mother as transmitter within the family of the social code. Freud, however, also wrote of the ego as the precipitate of abandoned object relationships showing that in the very structure of the ego it is deeply influenced by the experience of object relations. Even the id, once the daemonic untamed area of instinct and of primary process, is seen by some as being structured by society. I quote here both from Max Schur (Schur) and Talcott Parsons (Parsons) a sociologist deeply imbued with psycho-analytic knowledge as well as, from Foulkes. Parsons writes that given that superego and ego are seen to arise on the basis of internalisation of the socio-cultural environment, can even the id be completely exempt from the influence of object relations?

Schur agrees that as growth and differentiation occur, these processes must involve the id as well as the ego. Differentiation of the id and the ego from an undifferentiated phase occurs by interactions between innate experiential and motivation factors. Primitive structures, presumably residues of the earliest experiences of interaction between organism and environment, represent the earliest mental structures. The effects of the primary process form of organisation are evident in both id and ego. Primitive wishes, fantasies and defences indicate the presence of primary process contents of thought in the ego. That these processes have been modified by the use of perception and memory traces is indicated by the progress from impulse, from reflex arc to wish. The physiological need becomes the psychological wish. Thought processes organised according to the primary process cannot therefore be restricted to the structure of the id and must also be used by the ego. The primary process therefore is a continuum and mental functions organised according to it range from the most primitive elements that we attribute to the id, based chiefly on primitive perception and memory traces, to such relatively complex processes and fantasies, also I based on the memory traces of objects and word representations. The outcome of this from Schur's point of view is the assumption that the id is structural and has content. This leads then to a model of the mental apparatus as an open system with the id supplied by somatic sources, percepts and memory traces and also containing the repressed. Lichtenstein and Leowald are exponents of a similar point of view, that the very earliest interactional processes lead to laying down of a sense of personal identity, the ground plan of the self. Lichtenstein speaks of the "imprinting" by the mother upon the child of a basic sense of identity that derives from her modes of relating to the infant and her methods of handling of his impulsive and instinctual needs. By her responses to him, she organises his behaviour so that she can transform him into a need and pleasure satisfying organism for herself. Leowald in his analysis of the process of internalisation describes how the infant develops an internal map that charts the outside world and which gives to it a sense of familiarity and security against the primitive fears of loss and disintegration. (Slowly, security develops that the enraged self will not destroy the universe or disintegrate into particles of rage and fragmented objects and that the circle of mother of her breast, will not split into dangerous sharp explosive fragments, filled with dangerous gases and matter, with the infant's own weapons of urine, faeces and gases).

Leowald asserts that we need a concept akin to that of a force field for the organisation of stable structures that will hold the developing self together. In the interaction process between baby and mother there is an organism at one pole, which is at a low level of organisation, which is in constant interaction with a more highly structured and organised field of motivation that is at the other pole of the field. That is an abstract way of describing the mother-child relationship. A gradual equalisation takes place whereby the less organised system achieves more order. The organised disorder within that system, the child, is located in a part of the self that is now largely unconscious, barred from exerting its effects upon both the external world and upon its inner representative, the maternal imago, and upon the developing self-representation. The emerging self is now more protected from brute destruction. For continued growth to take place, the system as a whole, the personal system, must remain open to creative energy from within (the id) and to input from without, a continued process of experience leading to learning and to internalisation.

If we look at the group as a developing and emerging psychological system we can apply the same model though the participants are at a

much higher level of organisation than is a baby. The individual participants are relatively independent adults but however, within the system
and situation of the group the members become less organised. The
very creation of a group as a psychic symbol shows, as Scheidlinger
(Scheidlinger) has pointed out, a partial regression in all its members.
Something has to be given up from within oneself to create the group to
which all belong, that is Freud's basic model of group formation.

In this new system, the therapist is at the most organised pole of the
developing force-field and the patients at the least. A process akin to
the diffusion of a gradient takes place as the group processes develop
and will continue as long as the therapist does not try to hold on to
his original exalted position as a representative of the superego, as the
source of knowledge of control and of defence against internal danger.
De Mare (De Mare) has described this change in the structure of the
group as the move from hierarchical organisation to affiliative organisation. In the process of group development, which Foulkes described
as the growth of a group matrix, the group in effect develops into one
containing co-therapists and patients and each person combines in his
own person both these functions. What was originally projected into
and contained in the symbolic representation of the therapist and of
the entity group becomes part of each member. There is thus a cycle of
projection and introjection through which new internalisations can take
place at what I believe is a very basic and deep level.

The group matrix resonates at the same level as the basic matrix
itself, as laid down in the mother-child interaction, and therefore has the
power to dissolve very early cognitive emotional schemata, that form
its very basis of the sense of self. Psychoanalytic theory is now beginning to grapple with the psychology of the self. Though many writers
did so before Kohut, it is his recent work that has made the concept
almost respectable within the psychoanalysis. Before him, such writers
as Erikson, Jacobson, Winnicott, Spiegel, Sandler; more recently Schafer
and George Klein. It must be admitted that therapists outside the psychoanalytical association have been leading in this direction for three
generations or more. I refer to Sullivan and Horney amongst the Neo-
Freudians, Jung and Adler amongst the secessionists. And alongside the
Existentialists and before them all the great figures of William James and
the early American social psychologists, Cooley and G. M. Mead.

I want very briefly to present some of the views of George Klein
(Klein) who I believe has formulated the psychology that psychoanalysis

needs to link it with the basic constructs of group analysis which is from the start a psychology based on man as a social entity. Klein attempts to present a coherent psychology of self and of identity.

He points out that there are two essential aspects of self: 1. Self as an autonomous unit, distinct from others, as a locus of action and decision 2. One's own self construed as a necessary part of a unit transcending one's autonomous action. As he puts it, "we" identities are also part of the self. Identity must always be defined as having aspects of both separateness and membership in a more encompassing entity and as developing function that reflects one's role in a relationship to that larger entity. Psychoanalysis has an ego psychology but is also in need of a "we-go" concept to complement that of ego.

Klein emphasises our need for a psychology of the meaning of personal experience rather than the impersonal "a-meaning" psychology of drive theory. Repression, a term which he uses to cover in a broad sense all forms of mental defence, leads to gaps in comprehension of a person's self experience. Dynamically unconscious ideas become organised into schemata which are dissociated from the person's self conception, though the schemata still have organising and motivational influence on conscious thought experience and behaviour. However, because of their dissociation from the central self the effects of such behaviour are un-comprehended and cannot therefore exert a feed-back effect on the person's self concept. Repression as Klein points out is not solely the inhibition of the impulse; it is that the value of an action wish, encounter or relationship is inadmissible to a schema or acknowledgeable self identity. Attention is deflected from the meaning of the experience. The result is a form of ignorance. However, it is only comprehension that is removed and not the sought after gratification, which can be pursued because of the lack of comprehension of the meaning of the behaviour. If we look at psychological process from this point of view, we can see how in a social situation ignorance becomes the equivalent of repression within the individual. Information withheld has a similar dynamic effect on the processes of the group as does repression within the individual. There is a gap in experience. Foulkes (Foulkes) wrote that the dynamic equivalent of repression in the group is that which is not talked about. It is in this form that we see the operations of the forces of what he called the social unconscious "by which the individual is as much compelled and modelled by these colossal forces as by his own id and defends himself as strongly against their recognition without being aware of it but in quite different ways and modes."

The activity of these repressed schemata produces consequences but these consequences are not capable of being used for learning, thus the person does not learn from the experience. The person is unresponsive to his own experiences, i.e. to his own self awareness and to the responses he evokes in others and the consequences of such responses upon himself, on his self organisation, i.e. the self as locus of experience. We can look at this in terms of Piaget's basic schema of developmental learning processes. Experiences related to repressed schema is assimilative learning that is, learning which does not produce change in basic schemata. Change in such basic schemata takes place when the assimilative mode gives way to the accommodative, a way which is open only to the more highly organised central self.

In a very general sense the effect of psychotherapeutic influence is a feedback effect occurring in a particular state of consciousness of the individual which permits him to understand the meaning of his behaviour, to relate it to himself, to own it and to respond actively to his added knowledge and understanding.

The group analytic context favours conditions that allow such learning. Interaction takes place in a network of significant relationships where the effects of one's attitudes and behaviour are evident to all. Blocks to learning and to change are lessened because one shares the experiences with others. Individual narcissistic mortification, experiences of isolated shame and exposure are transformed into social approval for contributing to and facilitating the work of the group through allowing personal experiences to occur and to be revealed. Feed-back has eventually to be acknowledged for interpersonal relationships to remain significant and viable. The working of repressed schemata can more easily be glimpsed through insight into the behaviour of others who manifest either the same or closely related modes of experience or of behaviour. "I can see what I do because I can see and understand what you." This is Foulkes' basic mirror reaction. "Part of me is like part of you; part of you seems to me to be like my mother or my father and what you are and what you do evokes feelings in me that I can now look at and do some work." Indeed much of the work that people do in groups consists of silent reflection on personal experiences that has been evoked by situations in the group.

Group analysis and psychoanalysis are not identical. I have been talking about their similarities rather than about their differences. I believe that their similarities are more important than their differences. Why the similarities are greater than the differences, which are technical rather than basic, has been well put by Hans Strupp. Freud gave up a medical disease model of neurosis and redefined it as a universal problem which people had to learn to adapt to. In human life there is a renunciation of part of the instincts, a building up of discipline, of self regulation and of self direction. The basic problems of human mental and emotional life have to do with socialisation. The individual is in a continuous unconscious conflict with his social self and with society. Psychotherapy is a technology for re-experiencing these early struggles, for regression and progression through a possible re-emergence from these conflicts with a more adequate, resolution leading up to a resumption of emotional development to a more adult level. Therapy is an area of re-creation of conflict, for new resolution leading potentially to more satisfactory life experiences outside therapy. The therapist defines his role and his area and confines his activity to exploration of conflict within the space that he and the patient contrive together. The patient has to learn that in the long run he is on his own that he has to rely upon his own personal resources, which hopefully are now greater through the experience of psychotherapy which is basically a process of internalisation, making something truly one's own, not simply that of identification behaving as if one were now some other person. These considerations pertain both to individual and a group psychotherapy. Some early struggles will be evoked more clearly in one situation than in the other. Some early mechanisms are more clearly recognised in the one than the other. In both the space created by the setting is vital, as important as the processes that then take place within the setting.

References

Bion, W. R. (1974). Experiences in groups-and other papers. Oxford, England: Ballantine.
Burrow Trigant. (1927). The Social basis of consciousness. London. Kegan Paul, trench, Truber & Co.
Burrow Trigant. (1928). The Basis of Group-analysis, or The Analysis of the Reactions of Normal and Neurotic Individuals British Journal of Medical Psychology, 8(3): 198–206.
Ezriel Henry. (1950). A Psycho-analytic Approach to Group Treatment British Journal of Medical Psychology 23(1–2): 59–74.

Guntrip, H. (1968). Schizoid Phenomena. Object Relations and the self. Hogarth Press, London.

Redl, F. (1942). Group emotion and leadership. *Psychiatry: Journal for the Study of Interpersonal Processes*, 5: 573–596.

Rickman J. (ed) (1957). Selected Contributions to Psycho-Analysis The Hogarth Press, London.

Schilder, Paul. (1951). Psychoanalysis, man and society. Norton, New York.

Slavson, S. R. (1943). An introduction to group therapy. New York, NY, US: The Commonwealth Fund.

Winnicott, W. D. (1965). The maturational process and the facilitating environment. The Hogarth Press. London.

CHAPTER TEN

Some reflections on Bion's basic assumptions from a group-analytic viewpoint*

Dennis Brown

To one involved in training other group analysts, Bion's concept of basic assumptions has proved a provocative thorn in the theoretical flesh. It appears to have considerable descriptive and explanatory value when contemplating group processes in committees, community meetings and so on, but not those in therapeutic groups conducted on group analytic lines. Why is this? What does it reveal of the nature of the group analysis? And what light do group analytic concepts throw on Bion's formulations? These reflections offer some tentative answers.

Though a Kleinian psychoanalyst, Bion (Bion, 1959) stated that he tried to approach his experiences in groups free from the prejudices of individual analysis. Consequently, looking for analogies, he related his concept of basic assumptions to the functioning of social groups (the Church, Army and Aristocracy) rather than to phases of individual development. In brief, he described basic assumptions as primitive states of mind which are generated automatically when people combine in a group. These states are inevitable because of the dilemma created

---

*This chapter was previously published as: Brown, D. (1979). Some reflections on Bion's basic assumptions from a group-analytic viewpoint. *Group Analysis*, 12: 204–210.

by the dual pulls of man's individuality and of his groupishness. The phantasies and emotional drives associated with these basic assumptions unconsciously dominate a group's behaviour in a way that is apt to interfere with its explicit work task and so prevent creative change and development. In the case of a therapy group, the basic assumptions interfere with exploration by the group of the feelings and problems of individuals in it. While leaving open the question of how many basic assumption states there might be, Bion named three: dependence (expecting solutions to be bestowed by the therapist/leader, fight/ flight (fleeing from or engaging in battle with adversaries, particularly outside the group), and pairing (encouraging or hoping for a coupling of individuals which could lead to the birth of a person or idea that would provide salvation). The three states, Bion suggested, are institutionalised respectively in the Church, the Army and Aristocracy. In these social groups, the basic assumption states tend to foster their work task; respectively, to organise dependence on a deity, to defend the realm and to ensure the next generation of superior leaders.

Nevertheless, it is not difficult to relate Bion's ideas about basic assumptions to concepts originating in psychoanalytic theory. The relation between basic assumption groups can be seen as analogous to that between primary and secondary process thinking. It is possible to imagine the three basic assumptions of dependence, fight/flight and pairing as linked by phantasy systems associated with the oral-dependent, separation-individuation and oedipal stages of individual development. In terms of the erotogenic zones of early psychoanalytic instinct theory these would be related to oral, anal and phallic stages of development. However, modern psychoanalytic thinking is more concerned with the vicissitudes of the emerging self and "object relationships" (e.g. Jacobson, Kernberg, Kohut, Winnicott) and with motivational systems rather than instincts (e.g. G. Klein, Thickstun and Rosenblatt). As George Klein (Klein, 1976) (pp. 4–48) put it: "The essential *clinical* propositions concerning motivation have nothing to do with reducing a hypothetical tension; they are inferences of directional gradients in behaviour, and of the object relations involved in these directions. They describe relationships needed and sought out, consciously and unconsciously and how they are fulfilled through real and conceptual encounters, symbol and action. The key factors then, in the psychoanalytic clinical view of motivation are relational requirements, encounters, crises, dilemmas, resolutions and achievements—not a hypothetical 'tension reduction.'" Kurt

Lewin's field theory immediately comes to mind, but at the same time we are obviously nearer to what Freud proposed—a bio-psychosocial view of man. An attempt will now be made to point to some limitations of Bion's view, and to integrate the valuable essence of his concept into a wider scheme that is more in tune with group analysis and some of the modern trends in psychoanalysis.

The Kleinian interpretation tends to reduce all psychological processes to their most primitive infantile origins. It is apt to see the infant in the adult, not the person struggling to develop from infant to toddler to school-child to adolescent and onwards. Anna Freud's developmental lines and Erikson's psychosocial crises are reductively telescoped into what many would see as an oversimplified scheme. Although Kleinian analysts such as Jaques and Menzies have illumined the more primitive anxieties and defences active in institutions, "man's social existence needs to be viewed through eyes which look beyond the crib."

Again, as George Klein (p. 33) wrote: "Two components of selfhood must be recognised: a centrifugal assertion of personal autonomy, and a centripetal requirement for being an integrated and needed part of a larger, more encompassing entity or social unit. The reconciliation of this dual requirement as a condition for integrated selfhood itself creates one of the most basic sources of potential conflict." (It will be clear that George Klein has no connection with the school of Melanie Klein).

In a sense though, this is what Bion meant; but his decision to avoid viewing basic assumptions within the context of individual development blinds him in one of his two eyes, for man is both an individual and a social being. Bion decision accords with his emphasis on treating the group rather than the individuals in it. It also reflects his Kleinian id-psychology, with its seemingly sharp distinction between primary and secondary thinking. Because of this we read a lot in Bion's writings about "basic assumption groups," and virtually nothing about the psychological processes involved in the work of the "work group." (We ourselves might describe it in terms of enabling individuals to discern and overcome the remaining historical blocks to their continuing search for autonomy and relatedness). Bion seems to imply that if the group is told when it is not working, it will know how to and get on with it. But psychotherapy is a form of education in the fullest sense of the word. A good teacher would not be satisfied with only telling his pupils to get on with it; he needs to sustain the working process and in a sense embody it. Ezriel, the other main influence to the Tavistock Clinic approach to group psychotherapy, as described by Heath and Bacal (Heath and Bacal, 1972), at least includes "because ..." clauses with his interpretations. His interpretations of the required, avoided and calamitous relationships with the transference figure of the conductor, suggest to individuals why they may be behaving and experiencing in a certain way. Yet, as Heath and Bacal remark, restricting interpretations to the "here and now" and expecting individuals to make the link with their current life outside and with their past "presupposes capacities that possibly not all patients have."

Robin Skynner's (Skynner, 1979) ideas about the importance of modelling as well as of interpretations in therapy, especially for more deprived, non-verbal or chaotic people, are clearly relevant to this problem). One might add that the Tavistock approach—unlike that of group analysis which encourages analysis by the group—because it emphasises interpretation by the therapist, would seem to foster "basic assumption dependence." These factors may have contributed to the disappointing results found by Malan et al (see in their study of outcome of group psychotherapy conducted at the Tavistock Clinic), contrasting with the much better results described by Barbara Dick (Dick, 1975) who used a technique based on group analytic methods.

The fact that a concept, on its own, is a poor basis for effective therapy, does not invalidate it. How can the idea of basic assumptions be integrated into a more useful scheme? We would probably all agree that, as in a family, the reality of belonging to a therapeutic group demands that we face up to jealousy, envy and a considerable degree of frustration of dyadic dependency wishes. It also requires us to play an active role in our own salvation, and eschew the defence of blaming external agencies, including siblings and parents. Within the group matrix, both reality and phantasies can be discerned, talked about and eventually understood. What phantasies underlie basic assumptions? Bion (Bion, 1959) (pp. 163–164) traces the basic assumption states to defences against anxieties springing from an extremely early "primal scene," the archetypal provoker of feelings of exclusion. If the reality of belonging to a group does involve facing up to jealousy, envy and the frustration of dyadic dependency, it is not surprising that primitive phantasies and anxieties of this type are stirred up in an analytic group. If these are regarded as related to the narcissistically painful recognition by the child of separateness from mother and of the real relationship between the parents, then defences against recognition of the primitive oedipal situation can involve any of the (at least) three basic assumptions. Pain experienced by the self as a result of frustration or disillusion evokes rage and destructive and punitive phantasies along with associated paranoid or depressive anxieties. One might propose something like the following:

1. In the "basic assumption dependence," there is regression into the merging of the early mother-child nursing dyad, in which there is no room for the reality of an intruding father or sibling; it is denied. According to Mahler et al (Mahler, 1975) the psychological birth of the infant takes place in the second or third year of life, as he emerges from the symbiotic phase into a phase of separation and individuation. (This involves successive sub-phases: (a) differentiation and development of the body image; (b) practising of autonomous functions; (c) a rapprochement crisis in which attention is redirected to mother; finally, (d) consolidation of individuality and beginning of constancy of objects and of the self). It is in the space created by the realisation of separateness that the oedipal triad comes to be recognised and internalised, and the capacity to cope with the oedipal crisis laid down. This is also the beginning of the social birth of the infant.

2. In the "basic assumption fight/flight," an intruding threat is challenged or fled from. There is no time for maternal succouring, but equally none for passive contemplation of parental sexuality or "favouritism." It is as though separation and individuation are insisted on at the expense of less relatedness. Ambivalence is avoided through excessive use of projection.

3. In the "basic assumption pairing," the sexual theme is most nearly explicit, but passive contemplation is maintained through idealisation, in which a mood of hopefulness prevents the emergence of destructive rage, and each individual can identify with one or the other of the couple. This rarely includes a therapist, for coupling involving a therapist is more likely to evoke jealous rage and destructiveness. (This characteristic of the "basic assumption pairing" contrasts with more mature renunciation and resolution of oedipal rivalry through identification. As pointed out by the sociologist Talcott Parsons (Parsons, 1964): "The parents' erotic solidarity thereby forces him to a higher level of value internalisation than that governing any dyadic relationship within the family and prepares him, in his latency period and in subsequent orientations outside his family, to internalise still

higher-level patterns of value." Revolutionary zeal could also be viewed as a reaction to the fruitfulness of tradition, linked with the idea of parental fruitfulness; we often come back to traditional values when we in turn are challenged by the fruitfulness of our own children. In social manifestations of the "basic assumption fight/flight," such as war or political upheaval, the "reality" of external threats can overshadow the reality of internal phantasy).

The group dominated by a basic assumption is one which avoids reality testing of those elements in it which embody creative strength and self-reliance, as well as of those involving hatred and despair. In the dependency group strength resides in the leader, in the fight/flight group badness resides in the outside enemy and in the pairing group despair is kept at bay only by a hopeful illusion. In the dependency group there is no chance for integration of the group's own strengths because of "depressive anxiety," with fear of destructive feelings. In the fight/flight group the "paranoid position" avoids testing out the essential ambivalence of relationships. In the pairing group assertive feelings cannot be mobilised in a way that makes the defeat of despair less dependent upon hopeful illusion. I shall give an example of a dependency group:

A recent pre-break session in a group of patients, all originally referred because of psychosomatic disorders, was dominated by a mood of sullen isolation which left activity to the two co-therapists. It could be viewed as a group dominated by the "basic assumption dependence." This appeared to be confirmed by J. following a comment by one of the therapists that members seemed to be avoiding feelings about differences between them as well as about what they have in common at this time, admitting to disturbing feelings of jealousy which she had become increasingly aware of recently. She asked for "offerings" to explain their origin. This patient had originally complained of extreme lassitude which overlay an impenetrable repression of sexuality and of jealous resentment within the family, which had begun to lift as she came to realise her jealousy and envy in relation to a brother born when she was four. L. and M. began to talk of their hatred of each other because of things said on a previous occasion. R. described how she had recently asserted herself by finishing with an unsatisfactory boyfriend, but no longer needed the group which she felt to be unresponsive and dead like a brick wall. M. spoke of realising that depressed people were overwhelmed by fears, after he had left the last group session following a cathartic attack on L. for saying she did not care for him (or anyone in the group) and which he replied to at the time by saying that he would therefore never care for her. He had experienced this as a pain in the stomach. R. responded by saying that she had felt the same sort of pain when trying to hold things together with her boyfriend, and also at the age of four when she had seen her mother feeding her newly arrived infant sister. L., a compulsive eater, reported a bad week, cut off from feelings. She had a nightmare of being with a young godchild who was (in the dream) a diabetic like herself. She had to give it insulin, but "accidentally" gave it the same dose as she has herself, i.e. a massive overdose. Commenting on it, L. said the godchild was herself; she neglected herself by taking risks with her own diabetes-control. However, turning of aggression on herself could be linked with the birth of a sibling shortly after she was weaned at the late age of two.

The group finished with a recognition of each person's avoidance of strength out of a fear of omnipotent destructiveness, leading— until it was faced—to a regression to an undifferentiated state. When it was faced, L. was able to see a little more clearly that she avoided her own strength because of her fear of murderous jealousy and M. because of his fear that if he were to be an unqualified success in his life, this could lead to envious attacks by others. Recognition of their shared anger at the therapists for leaving them allowed them to repeat their resolve to have a session together during the break as they had discussed previously; disavowed destructive sibling and oedipal rivalry no longer blocked the path to co-operation. In retrospect it seemed that denying the reality of bad fee rivalry no longer blocked the path to co-operation.

In retrospect it seemed that denying the reality of bad feelings towards siblings and parents (fellow patients and therapists in the group) cut members off from the support and solidarity with the "good siblings and parents" in the group, and prevented their moving through ambivalence towards freer interchange and interaction with each other at a non-transference level. (The history of this slow-open group was marked by a striking difficulty in welcoming newcomers).

Both the interpretation described above and the therapists' style of not behaving like "brick walls" seemed to promote therapeutic change, and the ability to face differentiation and the fear of their own strength, so that defensive weakness could be transcended. Let us return to the questions raised in the first paragraph. Why are basic assumption states seldom observed or commented on in group analytic groups? And what does this reveal of the nature of group analysis? Firstly, the encouragement of spontaneous interaction and communication at many levels probably discourages the development of basic assumption states. Secondly, the group analyst is not a sphinx-like therapist. His flexible attitude conveys an analytic and democratic spirit through modelling as well as by interpretation. My impression would be that the mere interpretation of basic assumption could perpetuate them and not lead to group work on the basis of mutuality and joint endeavour. In fact, as stated earlier, it is striking how Bion fails in his writing to state what work a psychotherapeutic group should do. Following Foulkes we would say that developing members' autonomy and relatedness, within themselves and within the group, is fostered by working towards ever more articulate forms of communication—relating in both senses of the word; making oneself understood and trying to understand the communications of others. Though members are in the same boat, they are so for different reasons. Perhaps particularly in slow-open groups, individual members not only switch into and contribute to the group culture, they also to varying degrees hold back from it, consciously or unconsciously, for reasons of their own. They are at different points of individual development and group involvement. If this is not recognised, the individual is likely to feel coerced and depersonalised by an emphasis on group phenomena.

What light do group analytic concepts throw on Bion's formulations? The two-dimensional nature of Bion's scheme is highlighted by Foulkes' multi-dimensional view of the therapeutic task as one of *widening* and *deepening communication* at many levels: (a) the level of current adult relationships (or "working alliance"); (b) the level of individual transference relationships; (c) the level of projected and shared feelings and fantasies, often from early pre-verbal stages of development prior to separation and individuation from symbiotic merging; (d) a primordial level of archetypal universal images. "It will be seen that these levels range from the more conscious objective "everyday" relationships to increasingly subjective and unconscious phantasy relationships; from more to less clearly differentiated and individual relationships"; (Brown and Pedder, 1979 p. 229). Bion's relative neglect of the group's ego functions and its work task, and his failure to discuss where and how it is achieved, are pointed up by Foulkes' central concept of the matrix as the place in which group communications are made, distortions are corrected and group culture develops. It is in the matrix that the individual can question his boundaries and re-establish his identity. Foulkes' concept of *resonance*, through which group members react to what occurs at different levels of consciousness and regression, according to their needs and pre-occupations, seems an essential ingredient of group work; in order to co-operate in discovering their autonomy, individuals need freedom to discover themselves at their own pace. In contrast, having always to accommodate oneself to a group interpretation of basic assumptions must be like being coerced into a Procrustean Great Bed of Ware. After all, Foulkes always stressed treatment of the individual; "the individual is being treated in the context of the group with the active participation of the group"; (Foulkes & Anthony, 1957). Group analysis is "psychotherapy by the group, of the group, including its conductor." (Foulkes, 1975).

If Bion's basic assumption states exist—and I believe that something corresponding to them can develop in groups operating at Level c (v.s.)—the group analytic task is to recognise them in order to help the group to understand and transcend them, as in the group session described earlier. The same applies to projective identification and transference, and group analysis is well equipped theoretically and technically to do this. Perhaps we have here a final explanation of why basic assumption states are seldom seen and commented on by group-analysts. Foulkes understood the need for balance in man's paradoxical struggle for both individuality and meaningful belongingness. His background in psychoanalysis and interest in social forces brought new meaning to Gestalt observations of the interaction between figure and ground. The analytic group allows individual and group to discover that their complementarity is at least as real as the opposition stressed by Bion. Foulkes' view of the paradox is nearer to that of George Klein, and to that of Rabbi Hillel, who some 2,000 years ago wrote: "If I am not for myself, who will be for me? And if I am only for myself, what am I? And if not now, when?"

Acknowledgements

I wish to thank the students of the Institute of Group Analysis whose lively participation in the theoretical seminars stimulated these thoughts, and my colleague Jonathan Pedder, who stirred me to put them on paper.

References

Bion, W. R. (1959). *Experiences in groups*. Tavistock: London.
Brown, D. G. & Pedder, J. R. (1979). *Introduction to psychotherapy*. Tavistock: London.
Dick, B. M. (1975). A ten-year study of out-patient analytic group therapy. *British Journal of Psychiatry, 127*: 365–375.
Foulkes, S. H. (1975). *Group-analytic Psychotherapy: Method and principles*. Gordon and Breach: London: .
Foulkes, S. H. & Anthony, E. J. (1957). *Group psychotherapy: The psychoanalytical approach*. Penguin Books: Harmondsworth.
Heath, E. S. & Bacal, H. A. (1972). A method of group psychotherapy at the Tavistock clinic. In: *Progress in group and family therapy*, (ed. C. J. Sager & H. S. Kaplan), Brunner/Mazel: New York.
Klein, G. S. (1976). *Psychoanalytic Theory*. International University Press: New York.
Malan, D. H., Balfour, F. H. G., Hood, V. G., & Shooter, A. M. N. (1976). Group psychotherapy: a long term follow-up study. *Archive of General Psychiatry, 33*: 1303–1314.
Mahler, M. S., Pine, F., & Bergman, A. (1975). *The psychological birth of the human infant*. Hutchinson: London.
Parsons, T. (1964). *Social Structure and Personality*. Macmillan: London, Collier-.
Skynner, A. C. R. (1979). Reflections on the family therapist as family scapegoat. *Journal of Family Therapy, I*: 7–22.

CHAPTER ELEVEN

The theory of Incohesion: Aggregation/ Massification as the fourth basic assumption in the unconscious life of groups and group-like social systems*

Earl Hopper

Although I (Hopper, 2003) have developed my theory of the basic assumption of Incohesion: Aggregation/Massification or (ba) I:A/M in *Traumatic Experience in the Unconscious Life of Groups*, and have clarified and refined this theory in more recent publications (for example, Hopper, 2005a, 2009, 2010), I believe that this summary is the most lucid statement of it. The key text is *Experiences in Groups* (Bion, 1961), and further discussion and applications of Bion's ideas about groups can be found in, for example, "Bion's contribution to thinking about groups" (Menzies-Lyth, 1981), and *Tongued with Fire: Groups in Experience* (Lawrence, 2000), which include extensive bibliography.

The term "group" indicates a social system that is a group, and not some other kind of social system. Although all groups are social systems, not all social systems are groups. A group is not, for example, a committee, but a committee is a group. Similarly, a group is not a family, but a family is a group, and is sometimes called a "family group." Neither is a

---

*This chapter was previously published as: Hopper, E. (2012). The theory of Incohesion: Aggregation/Massification as the fourth basic assumption in the unconscious life of groups and group-like social systems, in E. Hopper (Ed.), *Trauma and organisations*. London: Karnac.

group an organisation, a society, or a village, etc. It is sometimes useful to refer to an "actual group" in order to indicate that a particular social system is, in fact, a group and not some other kind of social system.

Actual groups might be understood in terms of their work group dynamics and/or their basic assumption group dynamics, which is a matter of the frame of reference and the gestalt of the observer of them. However, generalisations about work groups are rare, primarily because there are so many different kinds of work group, and they evince such a vast range of variation in parameters, such as size and complexity. None the less, it is widely agreed that the effectiveness and efficiency of work groups are manifest in their social cohesion, which is expressed in the integration (as opposed to the disintegration) of their interaction systems, the solidarity (as opposed to the insolidarity) of their normative systems, and in the coherence (as opposed to the incoherence) of their communication systems, and in many other dimensions of their organisation, such as styles of thinking and feeling, and various aspects of leadership, followership, and bystandership.[1] Although the dynamics of work groups can be studied psychoanalytically (Armstrong, 2005), a more complete understanding of them is best served by the social sciences.

Although the work group might use the mentality of basic assumption processes in the service of its work, the basic assumption group is, in essence, both pathological and pathogenic. The pathology and pathogenesis of the basic assumption group are expressed unconsciously in terms of the dynamics of various so-called "basic assumptions." Using a Kleinian model of the mind, Bion (1961) conceptualised three basic assumptions associated with specific kinds of anxieties, processes, and roles: Dependency, associated with envy, idealisation, and the roles of omnipotence and grandiosity, on the one hand, and with the roles of passive compliance and low self-esteem, on the other; Fight/Flight, associated with envy, denigration, and roles of attack, on the one hand, and retreat, on the other; Pairing, associated with the use of sexuality as a manic defence against depressive position anxieties and the roles of romantic coupling, on the one hand, and their messianic progeny, on the other. I would suggest that there are two variants of the basic assumption of "pairing": one concerns the conception and birth of the new and desirable; the other, which I (Hopper, 2003) have termed "perverse pairing," concerns the use of pain under the guise of pleasure leading to stasis and an absence of fertility and creativity.

Many Kleinian students of basic assumption theory have argued that it is impossible to conceptualise more than these three basic assumptions, because the Kleinian model of the mind, from which the theory of these three basic assumptions is derived, does not permit the conceptualisation of a fourth. However, using an alternative model of the mind, I have conceptualised a fourth basic assumption in the unconscious life of groups. This model of the mind is associated with the work of many of the founding members of the Group of Independent Psychoanalysts of the British Psychoanalytical Society, such as Fairbairn, Balint, and Winnicott, and is shared by many sociologists and group analysts. Its central tenet is that, although it is important to study envy, it is more important to study helplessness, shame, and traumatic experiences within the context of interpersonal relationships, which are at the centre of the human condition. In this model, envy does not arise from the death instinct, but is a defensive or protective development against the fear of annihilation, and is directed towards spoiling the resources of people who are perceived as potentially helpful but who do not or will not actually help. In other words, envy might be more of a protective defence than it is a primary impulse.[2]

The basic assumption of Incohesion: Aggregation/Massification or (ba) I:A/M

Derived from this model of the mind, in which traumatic experience within the context of the relational matrix is privileged over envy and the putative death instinct, my theory of the fourth basic assumption provides a bridge between the Bionian study of "group relations" and Foulkesian "group analysis," and, in a way, between psychoanalysis and sociology. I call this fourth basic assumption "Incohesion: Aggregation/Massification" or, in the tradition of the literature concerning basic assumptions, "(ba) I:A/M." Although each of the three basic assumptions conceptualised by Bion is, in a sense, a source of incohesion in groups, this fourth basic assumption pertains specifically to the dynamics of incohesion. It indicates that the very survival of the group is in question.

The bi-polar forms of Incohesion are Aggregation and Massification. "Aggregation" and "Massification" refer to the processes through which and by which the group becomes either an aggregate or a mass. The terms "aggregate" and "mass" are taken from early sociology and anthropology. The underlying basic assumption is that the group is not really a group, but is either an aggregate or a mass. Although a mass seems to be more cohesive than an aggregate, in fact these two bi-polar forms of incohesion are equally incohesive. They are transitory and incapable of sustaining co-operative work.

An aggregate is neither a group nor merely a collection of people who have absolutely no consciousness of themselves as being members of a particular social system. An aggregate is a very simple social formation that is barely a social system at all. The members of it hardly relate to one another. They are often silent for long periods of time, and engage in various forms of non-communication in general: for example, gaze-avoidance. Among the metaphors for an aggregate are a collection of billiard balls or a handful of gravel. However, these metaphors are not quite right, because they utilise inorganic objects, and it is important to recognise that an aggregate involves a degree of libidinous interpersonal attachment. A better metaphor would be a bowl of whitebait, or a flock of ostriches, flamingos, or penguins, the flock having survival value. If sub-grouping does occur, it takes the form of contra-grouping rather than differentiation, specialisation, and co-operation.

A "mass" also refers to a social system that is not quite a group. However, whereas an aggregate is characterised by too much individuality, a mass is characterised by too little. Whereas an aggregate refers, for example, to a collection of people who are window shopping while strolling down a street, or who are walking through a tube station in order to catch many different trains, or heading for the exit, a mass refers, for example, to a highly charged political demonstration or rally in a confined location. In the former situations, people rarely touch one another, but in the latter they are so physically close that in any other situation they would be experienced as violating one another's sense of personal space, and might even be accused of frotteurism. Whereas in an aggregate people avoid one another's gazes, in a mass they are mesmerised through staring into one another's eyes or focusing on an object that they hold in common. Whereas the silence of an aggregate is one of diffidence, non-recognition, and noncommunication, the silence of a mass is rooted in a shared sense of awe and wonder in which people feel that they do not need words or even gestures in order to communicate. In fact, a mass of people prefers slogans and jargon to careful exposition, but most of all they prefer the silence of "true communication." Among the metaphors for a mass are a piece of basalt, a nice piece of chopped fish, or a *quenelle de brochette* (in which the fish from which it has been made can no longer be recognised as a fish, let alone as several fishes), a chunk of faeces, or a handful of wet sponges squeezed together. The metaphor of a herd of walruses is also useful.[3] Of course, during states of massification, neither sub-grouping nor contra-grouping is likely to occur, virtually by definition.

It is well known that Turquet (1975, p. 103) referred to the state of aggregation in terms of "dissaroy," which was his neologism for social, cultural, and political chaotic disorder, and that Lawrence, Bain, and Gould (1996, p. 29) referred to it in terms of "me-ness." Similarly, Turquet (1975) referred to the state of massification in terms of "one-ness," and Lawrence and his colleagues (1996) in terms of "weness." Although these neologisms are appealing, in fact most social scientists would favour the use of the terms "aggregate" and "mass," and, therefore, aggregation and massification. This is not merely a matter of semantics. In fact, these technical terms cover the confluences of interaction, normation, communication, and styles of thinking and feeling that characterise these polarised states, and go beyond the distinction that Bion made between narcissism and socialism.

Group trauma and the unconscious life of the group

Incohesion is caused by trauma and traumatogenic processes. Before outlining the main steps of these processes, I will stress that personal traumas are different from, but overlapping with, group trauma. Group trauma could occur in several interrelated ways: for example,

- through management failures on the part of the group analyst, or by other events that break the boundaries of holding and containment, causing the members of the group to feel profoundly helpless and unsafe;
- the members of the group regress to an early phase of life in which certain kinds of traumatic experience are virtually universal and ubiquitous;
- the members of the group share a history of specific kinds of trauma;
- processes of equivalence occur through which traumatic events and processes within the contextual foundation matrix of the group are imported and then enacted.

Group trauma provokes social and cultural regression and the collapse of boundaries between people and their groupings. Therefore, it is only in these circumstances that the language and concepts of personal trauma are really apposite for the study of group trauma. This is also why I try not to refer to the life of a group but to the "life" of a group, conscious or otherwise.[4]

Failed dependency and the vicissitudes of feeling of profound helplessness and the fear of annihilation[5]

The first step in the process through which trauma causes incohesion is that, through various combinations of strain, cumulative and/or catastrophic experience of failed dependency on parental figures is likely to provoke feelings of profound helplessness and the fear of annihilation. The phenomenology of the fear of annihilation involves psychic paralysis and the death of psychic vitality, characterised by fission and fragmentation, and then fusion and confusion of what is left of the self with what can be found in the object. Fusion and confusion are defences against fission and fragmentation, and vice versa: the fear of falling apart and of petrification is associated with fission and fragmentation; the fear of suffocation and of being swallowed up is associated with fusion and confusion, but the former offers protection against the latter, and vice versa.

Each psychic pole is also associated with both its own characteristic psychotic anxieties and its own characteristic modes of defence against them. Ultimately, disassociation and *especially* encapsulation occur as defences or protection against the fear of annihilation, which is characterised by psychic motion but not by psychic movement or psychic development.

These bi-polar intrapsychic constellations are associated with two types of personal organisation: one, the "contact shunning" or "crustacean," and two, the "merger-hungry" or "amoeboid." These two types of personal organisation have often been delineated in similar terms: for example, the crustacean type as a schizoid reaction against the fear of engulfment, and the amoeboid type as a clinging reaction against the fear of abandonment (e.g., Rosenfeld, 1965). Traumatised people tend to oscillate between these bi-polar intrapsychic constellations, and crustacean and amoeboid character disorders are very common among people who have been traumatised. Such disorders are apparent among people with gender dysphoria and in more narcissistic homosexuals, whose characteristic "not-me" psychic postures oscillate with fusionary

identifications as a way of protecting themselves from psychotic anxieties. Such disorders are also associated with perversions, which are often
characterised by early traumatic experience.

The traumatogenic and interpersonal origins
of the basic assumption of incohesion

Thus, the basic assumption of Incohesion: Aggregation/Massification or
(ba) I:A/M derives from the fear of annihilation and its two characteristic
forms of personal organisation. The second step in the process through
which trauma gives rise to incohesion is that, with respect to those states
of mind characterised by fission and fragmentation in oscillation with
fusion and confusion, traumatised people tend to use projective and
introjective identifications involving the repetition compulsion and trau-
matophilia (that is, the love and craving for traumatic experience) in
the service of the expulsion of their horrific states of mind, and in their
attempts to attack and control their most hated objects. These processes
are also used in the service of communication of experience that is not
available through conscious narrative. In fact, traumatised people feel
unconsciously compelled to tell the stories of their traumatic experience.

When they are unable to tell their stories, perhaps because they have
no one to listen to them, or when they are unable to tell their stories in a
particular way, perhaps according to ritualised procedures, traumatised
people attempt unconsciously to communicate through enactments,
which might be studied from various points of view in connection with
various forms of psycho-pathology. Enactments are of particular interest
to forensic psychotherapists, because they involve a failure of the symbolic process.[6] Within the context of a group, enactments also involve
processes of resonance, amplification, and mirroring. Thus, such enactments precipitate the emergence of the basic assumption of Incohesion.

Patterns of enacting the intrapsychic dynamics
of traumatic experiences

With respect to the bipolar forms of incohesion, the group is likely, in the
first instance, to become an "aggregate" through a process of "aggregation," in response to the fear of annihilation as manifest in the psychic
processes of fission and fragmentation. However, as a defence against
the anxieties associated with aggregation, the group is likely to become a
mass through a process of massification. This is partly in response to the

fear of annihilation as manifest in the psychic processes of fusion and confusion of what is left of the self with another. The process of massification also involves the "hysterical" idealisation of the situation and the leader, and identification with him and the group itself, as well as with its individual members, leading to feelings of pseudo-morale and illusions of well-being. However, the first group-based defence against the anxieties associated with massification is a shift back towards aggregation, thus precipitating the same anxieties that provoked the first defensive shift from aggregation towards massification.

Thus, a group-like social system in which the fear of annihilation is prevalent is likely to be characterised by oscillation between aggregation and massification. However, such oscillations are rarely total and complete, and, at any one time, vestiges of aggregation can be seen in states of massification, and vestiges of massification in states of aggregation. Moreover, each polar state can become located simultaneously in different parts of a social system, and even in different geographical locations.

Oscillations between aggregation and massification are not only a matter of the externalisation of intrapsychic and interpsychic processes. Such oscillations are also a product of the dynamics of these two sociocultural states, involving, for example, nomogenic responses to the anomogenic forces of aggregation, and differentiation and specialisation in response to the anomogenisation and homogenisation that are typical of massification (Hopper, 1981).

Sub-grouping characterises the first phases of the shift from aggregation to massification, in the same way that contra-grouping characterises the first phase of a shift from massification back to aggregation. Sub-groups and contra-groups can become more clearly demarcated in the service of attempts to purify the system-as-a-whole; their boundaries become more and more rigid and impermeable, and silence and secrecy prevail. Intrapsychic encapsulations are the basis of various kinds of subgroups and contra-groups. These groupings are the basis of various kinds of social–psychic retreat.

The emergent roles and their personifications
by crustaceans and amoeboids

During oscillations between aggregation and massification, many typical roles emerge. The role of whistle-blower is typical of states of massification, as is the role of jester or fool. The role of stable-cleaner,

characterised by a sense of mistrust, in-fighting, and refusal to cooper-
ate is typical of states of aggregation, as is the role of the endearing but
ineffectual peacemaker. More generally, "lone wolf" roles are typical of
aggregation and "cheerleader" roles are typical of massification.

Whereas Individual Members (Turquet, 1975) and Citizens (de Maré,
1991; Hopper, 2000) are likely to fill the leadership roles that are properties of the structure of work groups, Singletons and Isolates (Turquet,
1975) are likely to fill aggregation roles, and Membership Individuals
(Turquet, 1975) massification roles. In other words, traumatised people
with crustacean character structures are likely to become lone wolves,
and those with amoeboid character structures are likely to become
cheerleaders. As Foulkes would have put it, the former are likely to
personify aggregation processes, and the latter, massification processes.
As Bion would have put it, such people have *valences* for these roles.
And as Kernberg, following Redl, would have put it, such people are
exceedingly vulnerable to "role suction," because specific roles offer
them skins of identity. However, traumatised people are also likely to
create the roles in question. Thus, this process is recursive, and the basis
of the relations between personal systems and group systems.

Alford (2001) has provided a profoundly incisive analysis of whistleblowers, to which I would add moral masochism in the form of altruistic surrender (Freud, 1922). I would also suggest that it is only a matter
of time before someone is sucked into the role of whistle-blower.[7] Whis-
tle-blowers are often scapegoated in the search for people to blame for
aggregation, involving the splintering of relationships and the state of
mind associated with this, and the violation of the sense of perfect con-
formity and purity and the state of mind associated with this.

The role of jester allows its incumbents to speak the truth, as they see
it, sometimes outrageously, often with humour and irony. The incumbents of this role often have an attractive, adolescent quality, which carries a degree of self-protection for them, which tends to blunt the acuity
of their message.

The myth of Hercules is entirely apposite to a description of the role
of stable cleaner: there is so much to do in order to ensure the survival
of the organisation! The female incumbents of the role of stable cleaner
often become the housekeepers and cleaning ladies of the organisation,
roles that they have rejected within the realms of their own domesticity.
The male incumbents are more like workaholics who sacrifice themselves to the "firm" and to an older male mentor. Stable cleaners are not

always reliable, and might suddenly take revenge on their mentors and the organisations as a whole.

The role of peacemaker tends to suck in those who become the voice of platitude and homilies. The peacemaker idealises the need for compromise, but denigrates the recognition of the importance of taking tough decisions that is necessary for survival.

These roles and their incumbents have been described by Shakespeare with brilliance and acuity. Briefly: *Julius Caesar* is an examination of a traumatised society and its traumatised governmental organisations. I suppose that Brutus is the main personifier of the whistle-blowing role, although others in the group of assassins and saviours should be considered. With respect to the "fool," any of the plays in which Falstaff appears is relevant, but the fool aspect of the role of Caliban is also important. With respect to the peacemaker, consider Gonzalo in *The Tempest*, and Menenius in *Coriolanus*. So much horror follows the refusal to face reality (Hopper, 2003)!

Aggressive feelings and aggression

Aggressive feelings and aggression are especially important in the dynamics of incohesion. Both crustacean (contact-shunning characters) and amoeboid (merger-hungry characters) are likely to personify the processes of aggression associated with incohesion. They have great difficulty in acknowledging and experiencing aggressive feelings, not only in themselves but also in others. However, when crustaceans become angry, they become cold and over-contained; when amoeboids become angry, they become intrusive and engulfing, based on their tendencies towards vacuole incorporation.

The crustacean personification of the group's rampant aggressive feelings in states of aggregation is fairly easy to understand. It reflects a sense of one against all, and all against one, each and every one.

In contrast, the amoeboid personification of the group's aggressive feelings in states of massification is much more difficult to understand. It is important to recognise the forms of aggression that are typical of massification processes. One form of aggression involves the actual maintenance of massification processes: the manipulation of moral norms and moral judgements in such a way as to control the processes through which certain people and their sub-groups and contra-groups are labelled as deviant, immoral, and corrupt, which leads to their marginalisation and peripheralisation. Also important are anonymisation, rumour-mongering, and character assassination, if not actual assassination. Of course, processes of scapegoating and more general attacks on all those who are defined as "Others" or as "Not Me" support massification processes. In fact, the fatal purification of the system of all that is different, strange, and foreign is central to the study of traumatised social systems. Terrorism involves the use of violence in the service of purification.

Threats to personal and group identity

(ba) I:A/M is an acronym for the first three letters of the words Incohesion: Aggregation/Massification. However, I:A/M can also be read as "I am!,"[8] which is an assertion of personal identity when identity is felt to be threatened. As in the dynamics of exhibitionism, an assertion of identity is not as convincing as an expression of identity based on authentic feeling and belief. An assertion of identity is based on grandiosity and fantasies of omnipotence and omniscience, which come into being when dependency fails, that is, when our parents and our leaders fail us and disappoint us. Such affects and ideas are associated with traumatic experience.

The dynamics of the assertion "I am!" are closely related to the assertion "I am not!", as Winnicott (1955) realised in his discussion of the development of identity as a function of what he called "unit status," in terms of becoming aware of what is "not me," that is, of what one is not within a particular group context. It is in this sense that one develops a sense of being both a subject and an object simultaneously, a self and another, both from the point of view of oneself as a subject and from the point of view of another person as an "other." None the less, regression to this phase of development involves the experience that one's identity is threatened and, thus, is associated with either too much me-ness and too much not-meness, on the one hand, or with too much we-ness and us-ness, on the other.

Under conditions of optimal cohesion, the willingness and ability of the members of a group to refer to their sense of "we-ness" and "usness" indicate that a social system exists, as do notions of collective identity and of membership. We-ness and us-ness also develop in tandem with a sense of you-ness and other-ness. In this, there is a shared recognition of a boundary concerning who is inside and who is outside, or who should be included and who excluded from a particular social system (Stacey, 2005).

In contrast, the assertions "We are!" and "We are not!" suggest that the existence of the group is under threat, because otherwise there would be no need for the members of the group to assert their identity as members of it. "We are!" and "We are not!" might be statements by the members of a group during states of massification, but such statements are not possible during states of aggregation, because people lack a sense of we-ness and us-ness. The reason why these processes can be conceptualised in terms of a so-called "basic assumption" is that people who have regressed because their groups are under threat enact their fantasy that they are not a group but an aggregate, or a mass, both of which are states of collective being that offer protection from extreme anxieties.

Applications

The basic assumption of Incohesion occurs in traumatised societies.[9] Social traumas range from strain trauma, such as stagflation, to catastrophic trauma, such as economic and natural disasters. Massification breeds nationalism and fascism, which are always associated with racialism of various kinds. Fascism can be understood as a set of properties of interaction and normation systems. Despite their inequalities of economic and status power, all members of massified systems become equal with respect to their commitment to shared core values and norms. Fundamentalism can be understood as a set of properties of the communication system. Fundamentalism involves the transformation of words into objects, based on the ritualisation of language (Klimova, 2011).

Although the protection of socio-cultural diversity is essential for the long-term survival of the society as a whole, encapsulated contraformations are, in essence, enclaves and ghettos, which might be sanctuaries for those within them, but might also be sources of suffocation (Mojović, 2011). Although life within enclaves and ghettos might be culturally rich and nourishing, these social–psychic retreats might also be rubbish dumps that reflect processes of splitting and projection that lead to the depletion and distortion of the "cultural capital" of the society as a whole.

The basic assumptions of traumatised societies are likely to be perpetuated across the generations, recapitulated by macro-social systems and by their component micro-social systems, and vice versa. Based on projective and introjective identifications and other forms of interaction and communication between parents and children, teachers and students, etc., these processes occur within the foundation matrices of contextual social systems. In order for people to break these vicious circles and cycles of equivalence, adequate and authentic mourning and reparation are necessary. Yet, people rarely have or take opportunities for such work. Actually, unauthentic, ritualised mourning can make matters worse. Circles of perversion, in the sense of turning away from the truth, involve chosen traumatic events and the perpetuation of sadomasochistic experience (Long, 2008). After all, if the golden rule of civilised societies and mature people is to do unto others as you wish them to do unto you, then the leaden rule of traumatised and regressed societies is to do unto others as you have been done by.

Of special interest are those spontaneous communities that emerge after disasters of various kinds, such as floods and earthquakes. Although they are highly transitory, tending to become structured and institutionalised very quickly, they evince the defining parameters of large groups. Under certain circumstances, the members of these groups are extremely altruistic (Solnit, 2009), but I wonder whether this is an expression of massification as a defence against aggregation, and, thus, an example of how people make use of the basic assumption of Incohesion in the service of survival. Knowledge of (ba) I:A/M should inform the work of government agencies and local and community authorities in their interventions in the aftermath of natural disasters.

The fourth basic assumption of Incohesion is typical of traumatised organisations, and perhaps especially of organisations within traumatised societies. It is especially typical of prisons, mental hospitals, and, perhaps, even our professional societies and training institutes in which the capacity to suffer mental anguish is virtually a criterion for admission. Large, complex organisations are especially vulnerable to aggregation and massification, because they are, in essence, composed of units of various kinds, both with respect to their membership populations and with respect to sets of roles. This involves the paradox of complexity in which aggregation is characterised by excessive differentiation and specialisation of work combined with the greater need for co-ordination of it. Knowledge of (ba) I:A/M should inform the work of consultants to traumatised organisations. The basic assumption of incohesion is also typical of large groups, in which the trauma of regression is ubiquitous and often overwhelming. Large groups are especially vulnerable to aggregation, and, therefore, massification is also typical of them. However, although we work in and with large groups in conferences, large groups rarely occur in "social situ," with certain exceptions, such as certain kinds of audience, meeting, and rally. They can be constructed within organisations in order to facilitate the consultation process, in which case they tend to function as mirrors for the organisation as a whole, and, thus, as an important source of information about the organisation as a whole.

With respect to small groups in the context of traumatised organisations and organisations associated with trauma, the unconscious life of committees tends to be characterised by constant oscillations between aggregation and massification, which is why it is so difficult to accomplish their work agendas over a reasonable period of time. The members of such committees have difficulty in co-operating with one another, and in holding a sense of common purpose. Similarly, committees can become massified, as seen in the tendency of their members to agree with one another all the time, and to intrude into one another's work. Although patience in the chairmanship of such committees is certainly a virtue, it is often necessary to acknowledge the anxieties that threaten to overwhelm the members of them, and offer the space for discussion of the personal dimensions of the work.

The basic assumption of Incohesion also occurs in small groups that meet in order to study themselves or for the purpose of providing psychotherapy for their members, especially for the treatment of traumatised patients. In these treatment groups, all attempts by patients to express their individualities must be treated with care, because "individuality" might actually indicate schizoid isolation and an inability and refusal to co-operate with others, or be a step towards volunteering to become a scapegoat. The emotional life of treatment groups characterised by incohesion is likely to be either very cold or laden with affect. Intense demands are made on the group analyst and his use of countertransference processes (Hopper, 2005b). It is especially difficult to help clinical groups of forensic patients, who are often caught in the throes of enacting and perpetuating traumatic experience (Welldon, 2009). None the less, the personification of this basic assumption must not be met with containment and holding forever, but subjected to understanding and interpretation.

Yet, the basic assumption of Incohesion: Aggregation/Massification or (ba) I:A/M does not constitute a closed system. Incessant and eternal oscillations between aggregation and massification are not inevitable. People and their groupings can be resilient and can manifest mature hope. This depends on the development of citizenship and the recognition of the rights of others. It also depends on our making identifications with people who will be alive after we have died. These are the key elements of the transcendent imagination. I believe that pure and applied psychoanalysis and group analysis might be of help in the realisation of this "project," in the existentialist sense of the term.

Notes

1. The nature of social cohesion depends on the type of social system in question. For example, the main source of the cohesion of a societal social system is the integration of the patterns of interaction of its work group, whereas the main source of the cohesion of an actual group is the coherence of the patterns of communication of its work group. The reason why the cohesion of an actual group depends primarily on the coherence of its communication system is that so many of an actual group's essential functions are fulfilled by people and organisations within its social context. For example, an actual group does not have to provide for the economic needs of its members, because these needs are met through activities in its wider social context.

2. This is not merely a piece of esoteric meta-psychology. In his Introduction to *Traumatic Experience in the Unconscious Life of Groups*, Lionel Kreeger suggested that, in essence, I had repunctuated Turquet's work, and, in so doing, changed its meaning. In so far as it was Kreeger (1975) who extensively shaped Turquet's notes into the now famous "Threats to identity in the large group" in *The Large Group: Dynamics and Therapy*, Kreeger's comment was really a suggestion that I had repunctuated his version of Turquet's argument. I think that apart from using the sociological concepts "aggregate" and "mass," rather than Turquet's neolisms of "dissaroy" and "oneness," and apart from making several clarifications of his argument, my main departure from Turquet's theory was to emphasise the importance of trauma and the relational matrix. This slight turn of the kaleidoscope of psychoanalytical theory permitted the conceptualisation of the fourth basic assumption of incohesion,

which really should be regarded as the first of the four, because it is prior to Dependency. In other words, unless trauma is privileged over envy, it is impossible to conceptualise a basic assumption that is prior to Dependency, which is based on envy and idealisation, which, in the Kleinian model, are assumed to be primary.

3. It is hardly surprising that when I lectured on this topic in Dublin, several women in the audience suggested that whereas a bowl of boiled potatoes is the perfect icon for aggregation, a bowl of mashed potatoes is perfect for massification. Potatoes are a potent symbol of traumatic experience in Ireland (and in some other countries, too), involving starvation, on the one hand, and emigration and loss, on the other. During the discussion, an argument ensued about the best way to make mashed potatoes. I remember thinking that, in much the same way that a shift towards aggregation provides transitory relief from the pain of massification, a simple bowl of boiled potatoes would have settled the argument.

4. It is important to remember that although in the study of social systems it is sometimes useful to think in terms of organismic and "personistic" *analogies*, it is rarely useful to think in terms of organismic and personistic *homologies*. Social systems are *like* organisms and persons, but they are *not* organisms and persons. This distinction is especially relevant to the study of social systems that are changing, and when they are characterised by political conflict. (Incidentally, the same points can be made with respect to the use of "mechanistic" analogies and homologies, although they have the opposite implications). Although it is not entirely apposite to this outline of my theory of incohesion, I and Weinberg (2011) have discussed this issue in greater depth in the Introduction to *The Social Unconscious in Persons, Groups and Societies: Volume I: Mainly Theory*. Also, since writing this particular outline, I have read Weinberg's (2006) discussion of regression in groups, which provides a useful review of the literature on regression in social systems and some clinical illustrations of this.

5. I have learnt from Gordon Lawrence that more or less at the same time that I began to use the notion of failed dependency, Eric Miller (1993) also began to use this term, although we were working independently of each other. Gordon preferred to use his own notion, "thwarted dependency." This is typical of innovation in the community of intellectuals of London. Of course, we were all influenced by Winnicott's ideas about development from dependency to independent unit status.

6. Consider the masturbatory movements of traumatised patients in hospital settings, such as in the films that we have seen of Romanian orphans painfully and incessantly banging their heads against their cots, or the rhythm, cadence, and repetitions of "trauma poetry," for example, in Kipling's narratives of war, influenced by life in English boarding schools, or in Coleridge's *The Rime of the Ancient Mariner*, the hero of which was compelled to find a wedding guest to whom he could tell his story. It was hardly accidental that Coleridge knew something about addiction to opium: the use of addictive substances is ritualised, involving unconscious masturbation, often with other people, involving a tense balance between isolation and merger.

7. Actually, the perceived threat that the role of whistle-blower will soon be filled leads to the process of hiring a consultant from outside the organisation. In this context, the first task of the consultant is to be wary of processes of manipulation and seduction through which the existing management attempt to protect themselves from the shrill voices of those who are at the margins of power.

8. It is ironic and of more than passing interest that, as Martin Buber (1923) noted in *I and Thou*, when, as reported in the Old Testament, Moses asked God his name and what he wished to be called, God replied "I am." This highly condensed dialogue occurred during a period of massive social trauma, at the beginning of the attempts by Moses to lead the Jewish people out of slavery. However, "I am" was also used in the New Testament when Jesus referred to himself in terms of his personifying a number of essential qualities, for example, "I am the light." This, too, was a time of trauma.

As discussed in *The Times* (2010) by the Right Reverend Geoffrey Rowell, Bishop of Gibraltar in Europe, the poet Samuel Taylor Coleridge argued that

> If you begin with "it is"—that everything is reducible to the material—you have no place for the experience of being a human person. If you begin with "I am," with the experience of being a person, then that reality is as fundamental as the nature investigated and explored by the science of material things. So, too, if God is no more than nature then there is no source of transforming grace, of forgiveness... (p. 37)

Rowell continues, "The tension of explanation between 'It is' and 'I am' continues to challenge us in our own world, and in our own lives...

The language of 'I am' cannot be reduced to the language of 'It is'." I do not wish here to open up my argument to a consideration of the spiritual aspects of identity, but I would argue that when personal and group identities are severely threatened, the boundaries between the realms of the sociocultural, the psychic, and the somatic tend to be dissolved, and there is a very strong tendency to both doubt and explore one's relationship with both our neighbours and with God.

9. The Panel Report by Ira Brenner (2006) provides a useful but limited discussion of societal regression from a psychoanalytical point of view, most of which involves the implicit assumption that traumatised societies begin to regress, taking on the structure and functions of large groups. Some of these ideas can also be found in the work of Hannah Arendt (2007). Of course, the work on this topic by Vamik Volkan (e.g., 2009) has become obligatory reading.

References

Alford, C. F. (2001). *Whistleblowers: Broken lives and organizational power*. Ithaca, NY: Cornell University Press.

Arendt, H. (2007). *The Jewish Writings* (J. Kohn & R. Feldman, Eds.). New York, NY: Schocken Books.

Armstrong, D. (2005). *Organization in the mind: Psychoanalysis, grouprelations and organizational consultancy*. London: Karnac.

Bion, W. R. (1961). *Experiences in groups and other papers*. London: Tavistock.

Brenner, I. (2006). Terror and societal regression: A panel report. *Journal of the American Psychoanalytical Association*, 54(3): 977–988.

Buber, M. (1923/1958). *I and Thou*. (R. Gregor Smith, Trans.). New York, NY: Charles Scribner's.

De Mare, P. (1991). *Koinonia*. London: Karnac.

Freud, A. (1922/1974). Beating fantasies and daydreams. In *The Writings of Anna Freud: Volume I* (pp. 137–157). New York, NY: International Universities Press.

Hopper, E. (1981). *Social mobility: A study of social control and insatiability*. Oxford: Blackwell.

Hopper, E. (2000). From objects and subjects to citizens: Group analysis and the study of maturity. *Group Analysis*, 33(1): 29–34.

Hopper, E. (2003). *Traumatic experience in the unconscious life of groups*. London: Jessica Kingsley.

Hopper, E. (2005a). Response to Vamik Volkan's Plenary Lecture, "Large group identity, large group regression and massive violence." *Group Analytic Contexts*, 30: 27–40.

Hopper, E. (2005b). Countertransference in the context of the fourth basic assumption in the unconscious life of groups. *International Journal of Group Psychotherapy*, 55(1): 87–114.

Hopper, E. (2009). The theory of the basic assumption of Incohesion: Aggregation/Massification of (ba) I:A/M. *British Journal of Psychotherapy*, 25(2): 214–229.

Hopper, E. (2010). Ein Abriss meiner Theorie der Grundannahme der Incohesion: Aggregation/Massification oder (ba) I:A/M. *Die analytische Großgruppe. Festschrift zu Ehren von Josef Shaked*, 4: 55–76.

Hopper, E. & Weinberg, H. (Eds.). (2011). *The social unconscious in persons, groups and societies: Volume I: Mainly theory.* London: Karnac.

Klimova, H. (2011). The false collective self. In E. Hopper & H. Weinberg (Eds.), *The social unconscious in persons, groups and societies, Vol 1: Mainly theory* (pp. 187–208). London: Karnac.

Kreeger, L. (Ed.). (1975). *The large group dynamics and therapy.* London: Constable (reprinted London, Karnac, 1994).

Lawrence, W. G. (2000). *Tongued with fire: Groups in experience.* London: Karnac.

Lawrence, W. G., Bain, A., & Gould, L. J. (1996). The fifth basic assumption. *Free Associations*, 6(37): 28–55. Reprinted in 2000 in *Tongued with Fire: Groups in Experience.* London: Karnac.

Long, S. (2008). *The perverse organization and its deadly Sins.* London: Karnac.

Menzies-Lyth, I. E. P. (1981). Bion's contribution to thinking about groups. In: J. Grotstein (Ed.), *Do I dare disturb the Universe?* (pp. 661–666). Beverley Hills, CA: Caesura Press.

Miller, E. (1993). *From dependency to autonomy.* London: Free Association Books.

Mojović, M. (2011). Manifestations of psychic retreats in social systems. In: E. Hopper & H. Weinberg (Eds.), *The social unconscious in persons, groups and societies, Volume 1: Mainly theory* (pp. 209–234). London: Karnac.

Rosenfeld, H. A. (1965). *Psychotic states: A psychoanalytical approach.* London: Maresfield Reprints.

Rowell, G. (2010, March 20). Credo: Verses that lead us towards a greater understanding. *The Times*.

Solnit, R. (2009). *A paradise built in hell: The extraordinary communitiesthat arise in disaster.* London: Viking.

Stacey, R. (2005). Organizational identity: The paradox of continuity and potential transformation at the same time. *Group Analysis*, 38(4): 477–494.

Turquet, P. (1975). Threats to identity in the large group. In: L. Kreeger (Ed.), *The large group: Dynamics and therapy* (pp. 87–144). London: Constable (reprinted London, Karnac, 1994).

Volkan, V. (2009). The next chapter: Consequences of societal trauma. In: P. Gobodo-Madikizela & C. van der Merve (Eds.), *Memory, narrative and forgiveness: Perspectives of the unfinished journeys of the past* (pp. 1–26). Cambridge: Cambridge Scholars Publishing.

Weinberg, H. (2006). Regression in the group revisited. *Group, 30*(1): 1–17.

Welldon, E. V. (2009). Transference and countertransference in group analysis with gender dysphoric patients. In: G. Ambrosio (Ed.), *Transvestism, transsexualism in the psychoanalytical dimension* (pp. 81–106). London: Karnac.

Winnicott, D. W. (1955/1974). Group influences and the maladjusted child: The school aspect. In: C. Winnicott, R. Shepherd, & M. Davies (Eds.), *Deprivation and delinquency* (189–199). London: Tavistock.

CHAPTER TWELVE

"Holding" and "containing" in the group and society*

Colin James

"Holding" and "containing" are commonly used and even more commonly misused concepts from different theoretical psychoanalytical traditions. Their importance within psychoanalysis cannot be doubted as they are an integral part of the fabric of what is known as "object relations theory." They have achieved a major place in psychoanalytic theory and clinical practice as applied to the development of the individual. Here, echoing the discipline of group analysis, an attempt is made to apply these two concepts in order to understand the development of the person in relation to a group.

A second theme of this chapter is a natural and inevitable consequence of looking at group phenomena through these two concepts. It concerns the relationship of the individual's experience in the small group, to the larger group, and to the outside world; to areas of experience and behaviour of people in large groups and in society.

It is assumed as a starting point that the phenomena which these two concepts deal with are vital to the well-being of the mature individual

---

*This chapter was previously published as: James, D. C. (1994). "Holding" and "Containing" in the Group and Society. In: *The Psyche and the Social World*, (ed. Brown, D. & L. Zinkin), pp. 60–79. Routledge: London.

and are also important to the development of citizenship. It is implied that in looking at the theory of group analysis or of any other theoretical model dealing with this area, we have to be able to take in other people's points of view, however different they might seem from those to which we have become accustomed. This in some way resonates with the task of the mature adult having achieved an ability to integrate the value of the "other," and yet to maintain his individuality. (Winnicott, 1958; Winnicott, 1969).

Becoming a whole person is one aim: becoming a useful citizen is another. The two concepts studied in this chapter, "holding" and "containing," should help us to understand more of the development of the individual, and from there to be able to come to terms with the value of the "other," and from there, to that of "others." In a nutshell, people need healthy societies in order to be able to develop their full potential as human beings; healthy societies are made up of healthy people.

On the other hand, in order to be able to conceptualise holding and containing, one must have a rudimentary acceptance of the idea of object relations theory. Freud certainly implied an object relations theory and the work of Klein elaborated his ideas. The basic tenets of object relations theory have been most clearly depicted by (Winnicott, 1960), (Fairbairn, 1952), Balint (Balint, 1965) and (Sutherland, 1963). A very full exposition of this theory has been presented by Greenberg and Mitchell (Greenberg & Mitchell, 1985), and Kernberg (Kernberg, 1976) has written extensively and creatively on this topic.

The theory, especially as emphasised by Winnicott and Fairbairn, essentially implies that the human subject is object-seeking for its survival, development, and maturation.

The acceptance and utilisation of object relations theory and these two concepts within group analysis are relatively recent, and we can find historical and theoretical reasons for this.

Foulkes was sceptical of the validity of object relations theory, and yet he was the man who insisted on the social kernel of mankind's existence, the social focus which was able to make sense of man's relationship with his fellow beings, and brought from psychoanalysis a different view of group-process, and evolved and founded the groundwork of group analysis. In a communication to the business meetings of the Controversial Discussions on technique, of the British Psycho-Analytical Society, Foulkes (Foulkes, 1943) contributed a long-written contribution to the discussions. While, from his experience of

working with psychotic patients, acknowledging many of the phenomena which he had described, he was at pains not to give a primacy
to phantasies and the concepts of objects. He pleaded those words,
although originating as expressions of something emotional, when they
come to have meaning they are quite concrete, and become concrete
things in the mind. Yet at the same time he stated that "the whole of
mental life, conscious or unconscious is suspended between the two
material realities of body and mind, and always directed towards the
outside world, to which in a certain sense the body itself belongs." He
agreed that phantasies were important, but not that they were "primary
motors.' He considered that regarding inner objects and phantasies as
of primary importance was a mistake, and that one's primary concern
was to analyse these phenomena, and achieve rational and scientific
thinking in understanding them.

I feel that these two aspects of Foulkes' position, being sceptical of
the primacy of the inner world on the one hand, and yet being very concerned about relatedness to people in one's outer world on the other,
were arrived at as much from the intense political pressure engendered
at the time of the controversial discussions, and that the bifocal nature
of his thinking was the result of a social environment that was rather
frightened. (That is not to say that I believe that the whole of the controversies were about that point but, in my understanding, Foulkes' theory
of group analysis *and* his stance about object relations theory imply a
duplicity of thinking not entirely due to himself).

Later Foulkes (Foulkes, 1957), in a discussion of a paper by Fairbairn
on the critical evaluation of some basic psychoanalytical concepts,
agrees that the focusing of Freud's theory and concepts of the individual makes it difficult to study man within a purely one-person psychology, and agrees that man is a social animal, and best studied in a group
setting. Fairbairn's emphasis was that man was object seeking rather
than pleasure seeking and that his behaviour is determined more by the
reality principle than the pleasure principle.

Despite Foulkes' concern about the social context of man's experience, he does not, it seems to me, answer the essential question of
the internal representation of these relationships, and does not link
up the possibility of studying those social relationships in terms of
transference. I believe that this is partly a stance against the emphasis
of other analysts that all psychoanalytic phenomena are best understood from within the transference relationship. The very fact of man's

social nature must have an impact on the internal representations of experience from early life, and if one accepts any internalisation of the social world, there must be a sense of "internal" relationships, which would need some understanding in terms of object representations. Again, I feel that Foulkes did not answer the problem of how those social relationships are internalised, and again I think that this was a "sign of the times." I believe that we can match up these two focuses, and integrate the internal and the social by using the concepts of "holding" and "containing," but in order to do that, we have to examine the nature of the internal mechanisms in terms of object relations theory: a multi-object concept, resonating with a social focus. I have previously contended that they are important components of the methodology and utility of group analysis (James, 1984).

The concepts of "holding" and "containing" are very specific within the psychoanalytic corpus of knowledge of intrapsychic functioning, and owe this specificity to their origins: the first to Winnicott's theory of the relationship between infant and mother and its repercussions for future development; and the second to Bion's theory of containing, and its emphasis on intrapsychic experience and functioning, emanating from the work of Melanie Klein, elaborated by Bion (Bion, 1962b), and by Meltzer (Meltzer, 1978).

Kemberg (Kernberg, 1980), who has for some time, alongside Sutherland (Sutherland, 1963), studied and expounded Fairbairn's work, maintains that object relations theory is the crossroads where psychoanalysis and social theory meet.

Most people working with groups use ideas borrowed from this theory, and certainly there has been a tendency in the last decade or so within group-analytic circles to begin to use and explore object relations theory and its relevance to group processes. Let it be noted that this parallels another, paradoxical, tendency to move away from psychoanalytic theories and formulations as a whole, but I believe this is due to a generalisation of psychoanalytic concepts without attribution to their source.

There is, however, a dichotomy. This chapter is not meant to be a contribution to that debate, and yet by the very nature of the concepts dealt with here it may be seen as one, and a position statement would seem to be appropriate.

In the application of the concepts of "holding" and "containing" in individual analysis, the task is to use the associations and experience of the patient in the context of the relationship with the analyst, and these two concepts are best understood in that setting within the transference relationship. Likewise in a group setting, the conductor has to attend to the details of the moment, and the setting, and not actively attempt or even behave as if he or she is "holding" or "containing" the group, or the individual in the group. He certainly might bring that with him as his contribution to the work, but it is a position, a stance, an attitude rather than a magical quality that can cure all ills. The moment-by-moment task remains in the context of what he brings to the group to examine and think in the presence of the events in the group; to maintain a view of the group-as-a-whole, and to see the individuals in the context of that view.

My main aim is to use these two concepts to help us to understand the experience and development of an individual in relation to a group.

A second theme, which I believe is an inevitable result of the attempt to explore the experience of an individual in a small group, takes us to the implication of that experience for the person in relation to larger groups and to society and to the external world at large. The more we understand the experience of a person in relation to a small group, the more, I think, we are led to question the nature of the individual's experience in relation to the large group, the very nature of the behaviour of larger groups, and the individual's part in forging that behaviour. Along with Trist (Trist, 1987), I believe that it is increasingly necessary for us to examine and to be familiar with the processes in large groups for our social survival in our rapidly shrinking social world; shrinking, that is, in terms of the immediacy to our experience of events and phenomena far away. We are becoming increasingly familiar with them because of increased communication.

In parallel with this, Isobel Menzies-Lythe (Menzies-Lythe, 1981), writing about Wilfred R. Bion, refers to the group as the "natural extension" of psychoanalysis. She adumbrates the serious study of group phenomena, and sees this as important as is the understanding of the individual.

Within group analysis there is a tendency—some might say a regrettable and increasing tendency—to see group analysis as separate rather than as an extension of psychoanalysis and thereby to miss the contribution which both schools have to offer.

Instead of redirecting, or redescribing the theories differently, and seeming to regard the individual as split in two parts, one part as an individual, a unique but isolated individual, and the other part as a group-orientated social animal, we should, I think, view the person as having a continuum of experience which is constantly evolving and being influenced by internal object relationships, close relationships, group relationships, and large group relationships.

I wish to share what I see as a definite synthesis of the two concepts, which historically have been regarded as quite separate, and which in my view give deeper depth and meaning to the underlying phenomena when taken together as different aspects of the same view.

There are in this discussion several focuses which we have to keep in mind:

1. Foulkes' description of the matrix within group-analytic theory;
2. Winnicott's ideas concerning the relationship between mother and infant, and the importance of that experience for later development of the personality, and further, for the very perception and integration of social phenomena which are vital for the social functioning of the individual.
3. Bion's concern for a clear understanding of psychic functioning that leads to a capacity to think about the psyche and its relationship to the external world, especially in regard to people in one's external world.

As a student of group analysis, I was subjected to the then current view that, on the one hand, there was Foulkes' theory of groups, and on the other there was Bion's theory: they were seen as very different, and to be kept separate. At the same time, as a student of psychoanalysis, there was a theory of development in infancy, which laid great importance on the early interaction between infant and mother, and which was emphasised as being Winnicott's concept of "holding," while there was also a concept of "containing" which was attributed to Bion, and to projective identification and "thinking."

It was with a great sense of excitement that I discovered a link between Bion's paper "A theory of thinking" (Bion, 1962b), in which he clearly depicts the infant's need of the mother's capacity to "contain," and Winnicott's paper. The theory of the parent-infant relationship' (Winnicott, 1965) in which he asserts that the infant, in his utterly resourceless state, depends on the mother's "holding" capacity. These two papers, although published quite separately, had been given at the same conference, the International Congress of Psycho-Analysis in Edinburgh in 1962. I think that it was partly my awareness that these two papers had at least been given at the same congress that led me to explore links further. I must have had in the midst of my confusion some idea that there were links since I could not discern in my own behaviour nor in that of the people around me, especially in my patients, that profound a difference between what I regarded as personal and internal mental experience, and what I witnessed as social behaviour in therapy groups and more generally in other social contexts. Whereas I could acknowledge the separateness of "holding" and "containing" within their respective theories of origin, and whereas I could recognise and respect other different cm-phases and implications of those larger theories, I could not differentiate their importance for the infant's relationship to the mother at a crucial point in development. It is vital to grasp that there is an essential difference in the focus used in these two concepts.

"Containing" refers essentially to the mother's capacity to receive, through projective identification, primitive elements of experience (not of whole persons), and to make the "contained" available for the infant *to* take them back in a modified form into its awareness, in order for it, the child, to be able the more to understand its experience—modified, that is, by the mother's functioning. It is something of an anomaly, therefore, to think of the group as a container.

Whilst I appreciate that the group can be seen as the container as clearly described by Zinkin (Zinkin, 1989), I wish to distinguish that usage from the one implied here, since this process demands a more active commitment to the task of understanding than Zinkin implies. There are certainly resistances to this process in all of us, but if these can be clarified the likelihood of the group-as-a-whole becoming a container is enhanced. This difference of opinion is similar to that which I have with Brown (see below).

Winnicott's "holding," on the other hand, does imply a notion of "the total situation," and it is the binocular view of the minutiae on the one hand, and the "total view" on the other, which makes for a productive result, in using these two concepts together, provided that one gives due respect to the complexity and different emphases of the two concepts.

In relation to groups, Bion's (Bion, 1959) theory about the phenomena observed in groups is at first sight radically different from that of Foulkes' (Foulkes, 1964) work on these phenomena. The technique of each school seems quite different, and, of course, there are different aims in the techniques. The theories are different, and so different phenomena are emphasised. The methodology of using groups for therapeutic purposes is at first sight radically different. But let us suppose that while a Foulkesian group analyst is looking at the "matrix," and an observer with Winnicott's concept of "holding" in mind is attempting to evaluate the reconstruction in the group of previously deficient holding experiences, yet a third observer (and one steeped in Bion's notion of "containing") is seeing that task for the individual in using the setting to understand his or her own behaviour, and that of others, and is taking a view that the group is able to provide that function. Can we possibly conceptualise that all those things are going on? It would be folly to think that they were not, and many more besides, each with their own descriptive piece of theory somewhere.

I have elsewhere (James, 1981) drawn attention on the one hand to the well-recognised differences in emphasis between Bion's views of group phenomena and those of Foulkes, whilst also drawing attention to marked similarities and valuable overlappings. These two theories present the practitioner in group work and the participant in understanding his or her experience in a group setting, with the possibility of something "new" being discovered.

Bollas (Bollas, 1987) has written on object relations theory and early experiences with the object. Seen as a direct extension of Winnicott's work, it implies that early experiences cast a shadow as a record of early experience on the developing person. We might know something about this experience but might not have thought it. Bollas focuses on evidence for this phenomenon in individual work, but I would extend this to our experiences in groups, but we need the opportunity to learn how to think about that experience.

I hope to demonstrate that from the background of his psychoanalytic work which Bion brings to the group field, we see so many of the very basic elements of human development and experience in the very space of the group. There is something fundamental in being able to see the very earliest phenomena of development, repeated time and again in the group, and it is the difference of approach which makes the exploration of the theories of these three men so fascinating. The consensus suggests that group behaviour is not something that "just happens" in groups, but is of a primary nature, and implies as Bion (Bion, 1959) mentions, that the individual, for his or her fuller development, needs groups.

I shall attempt to tease out the elements from these various theories that depict a similarity of concern from quite different theoretical backgrounds and approaches. I shall outline the main hypothesis of Foulkes' theory, of Winnicott's theory, and of Bion's theory respectively, in order to enhance our understanding of a person's experience in a group set up to study such phenomena; but perhaps more importantly to understand the relevance of one's own experience in a group setting in terms of what it can tell us about the individual's experience in the social sphere. It is hoped that this exercise will enable us to get a deeper view of the individual's experience as a citizen of the world with all that that implies for the person concerned, but, as importantly, for what it implies for large-group and societal phenomena.

Both Bion and Winnicott describe the dependency of the baby on its mother, Winnicott emphasising the resourcelessness of the infant, utterly dependent for long periods of time. The interaction with the concerned and attentive mother strengthens the infant towards being able to deal with dependency on her, and her "containing" and "holding" capacities further the individual's development.

It might seem fanciful to think of the dependency of the infant as in any way related to the experience of an adult in relation to a group, and yet, if as Foulkes and Bion and many others believed, the essential milieu for the individual is the "social," then it would seem that just as the baby "needs" mother in order to survive and develop socially and personally, so adults would "need" to be able to function and relate in the group in which they find themselves. Here, I believe, there is a close relationship between Bion and Winnicott, and paradoxically between Bion and Foulkes. The ramifications behind each of their formulations to arrive at that point are historic and well known. What is sadly missed so often, is the fact that in recognising that common point, we might be able to understand the differences, not as polarised and in conflict, but very much as different emphases and aspects of a common whole.

To facilitate this I shall look at the central concept of the group matrix according to Foulkes, and then the development of the concept of holding according to Winnicott, and finally the concept of containing or container/contained according to Bion.

Whilst we may make links between these three theories, I wish to share my experience that only when I can view each in the context within which they developed can I see the similarities and respect the differences. I believe that only from that position can we make further progress in understanding group processes from a psychodynamic perspective.

Foulkes' group matrix

The interacting psychological processes taking place in a group involve the individuals in different specific ways and constellations: "Just as the individual's mind is a complex of interacting processes (Personal Matrix), mental processes interact in the concert of the group (Group Matrix)" (Foulkes, 1973).

Foulkes saw the essence of man as being social and not individual. This view has been extensively studied and elaborated by Behr and Hearst (Behr & Hearst, 1982), who point out that it is the group which is the basic psychological unit, though the biological unit is the individual organism. The matrix, as seen by Behr and Hearst, is the basis of all relationships and communication, a web of intrapsychic, interpersonal, and transpersonal interrelationships within which the individual is conceptualised as a nodal point. Foulkes thought that in group analysis what is reproduced is the matrix of evolving personality. He saw the group-analytic method as imposing within the group setting the individual's task of sorting out his or her relationship to other people, to the group-as-a-whole and to the leader. The group matrix is the operational basis of all relationships and communications. Foulkes conceptualised the individual as a nodal point in a network of relationships, borrowing an analogy from Goldstein of a neuron being the nodal point in a total network of the nervous system, which always reacts and responds as a whole. An aphorism of Foulkes' was, "As in the case of the neuron in the nervous system so is the individual suspended in the group matrix."

From what I have said already in relation to Winnicott's concept of holding and Bion's concept of containing, each with their emphases on the role of the mother at an early phase of development, I find it interesting to note that the Oxford English Dictionary refers to the origin of the word "matrix" from the Latin for "womb," and particularly to the definition of a matrix as "a place or medium in which something is bred, produced, or developed." I trust that this brief view of Foulkes' concept of the matrix, which can be compared particularly with Andrew Powell's (Powell, 1994) chapter, will be sufficient for the present time.

Winnicott's holding

An important aspect of Winnicott's concern about infant development is the emerging of a sense of the social, of the world outside of oneself, of oneself and mother as a pair in relation to other members of the family, but unquestionably also of a sense of a social sphere that is important. Throughout his work he is concerned with the differentiation of "self, a self in relation to an "other" and a self in relation to other people in the world. In both his papers "Psychoses and child care" (Winnicott, 1952) and "Transitional objects and transitional phenomena" (Winnicott, 1953), he talks of the need to recognise three areas of experiencing:

> It is generally acknowledged that a statement of human nature in terms of inter-personal relationships is not good enough even when the imaginative elaboration of function and the whole phantasy both conscious and unconscious, ... are allowed for.... Of every individual who has reached to the stage of being a unit with a limiting membrane and an outside and an inside, it can be said that there is an inner reality to that individual, an inner world that can be rich or poor and can be at peace or in a state of war.
>
> (1951: 230)

Winnicott pointed out that while being able to differentiate between an inner and outer reality, there was also a need to recognise a third area. The third part of the life of a human being is an intermediate area of experiencing, to which inner reality and external life both contribute. Winnicott's concept of the transitional object is the beginning of this exploration about this intermediate or third area of experiencing, and it is this statement that for me forms the link between Winnicott's ideas to those of Foulkes. In a previous paper (James, 1982), I attempted to draw similarities between Winnicott's descriptions of the experiencing of this third area and the links which Foulkes makes about the interrelatedness of people in a group, to emphasise the similarities of the extension of Winnicott's concepts of the transitional object and transitional phenomena, and their importance in the gaining of a sense of the "social," to a recognition of the importance of Foulkes' concept of the matrix as a construct with considerable explanatory power to describe the experience of a person in a group. On the other hand, in making this link between certain aspects of Winnicott's theory and certain aspects of those of Foulkes, I was mindful of the impact of development on the social sense on the one hand, and of the repetition of early experiences in group settings as portrayed by Foulkes' theory, on the other. It was also this seemingly similar emphasis with very different backgrounds which led me to attempt to make a further link with Bion's theories.

It is from the concept of a "shared illusory space" between infant and mother, which Winnicott studied and described, that later (Winnicott, 1965) led him to examine in more detail the relationship between parent and infant, and to develop the concept of "holding." He accepts that to begin with we have to see the baby not as such, but as part of an infant-environment unit, and goes on to delineate the relationship and the dependency on "mother" implicit in the infant's condition. His well-known phrase "there-is no such thing as a baby," comes from his assertion that the inherited potential of the infant cannot become an infant unless linked to maternal care. The concept of "holding" is used by Winnicott to denote not just the physical holding of the infant, but the total provision of physical and emotional concern which the ordinary mother gives to her infant. He implies a very important phase in development, subsequently leading to a relationship, in his phrase "the total environmental provision, prior to a concept of 'living with'" (Winnicott, 1960: 43).

In the earliest phases he saw the infant as being maximally dependent on the mother, and he described, in utmost detail, the delicate state of moving from utter dependency to relative dependency, stressing throughout the force in the individual always, normally, moving towards independence.

Winnicott saw that the infant was able eventually to clarify the boundary between inner reality and external reality *from a position of shared reality*; a deficit in the capacity to share from the mother's side or on the infant's part led to a deficit in the later development of independence, and interdependence. The latter term refers to the adult capacity to be able to "contribute-in" to relationships, as well as to receive from others. This feature of his work is pertinent to the task of an individual in a group relating to other members of the group, and to the group-as-a-whole. Quite often, people have difficulty in this task in group settings, because of earlier difficulties, which is not to say that relating in group settings is ever easy for any adult.

In his paper on transitional objects and transitional phenomena, Winnicott (Winnicott, 1953) was concerned with the earliest phases of human development, and maintained that the events in these earliest phases influence profoundly the organisation and development of the personality, referring particularly to the capacity for separation and individuation, and to the ability to develop a true sense of self. Winnicott was particularly concerned with the process involving the development of a sense of self, as opposed to a "false-sense" of self, which he saw as being present in many disturbed patients. A sense of self would be seen as a requirement for the capacity to relate to other selves, and this aspect of his work is particularly pertinent to our present task of understanding the nature of relationships with others, especially in a group setting.

Winnicott's concern with the intermediate area of experiencing, the shared illusory space, is of particular importance in our understanding of shared group experience.

His emphasis on the importance of the "carer"—namely, the mother—in the earliest phases of life, resonates into our adult social experience; we need to be part of that shared experience, and the adult "carer" part of us needs to guard and enhance the value of that shared space.

Another way to conceptualise the link is to say that in the holding phase the infant is maximally dependent, and this varies from absolute to relative dependency, and towards independence. Winnicott's sustained emphasis of the similarity between infant care and psychoanalytic care is a feature of his contribution to our understanding of the importance of environmental factors, from the earliest phases of life, in contributing to and maintaining the possibility of normal mental health.

In his extension of the concept of the transitional object, Winnicott (Winnicott, 1971) wrote of cultural experience as being located in the space between the individual and the environment. This lends itself to be looked at in the context of the group and also implies the importance of experiencing oneself as part of a group in order to be able to experience "culture."

Bion's containing

Wilfred Bion (Bion, 1959; Bion, 1962a; Bion, 1962b); (Bion, 1963; Bion, 1970; Bion, 1979) approached this whole area from a different background, and though he had more direct experiences with groups than Winnicott, there are some close links between the two theories. I do not wish to make these theories appear similar to each other. This would be a simplistic view, since the backgrounds from which these concepts originate are complex and quite different from each other. I am not in this presentation going to examine these differences in approach and theories between Foulkes and Bion in relation to phenomena in groups *per se*.

There is much work to be done in this area. Brown (Brown, 1985) has made a clear contribution to this task but looks at the differences between Foulkes and Bion in terms of approach and technique, whilst I believe that there are similarities and differences between Bion and Foulkes. Here I am trying to look at phenomena that might underlie those differences. Bion (Bion, 1952) stated his intention to show that the adult in his or her contact with the complexities of life in a group, resorts, in what may be a massive regression, to mechanisms typical of the earliest phases of emotional life, and pointed out that the adult must establish contact with the emotional life of the group in which he or she lives. He saw this task as *appearing as formidable to the adult as the relationship with the breast appears to be with the infant.*

I am going to look at the psychoanalytical background of Bion's theories in order to clarify links with Winnicott's theories about development and with Foulkes' theories about the matrix, in an attempt to extend and deepen our concept of the matrix not merely as something social and external but having profound roots in the inner world of the individual, involved in the matrix and in the earliest phases of development.

Central throughout Bion's work is the concept of projective identification (Klein, 1946). This refers to a group of phantasies and accompanying object relations having to do with the ridding of the self of its unwanted aspects and the depositing of those unwanted "parts" into another person, and, finally, with the "recovery" of a modified version of what was extruded. In his "A theory of thinking" (Bion, 1962b), Bion outlines a scheme that is at first sight complicated partly because of the language he uses, but which, inherited potentialities notwithstanding, implies that the capacity to develop a thinking apparatus depends on the interaction in the earliest phases of life with mother. Here there is a similarity to Winnicott's theory. The outcome, however, of Bion's formulations is radically different.

As a model, Bion uses the hypothesis that the infant has an inborn disposition, a preconception corresponding to an expectation, of the breast. When a preconception such as this is brought into contact with the realisation that approximates to it, the mental outcome is a conception.

Bion puts this in another way: the preconception of an inborn expectation of the breast, the prior knowledge of a breast, the empty thought—
this preconception mates with an awareness of the realisation when the
infant is brought into contact with the breast itself, and this mating is
synchronous with the development of a conception.

Bion further uses this model to serve for the hypothesis that every
junction of a preconception with its realisation produces a conception,
and that, therefore, a conception will be expected to be constantly con-
joined with an emotional experience of satisfaction. Bion, however,
limits the term "thought" to a mating of a preconception with a frustration. Thus he proposed that an infant whose expectation of the breast
is mated with the realisation of no-breast-available-for-satisfaction/
experiences a sense of "no-breast" or "an absent breast" inside. Then
the infant has to make a decision, either to evade the frustration or to
modify it, and this step depends on the infant's capacity for toleration
of frustration and on the relationship with the mother. If the capacity
for toleration of frustration is sufficient, then no-breast-inside becomes
a thought, and an apparatus for thinking it develops.

Although this hypothesis seems complicated, if we follow the idea
that a personality capable of maturity ultimately recognises a notion of
an absence and emptiness inside, or a "no-breast-inside" as a bad internal object, then this personality ultimately recognises the bad internal
no-breast as a thought. A capacity for tolerating frustration thus enables
the psyche to develop thoughts as a means by which the frustration that
is tolerated is itself made more tolerable.

If, however, the capacity for toleration of frustration is inadequate,
the bad internal no-breast confronts the psyche with the need to decide
between modification or evasion. The end result of this part of Bion's
hypothesis is that all thoughts are treated as though they were indistinguishable from bad internal objects. What should be a "thought," the
product of the juxtaposition of a preconception and a negative realisation, becomes a bad object indistinguishable from a thing in itself and
fit only for evacuation. Consequently, the development of an apparatus for thinking is disturbed, and instead a hypertrophic development
of the apparatus for projective identification takes place. If frustration
can be tolerated, the mating of conception and realisation, whether
negative or positive, initiates procedures necessary to learning by experience. Bion relates the development of the capacity to tolerate frustration as being intimately linked with the contact and perception of the

relationship and experience of, and with, the mother. If the mother can appear to contain the evacuated elements in this process, they can be re-experienced, re-integrated and a capacity for development of thinking grows. If, however, the mother cannot tolerate the projected elements, the infant is reduced to having to continue projective identification, instead of developing thinking, with increasing force and frequency.

In *Elements of Psychoanalysis* (Bion, 1963), Bion postulates that the most primitive experience is governed by what he calls "beta-elements," which are the raw elements of sensuous and emotional experience in which psychical and physical are indistinguishable, and which lend themselves only to projective identification. These elements are experienced in a concrete manner, as if they are lumps of faeces or bad emotions, which are evacuated into a breast that is not there. As the infant does this, the mother, the good object, turns no-breast into a breast and replaces, as far as the infant is concerned, the frightening, anxious experience into a more positive one by virtue of the feeding and holding situation which she provides. The infant experiences, according to Bion's postulate, that the beta-elements, the primitive-experience elements, are transformed by the breast, which is shorthand for the total experience with the mother at that point, into alpha-elements which have psychic meaning and which can be stored, repressed, elaborated further and symbolised. These are the elements of dream-thoughts, and the transformation from beta to alpha gives sense and meaning to the infant's experience, via the mother's response to the infant's projection.

Bion's conception of the container and the contained is a model for an object helping the infant to sort out those aspects of communication that are at first inchoately emotional. In order for projective identification to occur, there must be a conception of a container into which the projection can be sent. In other words (Grotstein, 1981), if the maternal response to the infant's need is adequate, the infant can re-introject the breast as a container capable of performing other functions, the function of converting beta-elements into alpha-elements. This model of the conjunction of the container and the contained extends the basic model for the development of thought, to the perception of relationship and to transference and countertransference interplay. It provides the basis for a differentiation between the psychotic and non-psychotic functioning of the personality. The relationship between the container and the contained can be symbiotic, providing a basis of fruitful relationships and learning from experience, or it can be experienced as mutually destructive.

The assumption from Winnicott's concept of holding is that the maternal preoccupation towards the needs of the infant supports and contains the inherited potentialities of the infant, towards the development and strengthening of the ego and towards the development of independence (which, of course, is never complete in any human life).

Bion's theory, on the other hand, focuses on the minutiae of the developments of either the capacity to tolerate frustration and to use benign projective identification to model on the mother's alpha-function towards the development of alpha-function independently, and from there to be able to develop thoughts about one's own experience of frustration; *or*, if the mother's containing function is deficient, then projective identification used by the infant remains or becomes excessive, and there is a distortion in the development of a capacity for containing thoughts.

In Winnicott's (Winnicott, 1969) article on "The use of an object and relating through identification," we arrive at a position very similar to Bion's, in which the development of a capacity to use the mother in order to develop oneself depends on the mother's ability to survive (the infant's hate). The holding function of the mother is very close here to the containing function of the mother, in Bion's terms.

The importance for group analysis of these theories, and the phenomena that they attempt to describe, is that, implied within Foulkes' concept of the social context of the individual's life, are elements of both Winnicott's "holding" function and Bion's "containing" function. It is my own contention that the psychoanalytic emphasis of Bion's theory and Winnicott's theory respectively will enable us to understand and utilise more fully our understanding of the individual's experience within the matrix.

The essentially psychoanalytic emphasis of each of these theories rests on the inner psychic experience of the individual in his or her task, within the group, of maintaining a balanced view of both inside and outside.

While these phenomena are universal in small groups, they are also prevalent in larger groups, whose very source and nature prevent initially their being regarded as anything remotely likely to lead to an understanding of these experiences.

It is interesting to learn from De Mare (De Maré, 1991) of his hypothesis that it is only in a median group or even perhaps a larger group, that true "dialogue" can take place. I assume that this is after the individuals have become accustomed to the threat of the more anxious aspects of larger gatherings. Friere (Friere, 1972) suggests that dialogue can only take place when the person on the receiving end of one's communications is regarded as a human being.

Friere's concern is with the releasing of human capacities which are otherwise repressed by societies, and particularly by a failure to communicate social experience in language. It is a contention of Trist (personal communication, 1987) that for our very survival in the world as it is today, we as human beings learn to communicate in larger and larger groups, and that our citizenship will be enhanced by the experience, and by our increasing capacity to serve as representatives for larger and larger groups. This resonates for me with the "carer" role of the participant in a small group, and is based on the divergence between being afraid and anxious of the "group," whilst at the same time being connected, and seeking group experience. Is this not in line with what Bion describes of the infant's experience with the mother (albeit represented initially by the breast), and Winnicott's contention of the infant's and therefore the eventual adult's dependence on the capacity of the mother to help the infant from the stage of being resourceless and dependent, to being able to use the "object" in order to enhance its sense of self, and to participate in experience with an "other" and "others" for its very own development?

But why are larger groups more anxious places, especially if we follow some of the lines of thought developed here? If there is a need for group and social experience, why are people anxious about it? Although the unconscious destructive forces in human beings must be accepted and worked with, is there not a problem in terms of organisation and development of human groupings which might not yet have enabled us to see the value of being able to be comfortable in large-group settings? The study of the large group can be fruitful (see Kreeger, 1975). Turquet (Turquet, 1975), wrote about the anxieties in the large group as being worthy of study for what one learns not only about the individual, but on the more positive side, what of value one learns of the large group, for itself, and for the individual's benefit.

In appreciating the impact of Bion's work, not so much on groups as in his prophetic sense of going to the heart of the matter, Lawrence (Lawrence, 1985) describes the frustrating work of "learning" in groups. In describing the learning experience, specifically in relation to working conferences, the emphasis is on the use of groups for learning—learning the dangers of some group phenomena and of the immense value of others, leading to a respect and valuing of the group as a necessary means of challenging the individual to trust the personal-group inter-action. There are echoes here, again, of the frustration which the infant experiences in Bion's terms when a satisfaction which is expected is not achieved.

Lawrence continues the theme to the learning about, or forging of, the capacity to overcome the anxieties and see further than one might dare imagine; of the value of the group, not as representing a mother-breast-container-comforter, but as a source of the capacity to strengthen one's resolve to understand immensely complicated issues concern-ing the interaction. There are a myriad links from this position to other aspects of large-group phenomena, and this links with De Mare's ideas referred to above.

This has been taken a step further in looking at the impact of dreams, not in small groups, but in larger gatherings (Lawrence, 1991). In follow-ing a theme which he discovered in the relevance of the use of dreams in a study group, his explorations led to investigation of the impact of local and more widespread interpersonal and social issues which impinge *into* one's very dreams. The residues of the day described by Freud might not be "just" residues; they may be deep manifestations of the impact of the social matrix on the more personal "manifest" content of a person's dreams. The "social dream matrix" is a pertinent way of exploring further the interaction of the person with the group, and vice versa.

Foulkes' notion of individuals being connected with a matrix in an ongoing group might be merely the start of our understanding of the importance of our interaction with the "social" environment, with what Foulkes called the "foundation matrix."

Turquet (Turquet, 1975) writes of his work in large-group settings. While he emphasises the difficulties and anxieties which people expe-rience in such settings, his overall view is of the value of the learning experience in such settings. Like Khaleelee and Miller (Khaleelee & Miller, 1985), Turquet reports his experience largely from training set-tings organised with the specific purpose of studying and learning about the difficulties of how organisations function.

Khaleelee and Miller report on their experience in the Group Rela-tions Training Programme of the Tavistock Institute of Human Relations (the Leicester Conference). There is evidence in their work in studying society and in consulting to organisations, from an organisation-as-a-whole perspective, of the concern which the individual has about society. They say that "by defining a task boundary it is possible to evoke, experience and observe societal dynamics in a group; society and the group are present in the individual." This resonates with Armstrong's notion of "the organisation in one's head": a notion that we carry in us a view of the organisation in which we find ourselves, which influences our perception of the phenomena (Armstrong, 1991a; Armstrong, 1991b; Armstrong, 1992).

The task of such programmes is to attempt to understand and encourage participants to understand this experience in large settings. The evidence is that the individual's understanding of themselves influences the actual phenomena experienced. Much of the time people are not consciously in touch with these phenomena. The anxiety due to the awesomeness and awareness of our deprivation if we are not in touch with this group element is an essential component of our existence.

Concluding comments

I shall finish by tracing, as I see it, the line of development from the most dependent infant to the most mature citizen. I do this in order to understand some of the things societies need in order to function optimally.

The sequence which Bion describes in his paper on the theory of thinking, involves modification of frustration by the individual. This, as I have summarised, depends on mother's containing capacity. The frustration which is tolerated makes way for the development of thoughts. Thoughts have, according to Bion, to be worked on to make them available. For thoughts to be translated into action involves "publication," which is regarded by Bion to be the making of sense-data available to consciousness. Because the individual is a political animal and, according to Bion, cannot find fulfilment outside a group nor satisfaction of any emotional drive without expression of its social component, so, as the infant can tolerate frustration and begin to "think" about his or her experience, so the citizen has to be able to understand his or her experience in relation to society. The more that this is achieved, the more effective and valuable society becomes.

Alongside our social needs we have our narcissistic needs and these have to be balanced in our roles as citizens. Whereas the individual depends on the group or society, society functions in proportion to the involvement of the individuals of which it is made up.

We would all agree that the aim of the individual is to develop an identity, a sense of self, and to be able to relate to others with optimum pleasure and responsibility. The parallel between the infant's relationship to its "container" or its holding environment on the one hand, and that of the individual to the group, on the other, is to my mind self-evident. I believe this analogy can also be applied to larger systems, and see a need for each "citizen" to be comfortable and responsible in that role.

From much of the work of the authors quoted in this chapter, one gets a sense of the interdependence of the individual, the group, and society. This was stated eloquently by Joan Riviere in 1936:

> Another point, which economists realise much better perhaps than other people do, is the degree of dependence of the human organism on its surroundings. In a stable political and economic system there is a great deal of apparent liberty and opportunity to fulfil our own needs, and we do not as a rule feel our dependence on the organisation in which we live—unless, for instance, there is an earthquake or a strike! Then we may realise with reluctance and often with resentment that we are dependent on the forces of nature or on other people to a terrifying extent. Dependence is felt to be dangerous because it involves the possibility of privation. An unrealisable desire for individual self-sufficiency may arise, and an illusion of an independent liberty may under certain conditions of life be indulged in as a pleasure in itself.
>
> (Riviere (1936) in Hughes (Hughes, 1991): 171).

References

Armstrong, D. G. (1991a). *The Institution in the Mind: Reflections on the relation of psychoanalysis to work with institutions*. The Grubb Institute: London.

Armstrong, D. G. (1991b). *Thoughts beyond and thoughts Free: Refletions on metal processes in Groups*. The Grubb Institute: London.

Armstrong, D. G. (1992). Names, thoughts and lies: The relevance of Bion's later thinking to understanding Group relations. In (Anonymous), p. 26.

Balint, M. (1965). *Primary love and psychoanalytic technique*. Tavistock Publications: London.

Behr, H. L. & Hearst, L. E. (1982). Group Analysis: A Group Psychotherapeutic Model Developed by S. H. Foulkes. In (Anonymous), pp. 1–13.

Bion, W. R. (1952). Group dynamics: A re-view. In (Anonymous), pp. 235–247.

Bion, W. R. (1959). *Experiences in groups*. Tavistock: London.

Bion, W. R. (1962a). *Learning from experience*. Heinemann: London.

Bion, W. R. (1962b). The psycho-analytic study of thinking; a theory of thinking. In (Anonymous), pp. 306–310.

Bion, W. R. (1963). *Elements of psychoanalysis*. Heinemann: London.

Bion, W. R. (1970). *Attention and interpretation*. Tavistock: London.

Bion, W. R. (1979). *A memoir of a future book 3: The Dawn of Oblivion*. Clunie Press: Perthshire.

Bollas, C. (1987). *The shadow of the object: Psychoanalysis of the unthought known*. Free Association Books: London.

Brown, D. G. (1985). Bion and Foulkes: Basic assumptions and beyond. In *Bion and Group Psychotherapy*, (ed. M. Pines), Routledge: London.

De Mare P., Robin Piper & Sheila Thompson (Eds). (1991). *Koinonia: From hate, through dialogue, to culture in the large group*. Karnac: London.

Fairbairn, W. R. D. (1952). *Psychoanalytic studies of the personality*. Routledge/Tavistock: London.

Foulkes, S. H. (1957). Psychoanalytic concepts and object relations theory: Comments on a paper by Fairbairn. In (Anonymous), pp. 324–329.

Foulkes, S. H. (1943). The second discussion of scientific controversies. In *The Freud Klein Controversies 1941–1945*, (Anonymous), The Institute of Psycho-Analysis and Routledge: London.

Foulkes, S. H. (1964). *Therapeutic group analysis*. Allen & Unwin: London.

Foulkes, S. H. (1973). The Group as matrix of the individual's mental life in group therapy. In *Group Therapy—An Overview*, (ed. L. R. &. S. E. K. Ed. Wolberg), Stratton: New York.

Friere, P. (1972). *Pedagogy of the oppressed*. Penguin Books: Harmondsworth.

Greenberg, J. R. & Mitchell, S. A. (1985). *Object relations in psychoanalytic theory*. Harvard University Press: Cambridge, MA.

Grotstein, K. (1981). *Splitting and projective identification*. Jason Aronson: New York.

Hughes, A. (1991). *The inner world of Joan Riviere, Collected Papers*. Karnac: London.

James, D. C. (1981). W. R. Bion's contribution to the field of group therapy. In: *Group and family therapy: An overview*. (ed. Ed. Wolberg & Aronson), Brunner/Mazel: New York.

James, D. C. (1984). Bion's "containing" and Winnicott's "holding" in the context of the group matrix. *International Journal of Group Psychotherapy*, 34: 201–213.

Kernberg, O. F. (1976). *Object relations theory and clinical psychoanalysis*. Jason Aronson: New York.

Kernberg, O. F. (1980). *Internal world and external reality.* Jason Aronson: New York.

Khaleeleee, O. & Miller, E. (1985). Beyond the small group. In: *Bion and Group Psychotherapy*, (ed. M. Pines), Routledge & Kegan Paul: London.

Klein, M. (1946). Notes on some schizoid mechanisms. In: *The Writings of Melanie Klein*, (Anonymous), Hogarth Press: London.

Kreeger, L. C. (1975). *The large group: Dynamics and Therapy.* Constable: London.

Lawrence, W. G. (1985). Beyond the frames. In: *Bion and group psychotherapy*, (ed. M. Pines), Routledge and Kegan Paul: London.

Lawrence, W. G. (1991). Won from the void and Formless infinite: Experiences of Social Dreaming. In: (Anonymous), pp. 259–294.

Meltzer, D. (1978). *The Kleinian Development: III The Clinical Significance of the Work of Bion.* Clunie Press: Perthshire.

Menzies-Lythe, I. (1981). Bion's Contribution to thinking about Groups. In: *Do I dare Disturb the Universe?*, (ed. J. S. Grotstein), Caesura Press: Beverly Jills, CA.

Powell, A. (1994). Towards a Unifying Concept of the Group Matrix. In: *The Psyche and the Social World*, (ed. D. G.Brown & L. M. Zinkin), Routledge: London.

Sutherland, J. D. (1963). Object relations theory and the conceptual model of psychoanalysis. *British Journal of Medical Psychology, 36:* 109–121.

Trist, E. (1987). *Personal Communication.*

Turquet, P. M. (1975). Threats to identity in the large group. In: *The Large Group*, (ed. L. Kreeger), Constable: London.

Winnicott, D. W. (1953). Transitional objects and transitional phenomena. In: *Collected Papers.* (Anonymous), Tavistock Publ., London.

Winnicott, D. W. (1958). The Capacity to be Alone. *International Journal of Psycho-Analysis, 39:* 416–420.

Winnicott, D. W. (1969). The use of an object and relating through identification. *The International Journal of Psycho-Analysis, 50:* 711–716.

Winnicott, D. W. (1952). Psychoses and Child Care. In (Anonymous), pp. 68–74.

Winnicott, D. W. (1960). Countertransference. *British Journal of Medical Psychology, 33:* 17–21.

Winnicott, D. W. (1965). *The Maturational Processes and the Facilitating Environment.* Hogarth Press: London.

Winnicott, D. W. (1971). *Playing and Reality.* Tavistock: London.

Zinkin, L. M. (1989). The group as container and contained. *Group Analysis, 22:* 227–234.

PART IV

GROUP-ANALYSIS AND SOCIETY

CHAPTER THIRTEEN

Group analysis: the problem of context*

Earl Hopper

Introduction

It is inevitable that when a psychotherapist speaks about psychother-apy, he speaks about himself. It is impossible to talk about our work in a "pure" way. In any case, an audience is usually more alert to the mood of the interaction between themselves and the speaker than they are to the content of his presentation. Thus, before I attempt to com-municate a certain amount of cognitive information about the problem of context in group analysis, I would like, straight away, to claim my own identity from within our matrix of professional and personal rela-tionships. I am a sociologist and a psychoanalyst and a group analyst. I am always all three, but, depending on what I am doing, I give more emphasis to one or another of these disciplines. Within myself, these disciplines are not in conflict. However, I am often constrained by the conflicts among them—or their representatives—within the real-world, but that is another issue.

---

*This chapter was previously published as Hopper, E. (1982). Group Analysis: The Prob-lem of Context. *Group Analysis*, 15: 136–157. The informal style of this paper is due to the fact that it is a slightly edited version of a talk given by Dr. Hopper at a AGPA conference in 1982.

It may be helpful if I compare myself explicitly to my two colleagues who will also speak this morning. I am more psychoanalytical than Dr. Skynner, who will speak about family therapy according to the group-analytic perspective. For example, the interpretation of the individual and the collective transference is my primary clinical preoccupation; however, I do not confine my interpretations to a particular school of thought, and I believe that the clarification and description of the transference in more or less everyday language is an essential first step—indeed, it often reduces the need for a formal interpretation subsequently. I also believe that "interpretative actions" or "interpretative gestures" (although Skynner does not call them so), e.g.; modulations in voice, raised eyebrows etc., warrant more careful consideration than psychoanalysts have given them so far.

I am more sociological than Dr. James, who will speak about certain aspects of Bion's later work in comparison to certain of the ideas of Winnicott and Foulkes. For example, the instinctual origins of psychic life and the projection and externalization of unconscious fantasy are, for me, less important than acts of imagination and various kinds of introjective processes—which I believe to be primary and prior to projection; moreover, Bion's theory of thinking, which was an entirely foreseeable extension of his preceding work, is merely a Platonist attempt to solve a problem that is iatrogenic to the Kleinian perspective—although it is elegant, it adds nothing to the "Allegory of the Cave." It is typical of those views which have emerged in a cyclical fashion throughout the ages, concomitantly with the importance which cultures have given to instincts as an important cause of psychic life. Thus, to be more precise, when I say "iatrogenic to the Kleinian perspective," I mean iatrogenic to any school of thought that suggests that psychic life is somehow immanent to the organism, and that does not make use of the axioms of the sociological perspective, which draws the boundaries of the person in terms of relationships with objects who may be experienced in the first instance through introjective processes rather than projective ones.

Incidentally, I am not a physician, but I am aware that people have bodies.

Now that I have said something about who I am—mainly in terms of who I am not—I would like to turn to the task at hand. I intend to discuss certain aspects of the problem of context, primarily in order to illustrate the distinguishing feature of group analysis or group-analytic psychotherapy,[1] namely: the clinical application of the axiom that, the nature of the "human" is social, and of the "social" human, at all stages of the life cycle and at all phases of history. I will try to state the problem in formal terms, and then illustrate it with a brief clinical vignette, which includes my interpretation and its aftermath. In the Conclusion, I will indicate very briefly a few of the implications of my approach and some of the literature associated with it. Although I will be talking about group process and group therapy, I believe that my more general remarks apply to dyadic therapy, including psychoanalysis proper.

The concept of "context"

"Context" refers to those parts of a text which precede and/or follow a particular passage, and which are sufficient in number to enable a person to determine the meaning or meanings which the author intended. In the first instance I would like to draw your attention to the etymology of the word "context." I can do no more than stimulate your intellectual curiosity, but certain verbal lineages warrant our attention. The prefix *con* is related to *cum*, meaning "together," "together with," "in combination" and "in union," and further, "altogether," "completely," and "intensive" or "in depth." It is closely related to such words as "community," "communion," and "common," which reminds us of the word "religion," meaning "to connect," "to bring together in entirety," "to make whole," etc., and connoting "being bound together through oath" or "being part of an altered whole." (Isn't it amazing how a good dictionary can make one seem intelligent and well educated?)

This line of association should not be surprising because the stem word "text" has at least two elementary but interdependent roots. The first, *textus*, means "tissue" and "style of a literary work"; later, *textus* was used to refer to the Gospel, precisely as it was written in all its authoritative glory. The second root is *texere*, meaning "to weave."

These two sets of connotations are infinitively suggestive, but especially intriguing is the implicit idea (or perhaps metaphor) to the effect that a thread and its properties will always be governed by its location within a larger whole, in this instance a fabric or textile. So, too, is the implication that logically the aetiological chain of any dependent variable will always stop with God, who will always be the hypothetical author of any definitive text concerning the Beginning, or the hypothetical weaver who has created the textile. In other words, in all schemes of thought the context of the context will always be some form of the Holy.

It follows that various properties of both material and nonmaterial things may be characteristic only of wholes, or in other words, only of contexts, which are woven together from their constituent elements. Properties of context are, therefore, emergent and irreducible to the properties of any of their elements. With respect to persons, the true Oedipus complex could be seen as an emergent phenomenon; and with respect to social formation, structures of authority or group morale would be in this category. The meaning of the word "context" is, of course, also related to the meaning of the word "understand." For example, in order to understand an event it is necessary to locate it within an abstract category of such events, and then to relate this category to at least one other such category, the existence and qualities of which are less puzzling. Usually, this will "cure" what Wittgenstein called a "disease of the mind"—referring to a condition of intense curiosity and questioning; but perhaps in deference to ourselves and our profession, we should also use the metaphor of an irritant between a live oyster and its shell which can, under certain circumstances, produce a pearl.

Communications are also events, although of a particular kind. Leaving aside a variety of problems in the philosophy of science, especially concerning the topic of hermeneutics, let us consider the phenomenon of transference. "Transference" refers to a repetition or a replication in the "here and now" of pain *and* defence as they have occurred in the past, and as they continue to occur elsewhere. As such, the transference contains a coded account of its own social and psychological aetiology. It follows that in order to understand the transference, it must be contextualised, that is, related to other categories of events which stand in specified relationships to the transference in terms of time and social psychological space. Theory offers a set of rules according to which the code of the transference can be deciphered or interpreted.

However, to contextualize the collective transference of a group and its individual or personal elements is easier said than done. After all, the boundaries of a group are not identical with those of its members, and the principle of apperception leads relentlessly back towards the Beginning and into the Womb. Thus, typically, but somewhat curiously, the contextualization of the collective transference is limited to two categories of events: those which are socially near and comparatively recent in the group's history (which means comparatively late in the life cycles of the group members); and those which are socially distant and pre-historical (which means during the early infancies of the group members, when it is assumed that. because biological constraints pre-dominate, people will have much less idiosyncratic variation in their experiences than they will have later on, and the content of unconscious fantasy will tend to be universal). Incidentally, this may be why so many of the psychoanalysts who work with groups seem to emphasise the determinancy of the first few months of life. In any case, this brings us to what for me is the problem of context.

The problem of context

A "problem" is neither more or less than a question that is hard to answer. Thus, I would now like to ask a few questions that are hard to answer. In attempting to contextualize the transference is it possible and is it therapeutically useful (and these are two separate questions), to explore a full range of events on the dimensions of time and social psychological space? How far from the so-called "here and now" should we go? Should we consider the later phases of the life cycle? Should we consider the structure and function of social institutions, not only now but also in a person's past? Might we take account even of events which occurred before a person was born, and which were located in another country? (I will not discuss here the notion of precognition, and will limit my enquiry to phenomena of replication; however, this does not mean that the transference does not contain information about what people anticipate and what they may even strive to make happen, a point which has not gone unnoticed in, for example, D. M. Thomas' *The White Hotel*, Gollancz Ltd. 1981, which could be taken as a case study for my perspective concerning group processes).

My answer to these questions is, on balance, yes, but very much on balance. In other words, I do not *confine* my attempts to contextualize the transference only to the infantile unconscious; I try to explore a fuller range of events on the dimensions of time and social psychologi-cal space, at least on some occasions and in certain circumstances. I only wish I could give you some general rules about when I go one way rather than another, but I have really not got that far in my own think-ing. Probably, I allow myself to be guided by my experienced intuition. However, I would like to remind you that even Dr. Bion did not give us much guidance on how to apply his cryptic statement—which is in effect the starting point of my thinking—that the "basic assumption group knows no time"—and, although he did not quite say so—"knows no space." (Incidentally, this statement is typical of Bion's work—after hours of reflection I am still not certain whether it is banal or an insight of genius; many in London respond to his written utterances as though they have come from a Buddha, thereby underestimating their own creative insights as readers of his text).

Finally, it would be as well to acknowledge that those of you who do not agree that the analysis of the transference should be our primary clinical preoccupation in group analysis may be wondering why I am making such a fuss. I can only stress that in my view the analysis of the transference is the basis of psychic change. (I would also like to remind you that this is the stuff that careers are made on!)

A brief outline of what i think is my clinical technique

In addition to training groups of various kinds, I conduct within my private practice one once-weekly group, one twice-weekly group, and one once-weekly co-conducted group. They meet for 40 weeks per year, and the sessions last for one and one-half hours. The therapy groups consist of from seven to nine patients, usually four men and five women, ranging from around 25 to 65 years of age, representing a cross section of neurotic and personality disorders, not including more than one really difficult patient or more than one of a really distinctive type, such as an addict, criminal, a depressive, a paranoid, etc. During the last few years, I have tended to see my group patients individually for at least a few months before they enter the group—this is in keeping with the evidence concerning favourable outcomes, but I work this way primarily because I enjoy it. By and large the patients are a cross section of the urban and suburban middle class, with a slight bias towards the professional upper middle class and the helping professions in general, but, somewhat surprisingly, Jews are not over-represented, as they are in most studies of the patient population in the urban areas of North America. The average length of stay is about four to five years. Incidentally, this often surprises people who do not know much about group analysis—and this may include our most severe critics within psychiatry and psychoanalysis—who assume that patients stay in treatment for a matter of months, if not a few weekends. In any case, I have what we call "slow-open" groups; they go on as long as I do, but new patients come in when old patients go out. Ordinarily, I speak after about 20 to 30 minutes, but I have no general rule. Sometimes, I start the group, and on some occasions I remain silent all the way through. My usual technique is to try to sense the common group tension (following the work of Ezriel), which almost always involves basic assumptions patterns (following the work of Bion), and then to interpret this collective transference from the group to the object or objects in question—usually, but not always, to myself; afterwards I try to help the group discover what each person has contributed to it as well as how each is affected by it. However, and I think this is very important because it distinguishes how I work from the approach of those who follow the conventional "Tavi" model, I might talk first to a particular person or to the partners in a sub-group, depending on how they may be *dramatizing or personifying* the more general theme. (As you know, "dramatization" and "personification" are two of Foulkes' early concepts; there is no reason why a conductor should avoid talking to an individual, especially if he is seen as a nodal point within the matrix, and if you recall that he is in the group as a patient and not as a student of group dynamics). I also try to be alert to the recapitulations within the group process of early family life (following the work of Schindler).

Several groups may go by before we (the group and I) have made anything like a comprehensive interpretation, and there are always an indefinite number of loose ends. Although I am obliged to see my patients essentially as *patients*, I do regard the group, and even use the group, as my co-conductors. I value their capacity to be holding and containing.

I rarely go beyond interpretations and "interpretative actions." I assume that this encourages the development of "psychic muscle," as well as the capacity for reflection. Nonetheless, I think of myself as a fairly spontaneous and warm type of therapist (of course, this is not really for me to say); certainly, I break rules more often than I abide by them. I try to communicate in an intelligent and organised way, but this should not be mistaken for being controlled and cold.

I am not particularly concerned about my own transparency, but I do not favour self-disclosure. Patients see what they see, and they make whatever use of it they wish and can, but this is different from telling them about myself. "Judicious self-disclosure" may be helpful, of course, but usually it is a therapeutic burden.

In my attempts to understand what my patients are asking me to understand, I allow myself to be guided by my counter-transference, based on experienced intuition, which I regard as akin to litmus paper in a chemistry experiment; although it can be a source of difficulty, it can also be a source of valuable information, as I will now try to indicate and to explain.

A brief clinical vignette

The passage which follows is from a session last autumn from one of my groups which meet in my consulting room at home, In its conscious and unconscious themes, it is fairly typical of the material from this group during the last few years, as it might be of material from my other groups, including some of the training groups and seminars which I take in various institutional settings, including the London School of Economics.[2] Of course we will have to trade off the accuracy of a tape recording for the communication of a mood, and we should remember that this passage is taken out of context. I would also like to prepare you for the fact that this material is very dense, and will probably make you feel flooded. It will suggest an infinite number and variety of interpretations, as it did to me at the time, and, in retrospect, as it does to me now.

1. I took a seat, the group continued to complain about the weather, it was cold and damp—"It's not the cold, but the damp"—and the rain beat against the window panes of my consulting room, which is in the attic of my house. Someone said, "Still, mustn't complain, it could be worse." The group drew closer together around our centre table. I felt that their sense of solidarity increased—not unlike what happens at the beginning of a "ghost story" or, I suppose, at the beginning of any ritualized story-telling event. It is not for nothing that so many stories start with storms.

I thought to myself that nothing changes—the first remarks I heard in England, 20 years ago, must have been "It's not the cold, but the damp," and "Still, mustn't complain." I also thought to myself that the weather in the late autumn was seldom different—for that matter the summer isn't either—and that I had rarely heard a group discuss the weather, at least not after I sat down, although they probably do talk about the weather while they are waiting for me to come into the room. So my antennae went out immediately.

2. The discussion shifted to a critical appreciation of my house and consulting rooms. They remarked upon its late Victorian style—"or is it Edwardian?"—the way I had converted it, especially the alterations to

the staircase, the general mixture of old and new (brick, pine and glass combined with high ceilings, old mouldings, large architraves, etc). and, turning to the room itself, the colours ("buttermilk, oatmeal, and earth clay," as one patient put it, "colours of trendy architects and feminist earth-mothers"); the two austere double-glazed windows set into the eaves, and the folding Habitat "director's chairs" (which members of the group set up for themselves when they come in after the other seats are taken). I should also add the two conformable chairs for which there is some competition, and the couch which comes apart into three seats for group work—items of furniture which pertain to my, work as a psychoanalyst, and which they neglected to mention.

I was feeling very uncomfortable, too closely examined, as though they were inspecting my private parts and parts of my private life. After all, they had been coming to my house once a week for four years. Why should they suddenly have become so preoccupied, ostensibly, with my room?

3. They returned to the weather outside, reassuring themselves that it was dry and warm inside. A woman said that the staircase on the side of the house, which they had to use in order to reach my consulting rooms, was too exposed—cold, wet, windy, dark, not at all safe—and she wondered why I had not enclosed it, since they had been complaining about it for as long as she had been in the group (over 5 years). Another said that this was obviously because my family and I didn't have to use it (which was probably correct). The group's Non-Complainer said, "Still, it's nice inside." I was thinking about my house as a symbol of Mother's Body, of my own body and of my own mind, of passages into and out of Mother's Body, but we can overlook the importance of the material surroundings of a group—perhaps as a transitional object—how early the Oedipus complex really begins, how ubiquitous and deep are the boundary problems concerning the inside and the outside, etc. I was also reminded of a lunchtime discussion I was having a few days previously at the London School of Economics about the history and scope of the literary usage of a ship as a symbol for Society and for the State.

4. The group came back to the consulting room. An older man spoke about the cost of housing and conversion work nowadays, and supposed that the Habitat chairs must have cost about £5 when I bought them, whereas they were now closer to £20. Another man said that everything goes up but his income. This remark was met with silence (partly, I suspected, because he is impotent; and I detected what the

author of *Brideshead Revisited* might have called a "bat-squeak" of anxiety). He then apologised for messing up the carpet with his wet, muddy shoes (which he did all the time anyway, for he really was an Archetypal Mess), and the group echoed that the carpet would be dry by the time the group was over, and the mud could be swept up. Another man asked me what did I expect, for surely this sort of damage was what the Estate Agents would call, "Normal wear and tear," and was probably taken into account in my fees, which was why I put them up every year.

I was feeling annoyed at the mess, and mildly guilty about the fees for "psychic-conversion work"—but I was also thinking that I was pleased with my house and consulting room. I was tempted to interpret certain aspects of their desires to intrude and to spoil in connection with their envy of me and of my relationships with my family and my "house," combined with their fear and feelings of guilt, and to show them how this was being manifested in various forms of splitting and projection. However, since I was vaguely aware that I wanted to punish them rather than understand them, I remained silent until I could sort my responses. I have learned that in this frame of mind it is best not to trot out the death rattles of correct interpretations, but to be silent in order to give myself space for reflection—not to defend myself from my patients by putting some theory between us. For example, I did not want to fall back on a "ritualized" interpretation which involves, for example, feelings of envy, fight-flight patterns, preoccupations with "Mother's Body," smearing attacks with faeces, etc.

5. The comment about fees prompted a young artist (who had never taken a conventional job in his life, because he had inherited several houses in London and an estate in the country, and of whom in this respect I was myself envious) to offer to paint a mural on my wall (which you can see was in part—but only in part—a continuation of the desire to smear my walls with faeces), but he thought that I was not the kind of person to spend money on art—at least not from an unknown artist. This was followed by a phase of pairing between two young females and him, and between the two females. The communication concerned the problems of careers and marriage nowadays, and their jealousy and envy of his young, anorexic wife who is also from an extremely wealthy family. Finally, one of the two women said to me in, a flirtatious way that my wife probably worked in the media—but didn't really have to, and that she was undoubtedly a kept woman—which the patient

wouldn't mind being herself, except that not only did she need a wife rather than a husband, but she also wanted a baby.

There is probably at least one such woman in all the groups which we conduct nowadays, and I suspect that it will sound as though it were taken from Margaret Drabble's notes for her next book, but, in any case, I had to struggle against my desire to become embroiled with this woman, a type for which I am an easy mark. I caught myself, and remained silent. I realise that I had begun to feel a bit bored, almost a little depressed—although "depressed" is too strong a term. I sensed that I wanted this flirtatious female to excite me. I was aware that the artist's insult had a grain of truth in it, and that I was hurt by it, but that this alone would not account for my feelings. I continued to monitor my feelings, but I was somewhat perplexed, and a little disturbed. You will realize that I remained silent, not because I had nothing to say, but because I could not identify the mood of the group.

6. My silence was rewarded. The painter commented that Prince Charles and Lady Di were going to live near his house in the country. Someone commented that Lady Di was pregnant, and another said that her tits would be enormous. The older woman said that Charles was very nice, more like the Queen, whereas Anne was a real cow, more like her father. Several joined in to say how marvellous the wedding was, and one said that she had heard that even the psychoanalysts had watched it on the telly in Helsinki last summer (she was right). The group began to discuss the pros and cons of royalty: the painter felt that although it cost the taxpayers quite a lot, it was one way to maintain these old country houses; others were concerned with snobbery, and felt that the funds for the Royal Family were being "sucked right out of their pockets."

Intellectually, I could follow the themes of gender confusion, a pre-occupation with my personal and family life, especially during the summer break, my family and the Royal Family and my fees and taxes, not to mention the basic assumption of pairing projected into the aristocracy, sexuality as a manic defence against depression, etc. In fact, I was tempted to call their attention to their depression which had been denied and which was being projected into me, but I decided instead to contain it for a while longer, mainly because I didn't know how to account for its apparent intensity. Also, I was feeling, by now, somewhat sluggish. I was thinking to myself that Bion would turn out to be right in all respects, that I had nothing of my own to offer, and that I was out of the group—I was uncertain whether I was being kept out of it or if I just felt out of it. I also felt lonely and isolated.

7. After a very brief silence, a girl who had the same name as a young female member of the Royal Family, who is usually silent and self-contained, began to cry. (Everyone seemed surprised but me; after all, they had been laughing and pairing in a manic way while I was feeling sad). Let us call her Elizabeth. Elizabeth had learned that the house in which she and her husband and daughter of two had their small flat was riddled with wet rot and dry rot and God knows what. The place was virtually diseased. The wet rot was mainly in the basement flats and in the joists below the ground floor flats, and the dry rot ran up one wall all the way to the roof timbers, and her flat had both. The insurance wouldn't cover it. Given the complex pattern of ownership among the freehold, the leaseholder, several sub-tenants, the banks and the building societies who held long-term mortgages—it was a real mess. She and her husband would have to go further into debt and borrow from her parents, who were retired and whose savings had not kept pace with inflation, and in any case they needed their savings because her mother's cancer was worse, and their expenses were greater. She and her husband agreed to negotiate with the freeholders and insurance company on behalf of all the tenants, *gratis*. When pressed about why, she said that it was because they didn't trust anyone else to do it, and they couldn't afford to pay anyone. She added that it might even lead to paid work; she didn't want to be a typist, her husband refused to drive a mini-cab, and they didn't want to emigrate.

The group knew that Elizabeth's husband had lost his job a year ago, and had set up a small financial services company which he operated from this flat, which was prohibited by their lease. She worked as a part-time secretary for him, but before she became pregnant she was about to become a stockbroker.

I was aware that I was being asked to provide psychotherapy free of charge, but I was fairly certain that the group were not more than pre-conscious of this. I was also aware that the group continued to be pre-occupied with "houses," and the problem of gender identity. Elizabeth was caught up in a defensive identification with me. Clearly, she needed some personal attention, but I waited to see if someone in the group would give it to her.

The group were moved by her desperate situation, and through their gestures and other noises of involvement and understanding, they gave the impression that they could empathize with it. She went on to say that the freehold was owned by Chassidic Jews through a maze of interlocking companies, and that they were being distinctly unhelpful. They were prepared to buy back all the leases at "current valuation" (which must have been at about a quarter of their cost). Several flats were owned by rich Arabs who used them to house their servants, and they were hard to contact. One flat was owned by a nice Iranian couple who had got out a few years ago, and who had put all their savings into their flat. The other English couples were also broke, and in one case the husband had just lost his job.

I began to feel drowsy, which usually means that I am defending myself against the experience of being envied and hated by people who are not fully aware of their feelings, and against my desire to confront and attack in response to my own hurt and, I suppose, fear. I was unable to concentrate on the details of how her life seemed to be collapsing around her, and realised that the group seemed more compassionate than I. They began to share similar experiences with Elizabeth. This might be seen as an example of how a group can function as a co-therapist, but in retrospect I believe that this was primarily a continuation of their attempts to make me feel excluded while at the same time to make themselves feel that they had something of great, exclusive value (an issue to which I will return).

8. Now, in our field details are everything, but I must begin to edit and condense my report: In the ensuing discussion, I noticed three related themes. The first was the malady of the building itself. An entire house could be eaten away by rot. From the inside you wouldn't even know that it was there until the house fell down. Timber could be turned to fungus. Like a dried-up leaf in which only a few stems held it all together. A debate developed about the origins of rot: whether wet rot comes before dry rot, or vice versa; was it best to keep it under control and live with it? Or would it be better to tear the whole thing down and start again, which would be painful in the short run, but better in the long run. It was necessary fist to stop all the leaks (from the roof, from the plumbing, rising damp, penetrating damp, etc)., but "dry" was not enough, "well ventilated" was also important. Be careful about modern building materials—they do not breathe.

I was aware that the group was concerned with the design faults of the female body. They were also deeply affected by what they imagined was the disintegration of the body of Elizabeth's mother. The problems of gender identity and its connection with Elizabeth's marriage to a man who was perceived to be a "wet" were also apparent.

The second theme concerned the type of people involved. Wasn't it ironic about the Arabs and the Jews? The Arabs were all over London. But the Jews really seemed to have survived, and now they owned all the property. They always come off best. Typical. Also the architects and lawyers. They always get their fees. Social parasites and prostitutes live off the misery of ordinary people.

I was aware that the group knew that I had been working with survivors of social trauma, and had been involved in bringing the Survivor Syndrome to public attention. It was reasonable to suppose that the group believed that I was a Jew.

The third theme was that things were not what they used to be. It was impossible to trust anyone in London today. The Chassidic Jews were frightening in their black clothes and hats, and they ought to try harder to fit in. If they wanted to live in England then they ought to act like English people. Someone remarked on the hairstyles of Chassidic Jews.

I sensed that I was being asked to explain this custom, but I remained impassive. I thought that this last remark might have been a veiled reference to my own change of hairstyle a few months ago from long to very short. This was, of course, the least of it. At this point I intervened. Before I tell you what I said, I would like first to tell you a little more about what I was thinking and feeling.

9. The group was almost over, and I was still silent. I felt anxious and flooded by the material. I had other, more specific feelings too, which I have mentioned to you. I said to myself that on such occasions the main thing is containment, and that although silence is not always rewarded, it is seldom wrong or destructive.

Nonetheless, I decided that the group were asking me to understand them. I, in turn, felt the strong pull to let them know what I did. I even said to myself that *this* was a defence on my part, and that it was probably stopping me from really understanding them. In fact, perhaps I understood too much! I had considered and discarded a number of interpretations concerning a variety of sexual and aggressive impulses and fantasies, as well as paranoid-schizoid and depressive anxieties, various personal and collective defences against them, including the three basic assumption patterns and combinations of them.

However, I decided to use my counter-transference as a source of data as to the nature of the transference process into which I was being sucked. So far, I had been able to contain the group's projected feelings without being overwhelmed by them or acting upon them, and this had given me space for reflection. I convinced myself, more or less, that my feelings were not primarily my own, in the sense that although I felt them, they were not in essence my own personal responses to the particular material and to the members of the group. I was holding feelings that were being split off, denied and projected into me. In order to identify the feelings and processes involved, I would have to take a risk in the negotiation of the psychic reality of the collective transference and its individual elements.[3]

An interlude

Let us consider this process in a little more detail. As the group continued and as their collective transference developed, I began to feel anxious, somewhat depersonalised, excluded, lonely, isolated, and somewhat drowsy, more or less in that order. I knew that some of these feelings were associated with my being an American Jewish Sociologist in England who subsequently became a psychotherapist, group analyst and, more recently, a psychoanalyst. I am familiar with feeling the feelings of an outsider and of a marginal man, because I have been one and, to some extent, remain one. However, I also know that some of these feelings were associated with my own early life experiences, and that some were associated with a mixture of both old and new experiences, in the sense that I remain influenced by the old and, on occasions, I am prone to provoke the new. Thus, how could I conclude that such feelings were *not* my own but primarily and essentially the denied, split-off and projected feelings of my patients? How could I be sure that I was not being prejudiced and paranoid or, at least, more paranoid than usual? It is impossible to answer these questions here (they require a paper or two in their own right) but basically I had to trust my trained intuition to the effect that the group was using me as a container for their own personal thoughts and feelings. I could recognise this because I am familiar with my own thoughts and feelings about the material under discussion; I like to think that I have come to terms with them, at least in part. But whatever I may think and feel in my personal life, I was able to trust my own deep conviction that I did not feel this way "usually" and "really" towards this group of patients. In other words, within the context of the situation at hand, these feelings were not familiar to me.

Thus, I concluded that unconsciously the group were feeling envious hatred towards me. In this connection, they felt themselves to be totally empty, and me to be totally full; they felt that I was keeping them out of my life, and controlling their access to my bountiful stores of all good things. Furthermore, I decided that through an unconscious process of denial, splitting and projection, they were, in retaliation, evacuating into me what they had been feeling themselves. In other words, they were making me feel towards them what they were feeling towards me. However, they were also trying to communicate what they had been feeling, and begging me to understand them and to help them understand themselves, and, in so doing, to relieve them from their pain. They did not want me to perpetuate a vicious circle of retaliation but to nourish them and comfort them with understanding.

In connection with the problem of context, however, the real issue is the origins of the group's envious hatred. This is the crux of the matter. Should I attempt to clarify their envy and their projective identifications in the service of attack and communication, and follow this with an interpretation or contextualization which connected their transference with those events which certain theory tells us are the original source of envy and potential envy within us all? Or, should I emphasize how envy can be used as a defence against other painful feelings, and in the service of passivity and inactivity with regard to attempts to understand and even to change the *external* sources of these feelings, and, thus, to reduce their feelings of pain and of their subsequent envy? You will see from how I have asked these questions that I lean rather strongly towards the latter alternative. The attribution of primary envy to all and sundry as though it were universally applicable and as though it really offered a basic explanation, prohibits our attempts to understand that some people are more envious than others, that some objects are envied more than others, and, therefore, that envy might be explained in terms of object relations *throughout* the life cycle and not exclusively or even primarily in terms of the universality of the so-called death instinct. All of which should not be taken to suggest that I do not have a healthy respect for the power of primary envy and the dreadful anxiety and general psychic pain which it involves.

You will see that I have now come full circle. I have returned to the initial questions with which I defined the problem of context. By now you will not be surprised to learn that *on this occasion* I decided to contextualize the collective transference in terms of the "far-away-there" and "now,' and in terms of the "far-away-there" and "then." In short, I decided to concentrate on the unconscious effects of various social facts, both those which were operative during their infancies—and even before some of them were born and which would only have indirect and highly mediated effects upon them—and those which were operative during their daily lives as adults in England today. Of course, it is beyond the scope of this paper to develop the view that since psycho-analysts, especially in the United States, have still not accepted the full implications of object relations theory (as opposed to instinct theory), they are unable to grasp the essence of the context problem, and, there-fore, they are also unable to appreciate the theoretical foundations of the group-analytic perspective.

The interpretation: the clinical vignette continued

Finally, I broke my silence. Unfortunately, since I had become anxious and had held back for so long (and perhaps even because I may have already been considering what I would present to you today), I made an interpretative speech, which usually I try not to do. Actually, I rather overdid it, as you will see, but I would not want this mistake to over-shadow the essence of the matter, namely a particular contextualiza-tion, not a particular aspect of technique.

I said that to feel helpless when one is helpless is not necessarily a bad thing. (Actually, this was an example of Hopper quoting Hopper, for I realised later that I had written this sentence in my last book—which indicates how I was using my thoughts and words as a "security blan-ket"). In fact, it may be the first step towards finding a good, construc-tive and realistic solution. If you can tolerate the anxiety of it all, you may have some time to think and you may be able to avoid making things worse.

Yet (I went on), I suspect that you may not be fully aware of what's really making you feel so helpless. Most of you know that you will be able to cope with dry rot and wet rot and all the difficulties that go along with it, and I suspect that most of you have been hearing what has been said in terms of disturbing desires and fears about everything that comes to your mind in connection with such words as "wet" and "dry," feelings which may have already begun to give us some trouble when you were talking about the rain and the mud, the painting, the Royal Baby, husbands and wives, males and females, etc., and I guess that you are *almost* aware of what this has to do with me and us here! But many of you have been denying *(the defence)* how frightened, helpless, and confused you feel *(the feeling of pain against which they were trying to defend themselves)* about the state of the nation, and in particular about the battles between the "wets" and the "drys" in Mrs. Thatcher's cabinet *(a source of the painful feelings)*.[4]

I will go even further (I continued). Some of you may be feeling something like what the Germans felt in the 1930s, when—like now—everything was so topsy-turvy and nobody knew who was who. These conditions make your feelings of fear, helplessness, and confusion even worse, but they may also be leading you to deal with these feelings by looking for scapegoats *(in this instance scapegoating is a form of instrumental adjustment to the painful feelings and to the sources of the feelings)*[5] You are very ready to blame Jews, professionals, and so on, including me—and maybe even especially me—an American Jewish professional who you think will be safe from all this because you think that I have two jobs as well as two countries. In other words, you are scapegoating me because you envy me, and you envy me because you think that I am free from the painful feelings that many of you are experiencing as a result of social forces which seem to you to be beyond your control, in the same way as you tend to scapegoat Jews and others whom you also envy—outside the group—and for the same reasons. We seem to be recreating before our very eyes the same sort of problems that are going on in our society. And they are not so different from what has happened at other times and at other places.

Following a brief silence I went on to say that it was curious that although the group knew that I would understand their feelings about this type of thing, they seemed to feel too ashamed to talk about them openly, almost as though they had fallen into a state of "group disgrace." I said that this may have had something to do with their fear that if they lost their jobs they would not be able to afford my fees, and that they would lose their contact with me in the group. Although many had owed me money in the past, it seemed that they had become reluctant to discuss this openly with me now. I suggested that perhaps they felt that I would go back to America soon, and reject them.

Finally, I concluded my interpretative lecture—and again I emphasise that this was essentially very poor technique—and said: Precisely because all this is so painful and confusing, you would like to throw me off the scent. You would like me to lose my sense of smell.

You want me to direct your attention to the infantile origins of your envious feelings, the ones against which most of you are fairly well defended at this very moment. You know so much about psychoanalysis nowadays that you want to explain everything away in terms of your mothers and fathers when you were babies. Tits, willies, bums, and pooh-poohs! You don't really want to go where it's hottest and smelliest tonight. But if we allow ourselves to be seduced in this way, we would be making a mockery out of what we have learned through our psychoanalytical insights.

The aftermath of this interpretative intervention

Following my intervention the group was silent. I found myself thinking that they were probably feeling chastised by my overly long and somewhat fervent comments. Yet, I also sensed that their silence was a thoughtful one. They seemed to be using the psychic space which my boundary-maintaining intervention had helped to recreate in order to reflect upon the many implications and meanings of what had transpired.

During this silence I found myself thinking about a public lecture which I had attended recently at the Tavistock Clinic. It was one of a series on the application of psychoanalytical ideas to community issues. The speaker was suggesting that young black men in Brixton were unable to trust older white men in positions of authority because they had failed to work through the anxieties inherent in the paranoid-schizoid position, and that they were poor and unemployed because they were unable to make healthy introjections of the opportunities available, or in other words, an unemployment rate in excess of 30% for over a decade was due to the experience which the male (but apparently not the female) community had "at the breast" during their first few months of life. I remembered that in the discussion which followed, I had said, as I would still say: unless we can acknowledge the reality of the helplessness which may confront people, we will be unable to help them to filter out their accurate perceptions of reality from their phantastic distortions of it; unless we can acknowledge our own feelings of guilt, we will be unable to help our patients find the most effective and efficient forms of instrumental adjustment available to them; and unless we can help them endure the pain inherent in feeling helpless, we may have to accept that paranoid fantasies and their attendant consequences are, inevitably, the only defensive solution available to them. To explain poverty and unemployment *primarily* in terms of the character traits of the poor and the unemployed is insulting and presumptious. It makes a mockery out of what we have learned from psyche analysis, and ignores what we have learned from sociology about how social facts affect psychic processes, and vice versa. One does not have to be a political activist to believe that psychotherapists ought to learn something about the nature of social processes, or a member of the hard, revolutionary left to believe that we should try to understand how our patients are constrained by social events. My remarks were met with silence and hostile embarrassment.

In retrospect, this event in my life may account in part for my having approached my group's communications in the way I did. It may also help to explain why I reacted in the way I have described, and why I spoke for so long—so long that the session had to stop soon after I did. However, the group took up my interpretation in depth and in detail during the next couple of months. The material which followed was characterised by a mixture of themes, but they were preoccupied with issues concerning sexual perversion and the perversion of power. In my experience, this combination is not unusual. In England, it is easier for a group to talk about their sexual perversions and even their most bizarre masturbation fantasies than about what their fathers did for a living when they were children, where they went to school, or about their current social class positions. In fact, if a conductor does not take this up more or less in the beginning, a group can go on for a very long time without ever knowing what its members do for a living. Why this should be so is a topic in itself, but it offers another example of the unconscious effects of social facts, which are denied.

Later that evening, while I was dictating my notes about the group process and the contributions of the various patients to it, I found myself ruminating that given the impossibility of ever giving a so-called "complete interpretation," whether it would have been better to go directly to the usual "there" and "then" origins of envy, rather than to the aetiology which I had chosen; or, in other words, whether giving emphasis to the infantile origins of their feelings would have been less defensive and more helpful than looking at the social constraints inherent in their adult lives? I am still uncertain about the answers to this question, and I am still without rules concerning the interpretative contextualizations of the transference. Moreover, I continue to wonder if I gave Elizabeth enough personal attention.

Some clinical and theoretical implications for further
discussion, and some references to relevant literature

I will now list a few points which warrant further thought and discussion. This will be no more than a set of brief notes concerning some of the implications of my paper for technique and theory development. However, by now you will have realised that I could not have presented a clinical paper which had not been theory-impregnated.

Clinical implications

1. Be prepared to go where it is hottest.
2. Be prepared to use your counter-transference, or your general affective responses to your patients, as a source of information concerning their transference:

   (a) Be prepared to "negotiate," at least with yourself in silence, the definitions of intra-personal and inter-personal reality.
   (b) Minimize self-disclosure, because it is usually a burden to your patients.
   (c) Beware of material which seems "topical" and "typical"; you may be eliciting it, and distorting your perception of it. Equally, be especially sensitive to such themes; they may alert you to the unconscious constraints of social facts.
   (d) Be aware of processes of projective identification as the group's mode of unconscious evacuation and communication of their most painful and confusing feelings.

3. Be prepared to contextualize the transference *and the counter-transference* in terms of a wide range of phenomena on the dimensions of time and social psychological space.
4. Learn about the structure and process of the "wider society" and its main institutions. Differentiate your knowledge of social facts and their constraints from your own political and social values.

Theoretical implications

1. Organisms, persons, and groups are not the same order of phenomena. Statements about one may not apply to the others, although they

must, be consistent. Psychic facts presuppose the prior and simultaneous existence of social facts as well as of organic facts.

2. Organisms, persons and groups may be viewed as open systems. This means that the personalities of the members of a group are elements of the context of a group, while at the same time the group itself is part of the context of the personalities of its members. It also means that the structure and process of a group will be a hologramatic expression of the configurations of its societal context.

3. Although basic personality pattern and character structure may be established during infancy, important elements of intra-personal and interpersonal functioning continued to emerge and to develop throughout the "life cycle," which is governed by the structure of the organism as well as by the structure of the society and which, therefore, may be considered in terms of the concept of "life-trajectory."

4. Let us reconsider Bion's cryptic statement that the basic assumption group knows no boundaries of time and space, for, despite its underlying emphasis on the instinctual origins of psychic life it may be the basis for a full understanding of a dynamic social psychology of group processes within their societal context. As such, it offers a line of thought which is at least as promising as Foulkes' tentative exploration of Jung's concept of the "collective unconscious," with its foundations in phylogenesis, the inheritance of ascribed characteristics, and such notions as "consciousness of race." In this respect it may be useful to recall Max Weber's work on "group charisma and group disgrace" and, more recently, Norbert Elias' work on the "civilizing process."

5. Let us reconsider Eric Fromm's neglected but highly ambiguous concept of the "social unconscious." It may be helpful to differentiate three of its central elements: that the impulses and attendant phantasies of which people are likely to be unconscious are governed by cultural beliefs, values and norms; that as a result, specifically. Of their fear of feelings of isolation, shame and helplessness, people are likely to become, and to remain, unconscious of those social arrangements which govern their power to control their own and other people's life chances; and that societies and their constituent social groupings have ways of ensuring that people remain unaware of their nonconscious processes, and, through repression and other more primitive mechanisms of defence, such as denial, become unaware of their unconscious ones. However, it would be misleading to use the term

"mechanism of defence" to refer to social and social psychological processes; for example, although the institution of education is an important agency of socialisation, it should not be regarded as a society's "mechanism of defence" any more than it should be an ego-based creative activity—which illustrates precisely why it can be so misleading to think about groups as though they were persons. In this respect it would be helpful for group conductors of all political persuasions to reconsider such phenomena as alienation and false consciousness as examples of group specific modes of defence.

In conclusion the following references may be useful to those who wish to explore these matters in more detail. Of my own work, especially pertinent are *Social Mobility: A Study of Social Control and Instatability*, Basil Blackwells, Oxford. 1981; "Sociological Aspects of Large Groups." in L. Kreeger. (ed.). *The Large Group: Theory and Dynamics*, Constables, London, 1975; "A Comment on Professor Jahoda's 'The Individual and the Group,'" in Malcolm Pines and L. Rafaelsen, (eds.), *The Individual and the Group: Boundaries and Interrelations*," Plenum, New York, 1982; and with L. Kreeger, "A Comment on the Large Group." and with Caroline Garland "An Overview" in Caroline Garland, (ed.). *The Survivor Syndrome Workshop*. Institute of Group Analysis, London, GROUP ANALYSIS *special issue November 1980*.

From among the works of my immediate colleagues, I have drawn upon S. H. Foulkes, *Introduction to Group Analytic Psychotherapy*, Heinemann, London, 1948; Colin James, "Transitional Phenomena and the Matrix in Group Psychotherapy" in Malcolm Pines and Lise Rafaelsen, op. *cit.*; Patrick de Mark, *Perspectives in Group Psychotherapy*, Allen and Unwin, London, 1972; and A. C. R. Skynner "An Open-Systems; Group Analytic Approach to Family Therapy," in A. S. Gurman and D. P. Kniskern, (eds.) *Handbook of Family Therapy*, Brunner/Mazel, New York, 1981.

I have also becn influenced immeasurably by W. R. Bion, *Experiences in Groups*, Tavistock Press, London, 196 1; H. Ezriel "A Psychoanalytic Approach to Group Treatment," *British Journal of Medical Psychology*, 23: 59 (1950), and "The Role of Transference and Psychoanalytic and Other Approaches to Group Treatment," *Acta Psychoterapeutica*, Supplementum of Vol. 7 (1959); and Walter Schindler. "Family Patterns in Group Formations and Therapy," *International Journal of Group Psychotherapy*, 1: 100–105; and, although they are not group analysts, by H. Guntrip,

Schizoid Phenomena. Object Relations arid the Self, Hogarth Press, London, 1968, and Eric Fromm, *The Crisis of Psychoanalysis*, Penguin, Harmondsworth, 1970, and *Beyond the Chains of Illusion*, Abacus, London, 1980.

Among the sociological works which I have found especially useful are Norbert Elias, *The Civillising Process*, Basil Blackwells, Oxford, 1970, Vol. 1, ar.d 1982, Vol. 2; The Frankfurt Institute of Social Research, *Aspects of Sociology*, Heinemann Educational Books, London, 1973; T. Parsons, "Social Structure and the Development of Personality," in N. J. Smelser and V. T. Smelser; (eds), *Personality arid Social Systems*. John Wylie & Sons, London, 1963; Max Weber, *The Theory of Social arid Economic Organisation*, edited by T. Parsons, O. U. P., New York. 1947; L. Seve, *Man in Marxist Theory*, Harvester Press, London, 1978; and E. Durkheim, *Suicide*. 1897.

Notes

1. I am really not bothered about the use of "analysis" of "psychotherapy"—which is often (but not always) an issue in the politics and sociology of the profession rather than a problem of theoretical and technical substance. Many in the helping professions need to emphasise "analysis" in order to assert their power over those who are not psychoanalysts or to assert some kind of identity for themselves within a jungle of confusing professional labels. In fact, when compared to psychoanalysis proper, group-analysis is "therapy." especially when practised by those-who do not have a psychoanalytic perspective. It is very much a matter for debate whether the term "group analysis" is pretentious, and whether it serves primarily to indicate that what we do is in essence different from what goes on in encounter groups and suchlike.

2. Incidentally, beware of material which seems too "typical" and too "topical." It may be a clue to the nature of your counter-transference, in that you may be creating the material; typicality and topicality are always danger signals. However, in this instance I am satisfied that I was not looking a gift horse in the mouth—except insofar as the group wanted to help me prepare this paper.

3. This happens whenever a conductor uses his counter-transference in order to go where it is hottest. It is impossible to know with certainty where projective identification ends and personal response begins. That psychic reality is always interpersonal and that psychic truth is always negotiable are at the basis of the "politics" of knowledge in the human sciences.

4. This very pregnant sentence refers to what may well be the essence of what a group experience is all about. In any case, you will notice how I have referred, on the one hand, to what is virtually protomental, and, on the other, to social factors which constrain the lives of adults. Thus, it could be left to the group to respond to my interpretation in whatever ways they wished. In this sense, a good interpretation should have the quality of an "image" in a good play or novel, but insofar as it comes from the conductor, it should reflect back to the group the image which they have created.

5. It is worth noting that an instrumental adjustment is more than simply a defence. It is a form of action which affects others, and which can also be assessed in terms of its effectiveness and efficiency. Since an action will almost always involve the actions of others, it becomes an interaction. which is a feature of a group process.

CHAPTER FOURTEEN

The language of the group: monologue, dialogue and discourse in group analysis*

John Schlapobersky

A man walks across this empty space whilst someone else is watching him, and this is all that is needed for an act of theatre to be engaged.

The Empty Space:
Peter Brook (Brook, 1990: xi)

A sleeping man is not roused by an indifferent word but if called by name he wakes.

The Interpretation of Dreams:
Sigmund Freud (Freud, 1900: SE 4/5)

Freud's hypothesis ... (was) that the process of becoming conscious is closely allied to or essentially characterized by the cathexis of word representation.

Therapeutic Group Analysis:
S. H. Foulkes (Foulkes, 1964: 116)

---

*This chapter was previously published as: Schlapobersky, J. (1994). The Language of the Group. In The Psyche and the Social World, (ed. D. Brown & L. Zinkin), Routledge: London/New York.

185

Introduction

Free-floating discussion is the group-analytic equivalent of *free association*. The term originates in Foulkes' own writing and describes a set of key clinical concepts in therapeutic practice that distinguish the group-analytic approach. The use of association in this approach differs from its use in individual analytic practice (Kris, 1990) and from the techniques used by practitioners of other group methods (Yalom, 1975). This chapter explores these clinical concepts and the theory that underlies them. It is focussed on the language of the group—the medium of free-floating discussion.

I shall differentiate between three primary forms of speech that arise in the matrix of any group. At the most basic-level *monologue*—speaking alone (with or without an audience)—is a form of individual self-expression. At the next-level *dialogue*—a conversation between two people—is the form of communication that distinguishes a bipersonal exchange. And at the third-level *discourse*—the speech pattern of three or more people—allows the free interaction of all its participants in a flexible and complex exchange that distinguishes the communication of a group (Moffet, 1968). These patterns of speech are universal cultural forms arising in all communication and are present in the life of every group, although in no set order. Monologue can be understood as a soliloquy; dialogue as the resolution of opposites or the search for intimacy; and discourse as the work of a chorus. The maturation of the group and its members involves a progression that begins with monologue in the individual's first encounter with themselves. It moves to dialogue in the discovery of the other and then to discourse when an individual's multiple inner objects are externalized and encountered in the group. As indicated, the progression is a logical not a descriptive one; the group process itself does not necessarily follow this pattern.

The group-analytic approach is distinguished from other group methods in that neither of the two earlier speech forms are disregarded. On the contrary, both monologue and dialogue are encompassed by and integral to group-analytic experience. True discourse remains the defining attribute of group communication because the complexity of communication between two people when the introduction of a third transforms them into a group, alters the nature of the original relationship in a radical and profound way. The use of free-floating discussion allows a pattern of exchange to move freely between these different speech forms, each of which constitutes a distinctive type of communication. It is through this movement—from monologue through dialogue to discourse and back again—that the group-analytic method comes into its own, creating an arena in which the dialectic between the psyche and the social world helps to refashion both.

The paper continues with a section that draws on relational theory to differentiate between *one-person, two-person and three-person psychologies*. I then apply to these psychologies material drawn from language theory and consider the speech forms each of them allows. This is followed by a series of clinical examples that illustrate the approach with descriptions and commentaries on these speech forms as they arise in different therapy groups. It is followed with an exploration of how the use of language in clinical theory has evolved from monologue to discourse, from the couch to the circle. It traces developments from the original idea of *the talking cure* in Freud's work to the first emergence of the term free-floating discussion in Foulkes' own writing and its subsequent development. The conclusion points towards a theory of discourse that will equip us to explore how:

> Psychotherapists are rediscovering that … The depths of the mind are reached and touched by simpler words that speak in images and metaphors … a universal, timeless language, pre-dating contemporary ideas…that touches the heart, the ancient seat of the emotions; (and) that speaks to the soul…
>
> (Pines, in Cox & Theilgaard, 1987: xxiv).

Psychological forms and the relational field

We are today witnessing the "the breakup of … psychology into categories according to the minimum number of persons essential to the study of each branch of the subject" (Rickman, 1950: 218). *One-person psychology* is concerned with what goes on inside a person; *two-person psychology* with reciprocal relationships and *three-person psychology* with the relational field of the basic family constellation—and with social roles and social relations derived from it. The first takes the nature of internal experience as its field and gives centrality to the mind as it is located in a body. Its psychological functions include sensation, perception, cognition, mood, memory, imagination, fantasy and the psycho-somatic link.

The second takes the intersubjective world as its field, gives centrality to relationships—a domain beyond but including the individual—and its psychological functions include bonding and attachment, exchange, affect and the inter-personal link. The third takes social relations as its field, gives centrality to the corporate world—a domain beyond but including both the individual and the pair-bond—and its psychosocial functions include social interaction, social role and social meaning.

I shall proceed on the basis of an assumption made here, that a truly group psychology incorporates one-person, two-person and three-person psychologies and that these three psychologies stand as an adequately differentiated range of categories to encompass all human experience. The group is a matrix of interaction, a relational field that arises between its members and between the interplay of these three different psychologies. Field theory is the discipline by which these different psychological levels are related. It provides group analysis with an integrative frame by which the higher-level functions in three person psychology are related to more fundamental functions in one person psychology (Agazarian & Peters, 1981). Skynner, applying field theory to group and family therapy, describes the isomorphic relationship between experience at different levels. Thus in a group changes in any one of its component psychologies will necessarily involve change in the others (Skynner, 1976; 1987).

Speech forms and the semantic field

Discourse, in one of its colloquial meanings, describes the communication of thought by speech, the exchange between someone speaking, someone listening and something that is listened to. It describes relations between narrator, listener and story (Moffet, 1968). The structure of discourse is this set of relations amongst first, second and third persons. When the speaker, listener and subject are each distinct (or potentially distinct) as persons, that is, when two people are speaking to each other in the presence of a third person, we have the rudiments of a group. For the purposes of this paper I am using the term *discourse* to describe only this kind of group communication. In a two-person situation, when only the speaker and listener are present as persons, we have dialogue. And when speaker and listener are the same person, we have monologue.

In one of its colloquial meanings—in de Marre's paper above for example—the term *dialogue* does not refer to an exchange between only two participants (de Marre, 1991). But for the purposes of this paper I am using the term in a more restricted sense to refer specifically to speech forms in which there are no more than two key participants who might be individuals, teams or—for example—gender groups. It thus serves to identify what is distinctive about a speech form based on an oppositional symmetry, reciprocity or duality in which the dialectic of the exchange is its key property. Where communication takes place between three or more participants, the term discourse is used to identify its more diffused properties.

Using a theory of language to examine group psychotherapy, we can see how the developing agency of the group's process begins at the first stage with the solitude of private encounters with the self that are allowed by the audience of the group. It leads at the second stage to greater agency for change when, through dialogue, others acquire psychic reality through conflicts over discrepant forms or levels of intimacy required of the same group experience. When the same experience has different meaning for its different participants, it exposes their different internal conflicts and can in due course help to resolve them. And this leads to the third stage—discourse—when the spontaneity of public exchange expresses individuals' primary process allowing the emergence of archaic anxieties and their reparative resolution. This is the kind of experience that has the most far-reaching consequences in terms of personal change. The most telling description of this kind of discourse is the way an individual's dream can be taken up in a mature group. As the last clinical example on pages xxx–xxx below describes, group members enter the dream together through a diversity of associations. In the discussion by which the dream content and its associations are explored in the here and now, we see the free play of words at work in the shared unconscious. As resonance in the group as a whole connects the one and the many, meaning is condensed and, in the sudden discharge of deep and primitive material, events happen in a moment that can last a lifetime.

Each of these speech forms can arise in a narrative form through the recounting or reconstruction of reported events; or a dramatic form in people's real experience of one another in the here-and-now of the group. The group's process is characterised by a fluid interaction between narrative and drama, between the stories people have to tell and the drama of their roles and interactions as they do so. Progress is seen in a shift from speech patterns that are initially dominated by narrative and description to more mature forms that include reflective dialogue and discourse; and then to a capacity to abstract and generalise from this experience, both inside and beyond the group. This progression recapitulates the child's primary pattern of growth in a decentering movement outward from the centre of the self. As Pines has described in this collection, the self-enlarges in the group, assimilating the matrix of group relations and "taking them in"; at the same time accommodating itself to this matrix and adapting to it. The paradox of this progression is that, as the intersubjective domain in deepened and enriched, participants become more themselves by moving outward from themselves.

The process of symbolisation originates with the most primitive sense of self in the representational schema of the infant as he differentiates for the first time between self and other. As the representational world is extended and externalised the infant's symbolising process is codified in a language whose semantic field is charged with forms of meaning that bear a close association to the individuals and experiences through which it originates. In this collection Eliott's, James' and Nitsen's papers all give careful attention to these early formative experiences. The way in which a child talks to itself, addresses its mother, relates to a friend, speaks to a doll or stands up to talk in the class-room can be different in each case. All these speech forms can arise in a dialogue between only two people for, as William James has said, relations are of different degrees of intimacy—merely to be with another, is a universe of discourse (James 1900). But whilst dialogue can generate an almost limitless range of meaning, the terms of a two-person psychology act as a constraint. Discourse in a group is extended far beyond this by a relational field that is almost as rich and indeterminate as its semantic field.

Through group interaction the relational and semantic fields—the matrix of interaction and the matrix of meaning—come to play upon one another giving new meaning to early symbolic and representational experience. Thus language is a form of behaviour in the group; a way of referring to experience in and beyond the group; and a way of transforming experience in the group.

Clinical illustrations: monologue, dialogue and discourse

Free-floating discussion proceeds through an interplay between narrative and drama, story and exchange, reconstruction and encounter. A reconstruction (by an individual or sub-group of some past event or trauma), or some other story in the group, might be a defense against the anxiety of an immediate encounter between its members. The drama of an immediate encounter might be a defense against painful stories about past or recent experience. *The examples that follow are designed to illustrate the gains to be had in clinical depth from the simple practice of establishing who is talking to whom about what?* As one speech form in either its narrative or dramatic form becomes evident as a defense, the therapist, or another group member, explores the defense to widen what Foulkes called *the common zone,* and this moves the exploration to another speech form through which it can be taken forward.

Monologue

A man sits in the group recounting the circumstances that brought him into therapy. He has been with us now for three sessions and is beginning to find his voice. But as he talks peoples' attentiveness diminishes. He looks at no one in particular; his narrative is delivered now to the floor, now to the ceiling; he is agonised but self-absorbed and the group's resonance is against his self-absorbtion rather than with his agony. Despite the distress in his story about his wife's suicide attempts; their loss of love and his concern about their children, the group of initially sympathetic listeners becomes increasingly disaffected.

Initially people had been eager to ask him questions and their responses were sometimes visible in exclamations and other reactions. But the speaker appears indifferent to his audience whose primary value, it seems, is to provide him with the space in which to talk to himself. He has not yet recognized others. They serve him primarily as narcissistic containers. They allow this for some time but after ten minutes one group member seems to be dozing off; another stares out of the window; another looks to the conductor. As his monologue continues, two members smile at each other and look away. After fifteen minutes the conductor asks the speaker whom he is talking to. Startled and in some consternation he looks about him and says, well, to the group, and falters as he does so.

It is as if he has found himself alone on a stage without an audience. The process of decentering has begun, initiated by a conflict between the content of his narrative, and the limitations of his role. He recognises the disengagement he has been responsible for but is as yet without resources to communicate empathically. His problem in the world has become manifest in the group. He has spent most of his adult life as a "marginal man" caring for others at his own expense and often colluding with them when, despite his care, they neglected or overlooked him. Now he wants it all back but, consumed by neediness that he has spent a lifetime disavowing, he has no resources to enter reciprocal relationships.

To find a voice through which to reach others he must also find himself; the group first provides him with space and permission to discover his own psychic pain. If the therapy is successful we can expect to see, some months after its commencement, changes in his communication patterns in the group. From these changes he will be able to generalise, to effect changes in relations with his family and social network. The group is the arena in which psyche and social world acquire their first distinction from one another. It is here then that they can be reconciled in the interests of altered social relationships which are his primary therapeutic needs.

On future occasions when he has something to say, he will learn from the group's cues how to make eye-contact; how to come out of himself and how to begin bringing people with him in a narrative that allows empathy—shared emotion. *To have an audience whilst he tells his story, he will need to learn a different role.* He will need to allow others time to respond; to establish evidence of others' interest in him and his story; and to offer a sense of collaboration in their arena of shared interest. Of course, he will not learn this all at once and there will be many future occasions when the group recoils from his monologue. He will again use others as narcissistic containers to give him the space in which to find himself. This process of self-discovery will proceed hand in hand with his discovery of the "otherness" of those around him. Other group members will keep him connected to integrative process, having themselves had cues from the conductor that his resources will allow him to tolerate the momentary discomfort and humiliation of a confronting interruption, in the interest of shared experience.

> Two years later the same man sits in the group with a lot to say about his inner conflicts; and about his problems in the world outside. In contrast to his earlier self-absorbtion, he now chooses his moment; speaks in shorter sentences; uses shared language; relates

what he has to say to what he knows others' preoccupations will interest them in; and allows pauses for response and interruption.

It is visibly evident that he is now able to use the group process to work on his internal one. In the progression from his early monologue to a participatory role in the group's pattern of discourse, the man is learning to overcome his isolation in the group and is being steadily equipped to do so in the world at large. What he is learning in the group about intercourse will steadily equip him to live in the world, rather than in its margins. He is now socially engaged and, whilst the nature and manner of his self-presentation continue to arouse resentment amongst other members over issues of control and detachment, his internal conflicts and anxieties are now an integral part of a shared process and are thus open to understanding and resolution.

Dialogue

This progression from autistic, private alienation towards an openly identified and shared social process lies at the heart of the group-analytic enterprise. The distinctive speech form that arises through dialogue at the second level is illustrated by exchanges in two different groups that arise between two members in each case. The first describes the concepts of *valency* (Scharff, 1991), and *mirroring* (Pines, 1982) and the second, those of *projection* and *projective identification* (Sandler, 1988).

A: Valency and mirroring:

> A man in his mid-forties who has been using the group to come to terms with his divorce, shares with us towards the end of the session a poignant moment in his relationship with his teen-age daughter visiting him for the week-end. He tells us of how she has begun to talk to him about her menarche. He recounts in the group what she said about it and how she did so. People comment on how touching they find her openness with him, and on how moving they find the trust between them. He tells us his daughter has had mixed feelings; she was pleased but also awkward and embarrassed. Her mother—his former wife—has supported her practically and emotionally and this too he is pleased to acknowledge as he relates his daughter's narrative to the group. Sitting opposite

him is a woman in her late 30's who—like him—has been in the
group for some years. She is the only one of the 7 who says nothing
at all. But she does not take her eyes off him as his narrative unfolds
whilst different members engage with him at different levels and
in different ways. She watches and listens attentively and in tears
but will not be drawn out about her reaction. At the next session
a week later, she initiates the discussion by telling us that she has
not been able to get the picture of this man and his daughter out of
her mind.

She wishes she had a father like him. She had not believed it
possible that a young girl could trust her father so intimately with
her developing sexuality. She wants to know more about their relationship and as he tells her she replies with detail—long known in
the group but never explored in quite this way—about her relationship with her own father who abused her violently and sexually.

In the course of this dialogue the man opposite her becomes confirmed
as the transference object for the good father she had always longed
for and never known. She in turn furnishes him with the opportunity
to reach and recover in the group a lost aspect of his self that can be
benevolent and tender towards women. The benign quality of his generosity, as it emerges with increasing evidence of his resources as a good
father, stands in dramatic contrast to the destructive person we have
known about, in his relations with his wife. The emotional charge—the
valency—between the two of them becomes the group's object of interest. One other woman, in particular, whose own history involved an
unresolved Oedipal conflict, becomes excited and animated by what she
sees happening between these two. She makes herself available to them
as a facilitator and, as they talk to each other across the group, she moves
their discussion forward at those points at which they reach impasse.

They are each, of course, talking to the group as a whole but they
do so by addressing each other. They generate emotions in the group
as a whole but they do so because of the emotions they arouse in the
encounter with each other. These two people each find reflected in the
other, the lost ideal of their respective parental introjects. They select
each other for an exchange that involves, temporarily, more intense
emotion than arises elsewhere in the group and through this they
each provide a reparative mirror for a lost aspect of the other. In both
these cases, however, each person's sense of the other is derived from

a principal relationship with themselves. She experiences him as her idealised father and he, similarly, relates to her as the mirror image of women familiar to him in his own life experience.

"Otherness" for each of these people is derived from their unconscious primary preoccupations with their own internal objects. There is work to be done before they can each relate to another of the opposite sex as a genuinely "other" person, rather than as some reflection of their own internal imagery. The next example describes an interaction through which a conflict between two individuals in a group (over discrepant requirements for intimacy), at the moment at which longstanding internal conflicts acquire some resolution.

B: Projection and projective identification:

Two people are closely connected in a group by complementary roles in their life outside. She has a son like him with whom she is engrossed. He has a mother who, like this woman in the group, he finds strident and intrusive. The valency that emerges involves an antagonistic preoccupation between them. He reports a dream to the group in which she, clearly recognisable, suffocates his father. As the story of the dream unfolds in the group she becomes increasingly angry and distressed. She is furious at the role in which he has cast her in his dream life and treats the dream—in so far as it describes her—as if he had chosen its content as a conscious attack on her and could be held responsible for it. She rounds on him and, as he defends himself against her attack, he becomes increasingly aggressive himself. The therapist eventually intercedes with a modest observation about her that has an astonishing effect on her. "It's his dream which you can learn from if you wish to, but in the last analysis it's *his* dream." In the discourse that ensues the whole group explores the hostile dialogue that followed the reported dream and she struggles with the realization that she has been trying to control the content of his psychic life.

The understanding this generates eventually leaves her in tears as she takes back the projections by which she has maintained this man—in her mind—as if he were her son. The hostile cathexis between these two—what Zinkin calls malignant mirroring— is being undone. It helps to resolve his anxiety that she will damage him with her projections, as his mother damaged his father. And it helps to resolve her separation anxiety about losing her own son.

Zinkin uses the term malignant mirroring to replace, with a single process, the experience of two distinct projective identifications that have a symmetrical relationship with one another (Zinkin, 1983). As we can see here, it is the experience of dialogue that links the two individual's experiences and resolves the valency they hold for one another. The dream illustrates how he lived with the fear of damage—the fear of what her projections could do to him—and identified with this fear. Projective identification has been the basis of their valency, in this case malignant mirroring, a hostile cathexis.

At the point of this confrontation she experiences him for the first time as a genuinely "other" person and is freed by this realization although she is shocked by it for some time. And he undergoes a comparable experience. These events allow her to generalise from the group to her life in the world and in particular to the relationship with her son whom she has bound with her projections for much of his life and is fearful of losing.

She is distraught as she begins to take all this in and for some weeks is depressed in the group. This in turn arouses compassion in the man who, witnessing her distress over the way in which she mis-related to him, appreciates her—for the first time—as a genuinely "other" person, rather than the projected representative of his damaging mother. So he appreciates her as a genuinely different person and can relate constructively to her needs. And this in turn helps her consider how, by relinquishing control, she might gain rather than lose.

Discourse

The examples above illustrate the free-floating nature of group discussion as it moves between them all three speech forms, with the conductor providing a minimum of direction. Rather than seeking to press the group's exchange towards one pattern or another, the conductor regards the speech form expressed by the group as a source of information as to what is happening in the matrix. In the example below discourse is initiated by information from one of the group's members, but there is neither monologue nor dialogue. Discussion is maintained by the group as a whole and, in our attempt to analyze it, individualistic concepts are of only limited value.

In a twice-weekly group of many years standing, events are dominated by increasing evidence of peoples' development and differentiation. One evening one of the members, a man who has struggled against his parents' envy of his youth and their attacks on his individuation, discloses that he has finally reached a crucial financial target in the business he established. The figures are startling and unexpected but—for the moment—his achievement does not earn the regard it merits in the group.

One of the men, facing major financial dilemmas in his own company, is withdrawn and unresponsive; another, successful in his own career, explores the issue constructively, but for some time there is a limpness about the group's responses and, in their reluctance to confirm evidence of this man's progress, they behave like his parents who resent the fact that he has been successful on his own. Discussion moves round to one of the women who is expecting a baby. She is finding her position in the group sometimes difficult to protect.

What is most striking is the reaction of the two other women to news of the pregnancy. She has struggled to conceive and has finally been rewarded by a healthy pregnancy. Since then one of the women has left the group unexpectedly, and now the other woman, the mother of a small child, offers a disproportionate amount of advice, punctuated with references to ectopic pregnancies and other disasters.

The issue of envy lies beneath the narrative. All seven members participate in different ways and the atmosphere is coloured by tension between affirmation on the one hand, and anxiety and antagonism on the other. People have struggled for years together and are really very close—they do wish to affirm one anothers' success. Despite their affirmative desires, they experience serious problems of envy. After 45 minutes the conductor offers an interpretation of the tension, suggesting that people are anxious about each other's envy of their own progress and, perhaps, ashamed of their own envy of others' progress.

The quality of the exchange alters, relief allows disclosure and the second half of the group session is taken up with a wide-ranging exploration of envy and jealousy in intimate relations.

It is not a new subject in this group and people are accustomed to exploring the less acceptable aspects of their own personalities with one another. It ranges over mens' envy of womens' creativity aroused by the prospect of a woman bringing a new baby into the group; and womens' envy of mens' penises or potency in their reaction to the financial and career success reported on at the outset. Neither of these envious forms is exclusive to either gender and this too is recognised and discussed, as is the acute anxiety that a number of members acknowledge about the prospect of envious attacks from those closest to them as they progress through their therapy.

The group's exploration is open and diffuse; there is no exclusive narrative line, and no single contributor. To understand the group we should have to consider the texture of its discourse rather than merely the text of its narrative. In a mature group at this stage we see that the "the conductor strives to broaden and deepen the expressive range of all members, while at the same time increasing their understanding of the deeper, unconscious levels (Foulkes, 1964: 112). In the texture of the discourse we discover what Foulkes called,

> A *common zone* in which all members can participate and learn to understand one another. *The zone of communication* must include the experience of every member in such a way that it can be shared and understood by the others, on whatever level it is first conveyed.
>
> (Foulkes, 1964: 112)

The zone of communication in this group now incorporates the shared fear of others' envy and the shared sense of shame at acknowledging envy of one's own. It leads on to the recognition that developmental arrest and some of the other forms of neurosis discussed in the group are attempts at envy pre-emption (Kreege, 1992). What concerns us here is the way this recognition is arrived at. One member provided information about his success at work which led through group association to another's reference to her pregnancy. The first introduced a subject—ambivalence about progress associated with internal conflict and the fear of external attack—to which another resonated. This theme was amplified by resonance in the group as a whole which extended the exploration. From the introduction of this theme to its amplification, exploration, analysis and resolution there was one focussed but brief interpretation by the conductor which set him apart from the others but, for the rest, discourse in the group to which the conductor contributed like the other members, was responsible for its progress. The theme that provided the group's focal conflict (Whittaker & Lieberman, 1965) in this session rested on an anxiety as to whether the group could relate to its members as a generative rather than envious parent and provide them with confirmation for their progress. For the group as a whole to be experienced in such positive terms each of its members needed to find their individual part in the destructive envy anticipated from the others.

We would fail to take advantage of the real benefits of group-analysis if we confined our attention to content analysis of the text. An attempt to characterize a discussion like this requires concepts that describe context as well as content; texture as well as form; ground as well as figure; and group atmosphere as well as the dynamics of the individual. The development of group-analytic theory has not, regrettably, developed to characterize group process in this way because of the difficulties we continue to experience in characterising the complexity of such exchanges (Skynner, 1987). "Our concepts and technical terms," says Balint, "have been coined under the physiological bias and are, in consequence, highly individualistic; they do not go beyond the confines of the individual mind (Balint, 1985: 228). A theory of discourse should help to clarify how "inner (mental) and "outer" reality merge inside the common matrix of interpersonal social reality, out of which they originally differentiated." (Foulkes, 1964: 98) Our attempt to conceptualise change is now assisted by the distinction provided in this account between the relational and semantic field. By exploring their interplay,

> It becomes easier to understand our claim that the group associates, responds and reacts as a whole. The group as it were avails itself now of one speaker, now of another, *but it is always the transpersonal network which is sensitized and gives utterance, or responds. In this sense we can postulate the existence of a group "mind"* in the same way as we postulate the existence of an individual mind.
>
> (Foulkes, 1964: 118)

The group "mind" can now be understood as the composite of its semantic and relational elements.

From the couch to the circle: the evolution of technique

Freud's talking cure and the first fundamental rule

Brown (Brown, 1994) gives a comprehensive account of how the metapsychology of psychoanalysis has been revised by object relations theory. I am here concerned with the implications of this change for clinical theory. In his early collaboration with Breuer, Freud recognised that the crucial ingredient in their treatment of hysterics was free word association—what one of his patients called "her talking cure"—rather than hypnosis. His original idea "that whatever comes into one's head must be reported" (Freud, SE12: 107) was later set out as the "fundamental rule of psychoanalytic technique" (Freud, SE12: 107):

> A rule which structures the analytic situation: the analysand is asked to say what he thinks and feels, selecting nothing and omitting nothing from what comes into his mind, even where this seems to him unpleasant to have to communicate, ridiculous, devoid of interest or irrelevant.
>
> (Laplanche & Pontalis, 1983: 179)

The analytic relationship dictated by this rule emphasises its linguistic content, establishes the neutrality of the analyst and helps to foster the regression of the patient. It has a further consequence which, like the use of the couch, is a remnant of the hypnotic method out of which it evolved—it confines the work of psychoanalysis to the patient's monologue.

Freud's original paradigm was an intrapsychic drive psychology whose formulations are those of a one-person psychology concerned with the individual in isolation. He maintained the use of the couch for the protection it afforded him from uncomfortable interaction with and exposure to his patients; and for the benefits it brought to treatment, minimising the extent to which free association was contaminated by dialogue. (Freud, SE12: 134)

The critique of classical theory took issue with these limitations. Balint, "for want of a better term" but in language that has had momentous consequences, introduces "the *object* or *object-relation* bias" on the grounds that "all our concepts and technical terms" except these two "have been coined under the physiological bias and are ... highly individualistic; they do not go beyond the confines of the individual mind" (Balint, 1952: 226, 228). Today the concept of counter-transference has been recast as a valuable clinical tool; the analyst's subjectivity has been brought into the therapeutic arena as an acknowledged resource, rather than as the troublesome intrusion Freud had earlier believed it to be; and free association, stripped of its unnecessary drive theory, has been reconceptualised in the context of a two-person psychology focussed upon the dialogue between patient and analyst (Lewis, 1990), "an interrelation between two individuals … a constantly changing and developing object-relation," a "two person situation" (Balint, 1952: 231).

Foulkes' development of free-floating discussion

Foulkes' work has taken the same line of development one stage further, providing us with a clinical method that allows the participation of three psychological objects in the associative process. Free-floating discussion rests on what he called his "model of three." Although the maximum composition of what could be properly called a group is indeterminate and controversial, its minimum number is three. Between the dyadic experience of a pair and the group experience of three there is a transition just as radical and profound as that between one and two. Whatever the size of a small therapy group, the model of three gives it its underlying emotional structure. There is an indeterminate maximum in the number of individuals that can be present in any group, and there may be more than one conductor. But there are only three categories of psychological object—the individual, the conductor, and the group as a whole. In the bounded space between these three objects, we find a three-person psychology at work.

Like Freud before him, Foulkes worked towards and arrived at his method before naming it. Described initially as "a kind of group associative method," the term enters his primary text well after his first descriptions of its use. He then returns to it frequently, refining and redefining his descriptions and, in explaining how it evolved, recounting how he initially treated peoples' associations in the group individually. Only later did he become "aware that it was possible to consider the group's productions as the equivalent of the individual's free association *on the part of the group as a whole.*"(Foulkes, 1964: 117)

> If one allows one's "floating attention" as Freud termed it, to record automatically its own observations, one begins eventually to respond to "pressures and "temperatures" as sensitively as any barometric or thermometric gauge with something akin to an internal graph of change on the cerebral "drum" of the therapist.
>
> (Foulkes & Anthony, 1968: 142)

The group matrix is the "operational basis of all relationships and communications" (Foulkes, 1964: 118). It has both a relational and semantic field. Through the interplay of these two fields, free-floating discussion allows "the construction of an ever widening zone of mutual understanding within the group," (Foulkes, 1964: 116) which Foulkes regards as its manifest content. This is understood to relate to the latent meaning "as a manifest dream relates to latent dream thoughts" (Foulkes, 1964: 118). In the course of group discussion symptoms (manifest content) are translated into their meaning (latent content) and this:

> "Transforms the driving forces which lay concealed behind them into (new) emotions ... embers learn a new language ... previously spoken only unconsciously," in the course of which "they (become) active participants in their own healing process" and undergo change at a number of levels.
>
> (Foulkes, 1964:176)

The group analyst works both as therapist and as group member beginning with the dynamic administration of the group and the initiation of free-floating discussion. He assumes a more active role in a new group and allows the "decrescendo" of his own role as the group gains authority. He is responsible for identifying disturbances in the group's process—what Foulkes calls location—and for providing a balance between analytic (disturbing) and integrative forces, as the manifest content is translated into language that describes the unconscious. Transference is prominent but the work is undertaken in the dynamic present. One of Foulkes' own descriptions of the conductor at work gives a vivid account of the clinical role which contrasts dramatically with Freud's account of the psychoanalyst at work behind the couch (Freud, SE12: 134).

> He treats the group as adults on an equal level to his own and exerts an important influence by his own example. He sets a pattern of desirable behaviour rather than having to preach ... puts emphasis on the "here and now" and promotes tolerance and appreciation of individual differences ... (He) represents and promotes reality, reason, tolerance, understanding, insight, catharsis, independence, frankness, and an open mind for new experiences. This happens by way of a living, corrective emotional experience.
>
> (Foulkes, 1964: 57)

In contrast to the first fundamental rule in individual practice described above, the group analyst is supportive as well as analytic and the linguistic content of the therapy relationship is not so paramount. Regression may occur but it is counterbalanced by a progressive role through which group members become active participants in their own healing process. Finally, the group analyst's role is neither neutral nor detached. The quality of his engagement is evident, as is his readiness to maintain a human position that will serve the group's members as a model. *Foulkes' clinical recommendations to the conductor can be summarised as a responsibility for promoting discourse* (Foulkes, 1964: 57).

Conclusion; towards a theory of discourse

A twice-weekly group meets for the first time after the Christmas break. Its members have common difficulties making or sustaining relationships. Joan reports that she had a terrible time over the holiday. It was like the roof caved in. Susan says she was also pretty shitty. Adam says he was fantastic. He had no contact at all with his recent girl-friend but went abroad on a working trip with a different girl, an old chum who doesn't mean much to him and with whom there is no intimate relationship. He no longer finds his current girl friend attractive and, although they speak every day on the phone, he was pleased not to have to see her over the break. Whilst abroad with the new one, they got on like a house on fire. Anne takes up the image of the house on fire in one case, and the collapsing roof in another. She finds parallels between them; others agree. Adam is directed by the group to look at how he was now treating this girl-friend as an earlier partner had once treated him. The attraction he once described to us is now replaced by repulsion. He couldn't bear the thought of being close to her body. He talks a lot about attraction and repulsion. Susan knows only too well what he meant, she says, referring to her loss of sexual desire, and when she feels this way there is nothing her husband can do about it. They just have to wait until her sexual feelings return.

Joan had described to us in the last group (before Christmas) how loved she felt by her partner. He had sent her flowers and a lovely note whilst he was away on a business trip. But once they were together over Christmas, the roof caved in. He just wasn't there with her. In the group people know her well and question whether she wasn't the one who vacated the house first. As the subject of attraction and repulsion, intimacy and withdrawal is taken up around the group, a new sense of acceptance and recognition enters the discussion.

Adam is ready to consider how he will find someone attractive providing there's nothing whole-hearted in how they find him. If they're genuinely attracted to him, in ways that reflect his own attraction towards them, he loses his feeling for them. His own sense of desire becomes repulsive. He can't tolerate two whole-hearted people in the same relationship. If they get on too well, the house on fire brings the roof down.

The group is not dealing with Adam's manic flight; nor with Joan's depression, nor Susan's disorder of sexual desire nor the reaction of the group as a whole to the recent Christmas break. Nor is it dealing with the common relational problems they mirror to one another. It is dealing with all of this simultaneously and as the relational matrix generates a semantic field this in turn helps to transform their relationships inside the group and beyond.

In this semantic field, meaning is condensed by a number of key images which enter the word play of the discussion. A disorder of sexual desire is an empty house; passion can bring the roof down; desire can become its opposite; two whole hearts can produce an empty house. The group's subject is not simply the series of static images by which it is reproduced here. A sense of profundity accrues as the process of discourse—now a chain reaction of associated images—develops a symbolic language by which the tension between hope and fear is brought out and, over time, resolved.

In a couples group of some years standing, with three couples and a therapist, one partnership was under discussion for some weeks. Prior to joining the group they separated and came together several times in a seemingly intractable pattern of conflict and reconciliation. The session reported here marks the turning point in their conflict. He has been convinced for some time they should separate and he wants her to leave the house.

He brings a dream to the group in which he is with her on a luxurious ocean liner. He leaves her inside and climbs a gangway that looks as if it is going somewhere but it leads him over the side; he falls into the sea and the boat sails away. There is a much smaller

boat nearby which he swims towards. As he struggles in the water
he then sees a red flag floating nearby. He tries to secure the both
the red flag and the boat but the current keeps them apart and in
the attempt to have both he loses everything and knows he will
now drown. One of the other men invites the dreamer to offer his
own associations to the dream. As he begins to do so, the third man
enters the discussion with his own associations based on different
imagery. The three women then enter the discussion. The woman
who fears abandonment is barely interested in the dream and much
more concerned with where she will live if he insists she should go.
The two other women are closely identified with her. A dialogue
develops between the men and the women as to where the discussion should go; the men want to discuss the dream's imagery but
the women address the relationship conflict at a concrete level.

After a prolonged and fractious exchange that includes material
from the two other couples, we are reminded by the partner that the
dreamer's son recently sent this couple some red roses as a token of
hope for their reconciliation. There is a sense of startled recognition
in the group as everyone see these roses as the warning flag in the
sea. The discourse acquires a new vitality and, towards the end of
the group, the therapist offers an interpretation that extends this
recognition. He suggests that the dreamer, like all the group's members, is deeply bound to his partner and has discovered in his dream
that if he gets her to walk the plank, he'll end up in the sea himself.
The man laughs with relief at being understood but she doesn't
know whether to laugh or cry and looks from him to the therapist
saying "Yes, yes, yes." The discussion continues with humour and
appreciation to the end of the session. In the weeks that follow this
imagery is returned to repeatedly as the couple emerge from their
conflict and bring their new-found affection and good will to bear
on the other couples' conflicts.

The exchange moves between monologue, dialogue and discourse.
There is both narrative and drama in each of these speech forms as
we move between real and reported experience. Language is working
here to generate mutative metaphors that come in a moment that can
last a lifetime. At such a moment, "a sense of mystery, astonishment,
and uniqueness ... transcends any descriptive technicalities."(Cox &
Theilgaard, 1987: 17) As Cox describes it,

We have a fragmentary glimpse into therapeutic space. It emphasizes the universal pull of the primordial. It is an intrinsic part of
the psychotherapeutic process in which a patient comes as close to
his true feelings as he dares … Metaphor affords the possibility of
engagement with those primordial themes to which all our experience gravitates.

(Cox & Theilgaard, 1987:9)

In this group the dream is first a soliloquy, a way of thinking aloud
about the viability of the partnership and the fear of separation. Then
it becomes the subject of a dialogue, initially between this man and his
partner and then between the men and women in the group as they are
all drawn into a review of their relationships. Throughout the session
it is the subject of discourse, yielding moments of profundity in which
the group works like a chorus in an ancient drama, challenging private
deceits with public recognition and confirming private recognitions
with public affirmation. Free-floating discussion thus encompasses all
three speech forms but it provides more than simply direct access to primary process. It is also the means by which associative patterns are ana-
lyzed and explored, new forms of meaning are constructed and a new
sense of the individual emerges in the widening cycle of the whole.

References

Agazarian, Y. & Peters, R. (1981). The visible and invisible group, London:
    Routledge.
Brook, P. (1990). The empty space, London: Penguin.
Brown, D. G. (1994). Self-development through subjective interaction: A fresh
    look at "ego training in action." In: *The psyche and the social world*, (ed. D.
    Brown & L. Zinkin). pp. 80–98. Routledge: London and New York.
Cox, M. & Theilgaard, A. (1987). Mutative metaphors In psychotherapy:
    The Aeolian mode, London: Tavistock.
de Mare, P. et al. (1991) Koinonia: From hate through dialogue to culture in
    the large group, London: Karnac.
Foulkes, S. H. (1975). Group analytic psychotherapy: Method and princi-
    ples, London: Gordon and Breach.
Foulkes, S. H. & Anthony, E. (1968). Group psychotherapy: The psychoana-
    lytic approach, London: Pelican.
Foulkes, S. H. (1964). Therapeutic group analysis, London: George, Allen
    and Unwin.

Freud, S. (19??) The Dynamics of Transference, in SE XII, London, Hogarth Press.

Freud, S. (19??) On Beginning The Treatment: Further Recommendations on the Technique of Psychoanalysis, in SE XII, London, Hogarth Press.

Freud, S. (1900). The interpretation of dreams, SE IV/V, London: Hogarth Press.

Freud, S. (1911–1915). Papers on technique, in SE XII, London: Hogarth Press.

Gay, P. (1989). Freud: A life for our time, London: Papermac.

James, W. (19??). Varieties of Religious Experience ????

Kohon, (ed.) (1986). The British School of Psychoanalysis: The independent tradition, London, Free Association Books.

Korzybski, A. (1933). General semantics, Pennsylviania USA: Science Press.

Kreeger, L. (1992). Envy preemption in small and large groups: 16th. S. H. Foulkes Lecture', in Group Analysis, ??.

Kris, A. O. (1990). The analyst's stance and the method of free association: Sigmund Freud Birthday Lecture of the Anna Freud Centre, 1989, in Psychoanalytic-Study-of-the-Child, 45: 25–41.

Laplanche, J. and Pontalis, J.B. (1983) The Language of Psycho-Analysis, London, Hogarth Press.

Lewis, A. (1990). Free association and changing models of mind, *American Academy of Psychoanalysis*, 18(3): 439–459.

Lewis, A. (1990). One person and two person psychologies and the method of psychoanalysis. *Journal of Psychoanalytic Psychology*, 7(4): 475–485.

Moffet, J. (1968). Teaching the universe of discourse, Boston USA, Houghton Mifflin.

Pines, M. (1982). Reflections on Mirroring: 6th. Foulkes Lecture', in Group Analysis, 1982, 15, suppt.

Pines, M. (1987). "Introduction," M. Cox & A. Thielgaard, Mutative Metaphors In Psychotherapy, op. cit.

Rickman, J. (1950). The factor of number in individual and group-dynamics, in John Rickman's Selected Contributions to Psycho-Analysis, London, Hogarth Press 1957.

Rycroft, C. (1985). Psycho-analysis and beyond, London: Hogarth Press.

Sandler, J. (ed.) (1988). Projection, identification, projective identification, London: Karnac.

Scharff, D. & J. (1991). Object relations couple therapy, New Jersey USA, Jason Aaronson.

Skynner, A. C. R. (1987). Group Analysis and Family Therapy in Explorations with families: Group analysis and family therapy, London: Methuen.

Whitaker, D. S. & Liebermann, M. A. (1965). Psychotherapy through the group process, New York: Atherton.

Yalom, I. (1975). The theory and practice of group psychotherapy, New York: Basic Books.
Zinkin, L. (1983). Malignant mirroring. *Group Analysis*, *16*(2): 113.

CHAPTER FIFTEEN

The psyche and the social world*

Dennis Brown and Louis Zinkin

In our discussions as a group of authors, there has been much questioning of one another's theoretical preoccupations or biases. At times there has been agreement and at others sharp disagreement. Where disagreement has occurred, it has not been about the value of one another's ideas in their own context, but about the extent to which they can be brought into a group-analytic model without violating some of the basic principles of group analysis. This, in turn has led to questions as to how far group-analytic theory can be extended.

For example, can an intersubjective theory be reconciled with an object relations one? Can a model which regards the individual as an abstraction be reconciled with theories based on the primacy of the individual and of the internal world of the person? By extending psychoanalytic theory, are we in danger of watering it down? In rejecting reductionism, is there a danger of inflating our theory to such an extent that important distinctions become blurred? Is it possible to speak of a "group mind'" or even a "world soul" as we move into cultures and across cultures, seeking unification of diverse

---

*This paper was originally published as Chapter Fifteen in Brown, D. & Zinkin, L. (eds) (1994) The Psyche and the Social World, London. Routledge.

ways of looking at the world and invoking transpersonal processes? Can attachment theory, quantum theory, systems theory, or linguistic concepts all be brought together into some all-encompassing mega-theory which would provide support to a generally accepted model of group analysis? Not only can we not agree on whether this might be possible; we cannot even agree on the desirability of such integration.

These problems are not, of course, unique to group analysis. They are of concern to all the human sciences in this postmodern age, which attempts to avoid the problems created by all-embracing, total theories. We believe, though, that group analysis is not only especially prone to these agonising questions but has a special contribution to make to understand their nature. Seeing people in groups, trying to achieve a common understanding in an increasingly fragmented world, not only exposes seemingly incompatible differences of viewpoints but also provides possible solutions.

As editors reviewing the book as a whole , we have a similar problem to that facing the group conductor trying to understand the group-as-a-whole. We can see both a unity and a great diversity. Any representation of the whole which we make resembles a group interpretation, which may or may not resonate with the views of any individual member. So we must emphasise that we are presenting only our own provisional understanding. Also, in attempting such an overview, we can draw out only certain features of varied and complex contributions. In no sense is this intended as a critical review of the value, the merits, or demerits of any individual thinker.

We shall look first at the problems and contradictions as we see them, then attempt to integrate the contributions, and finally take a tentative look to the future.

Problems and contradictions

Although each contributor to this volume is attempting to develop group-analytic theory within a Foulkesian framework, it is inevitable that others will question whether extending the theory alters its fundamental tenets. This is particularly liable to happen when the author brings in a new frame of reference.

It will be convenient in this section not to follow the order of chapters but to group them in four main divisions:

1. *Psychoanalysis*. Problems here include divergences within the psychoanalytic community as well as difficulties of stretching theory beyond its clinical orientation. Psychoanalytic concepts are particularly prominent in the chapters[1] by James, Brown, Nitsun, Elliott, and Marrone.
2. *Systems theory*. Family therapy is allied to group therapy but usually does not make any use of unconscious phantasy (Behr & Blackwell).
3. *Social sciences*. This is a field of study not easily delineated, but including sociology, anthropology, linguistics and political theory (Zinkin, Schlapobersky, & Le Roy).

> *General, more abstract philosophical theories*. These include religious and moral standpoints, particular views of the philosophy of science, and cosmology. Naturally, this category gives rise to the greatest degree of controversy, and especially to attacks of being vague and "unscientific" (Powell, Pines, & De Mare).

These categories stem from the theoretical framework of each chapter, which in turn usually reflects the professional background of the contributor. The comments on our own contributions arise from joint discussions and reflect the difficulties we ourselves acknowledge.

Psychoanalysis

The question here is whether the joins made between various analytic theories, as well as between individual and group analysis, are as seamless as they appear.

Dennis Brown sees, in the development of object relations theory, a trend from object to subject which seems to correlate with much of Foulkes' conceptions of group analysis. He points out the limitations of Foulkes' own psychoanalytic position, which has been transcended in later developments of theory. We anticipate that few would quarrel with his description of these trends towards intersubjectivity, but we do not, of course, know whether Foulkes would have been happy with Brown's re-wording of "ego training in action." There is an ongoing debate concerning the impact of infant research on psychoanalytic theories of development, which seriously questions many assumptions, particularly affecting primary narcissism and the early projective mechanisms of internal objects posited by Klein and her

followers. Since these notions are quite basic for most psychoanalytic theorists, it is questionable whether the problems inherent in
the notion of internal objects (originally conceived as the objects of
instinctual drives) can be overcome without so radical a revision of
Freud that many would not recognise the theory as psychoanalytic.
A revision in this direction is at present being undertaken in self psychology following Kohut, where intersubjectivity is indeed coming to
the fore. But should it be taken to the point where drive theory is altogether abandoned? If not, how can it be modified? Again, the reader
will have to decide after carefully considering Brown's arguments, but
it should be remembered that there is by no means a general consensus within psychoanalytic circles on these questions. Most group analysts faced with this issue would probably want to retain a place for a
subject-object theory as well as wanting to incorporate the more relational concepts implied by intersubjectivity, but there remains room
for considerable disagreement.

In his chapter on attachment theory, Mario Marrone persuasively
argues for the importance of Bowlby's work. However, his place in the
psychoanalytic movement remains extremely problematic. In broad
conceptual terms, Bowlby's thinking is based on his strongly held view
that psychoanalysis is part of natural, rather than hermeneutic, science.
Basically, though subjectivity is acknowledged, the whole thrust of the
theory is biological and behavioural, and his notion of the working
model is simply not the same as what most analysts mean by the internal world. Though analysts do speak of self- and object-representations,
their idea of the phantasy-life of their patients would not have been
acceptable to Bowlby. As Marrone points out, the concept of a behavioural system is a key issue in attachment theory. Not all group analysts
would agree that behavioural systems are an object of study in group
analysis and would not accept the epistemology implied by such a term.
It is difficult to integrate with Brown's movement towards intersubjectivity, the notion of coherence as developed by Pines and the dialogue
of De Mare, Zinkin, and Schlapobersky. In anthropology, as shown in
the chapters by Le Roy and Zinkin, there are limitations to its objectivity, to the extent to which a fieldworker can be a neutral observer. Similar problems are raised by Blackwell and Behr through family therapy
and the use of cybernetic models. There are also technical problems in
the kind of active enquiry that Marrone advocates on the part of the
group conductor.

Barbara Elliott's contribution is perhaps the most original and controversial in this volume, in that she proposes that certain experiences in the group can be explained only on the assumption that some sort of memory traces exist of pre-natal experience in the womb, and that both men and women have phantasies of having a womb inside them. At this stage such suggestions must remain somewhat speculative, but Elliott at least points out that her suggestions are compatible with research findings and gives vivid clinical arguments to support her thesis. However, few group analysts would make the interpretations she does, and most would deal with phantasies of fusion and of absence of true object relations differently. Nevertheless, many will find her arguments and suggestions wormy of further consideration, and her idea may represent the sort of contribution to our understanding of human development that can be found more readily in a group-analytic setting than in an individual one.

The chapter by Morris Nitsun puts a "psychoanalytically based'" phantasy firmly on centre stage: the primal scene. In doing so, he raises considerable problems. First, there is the centrality of the Oedipus complex in Freud's theory. To various extents, psychoanalysts have increasingly paid attention to the pre-Oedipal stages of infant development, even though, as Nitsun points out, the Oedipal stage is placed much earlier in Klein's theory than in Freud's. Second, there is the vexed question of whether the Oedipus complex is universal. It is not generally agreed that it occurs in the same form or is equally important in all cultures. Third, in Jung's account of the "coniunctio" (the alchemical picture of the union of male and female), as depicted in his essay. "The psychology of the transference" (Jung, 1946), he does not pay much attention to it as a historically determined intrapsychic phantasy. Instead, he regards it as one of many archetypal patterns concerned in the union of opposites. As an archetype, this pattern would transcend cultural differences. Last, there is Nitsun's main thesis. He sees the primal scene as so central to group analysis that he metaphorically puts it in the centre of the circle of the group, the place physically taken up by the small table that most group analysts use. His arguments to support this idea are quite involved, but would surely be contested by other group analysts who contribute to this volume.

Beyond the objections within psychoanalytic theory or even those within analytical psychology, Foulkes' idea of the matrix would be considered by many to regard all phantasies as arising from a relational network, rather than any one being central. Most people would not imagine the matrix as having a centre in this sense. This is not, of course, to deny the importance of primal scene phantasies in the group, but the underlying theory of-how they should be understood in the group context remains sharply controversial. Moreover, maternal, paternal, and sexual elements pervade everyone's thinking at all levels, including that of group members and the conductor. As well as "maternal" nurturing and "paternal" law-giving, their *relationship* permeates the foundation matrix land personal matrices of the group, and therefore the dynamic matrix of the group.

Colin James's chapter makes a strong claim for the integration of group analytic with object relations theory, using Bion and Winnicott as his main exemplars of that theory, challenging the usually held view that there is a great gulf between Foulkes' and Bion's group theories. This involves him in making links between holding and containing, with repeated warning of the difficulties in tearing concepts from their theoretical contexts. Despite the fact that both analysts presented these ideas at the same conference, many readers might question whether the abstract formulations of Bion on thinking are compatible with Winnicott's notions of maternal holding. Certainly these two men did not embrace each other as though they had arrived at the same idea by different routes, and it remains doubtful whether each regarded the other's ideas as congenial. This doubt is furthered by James's subsequent quoting of the group relations authors: Turquet, Trist, and Lawrence, who are strongly influenced by Klein and Bion, rather than by Winnicott. This bias might explain James's dismissal of Zinkin's (1989a) proposition that there is a creative ambiguity between what is container arid what contained: the group acts as container for its constituent members, who come to contain the idea of the group, and the group initiates inter-member processes. However, this view accords with James's interpretation of Bion's ideas that meaning is created in, through, and by the group, as by the containing and meaning-creating responsiveness of the early mother.

As for the integration with Foulkes, it is highly questionable whether, as James contends, Foulkes' differences were simply a sign of the times. Can man as a social being be entirely explained by the externalisation of object relations as James, following Bion, tries to show, or might it be that this attempt misses what is essential in Foulkes' position—namely, that no individual can be understood outside his or her social world at any given time (Brown, 1985). The question here is a fundamental one for psychoanalysis: should we take the inner world of the individual as the primary object of study? The reader has to decide after examining James's detailed analysis and the logic with which he proceeds from the individual to the dyad, to the small group, to the large group, and to the larger society. Whatever the implications for psychoanalytic theory, the question for the group analyst is: can psychoanalysis provide an *adequate* model or does it need to be supplemented by others which do not start with the individual?

Systems theory

The issue of systems theory and its relevance or compatibility with group analysis is taken up by Dick Blackwell and Harold Behr. They both deal with ways in which systems theory needs to be modified in the light of group-analytic technique. These authors share both a group-analytic background and experience with family therapy. They both see considerable problems with integrating the two disciplines.

Behr draws attention to certain fundamental differences between the two disciplines. Can the same technique be applied to a standard group-analytic group where the conductor is less of an outsider, more part of the group from the outset, more continuously present throughout all its communications, less concerned about "symptoms," less in a hurry, less embattled with the group in a bid to change the system than in family therapy? He brings out, too, the conductor's function in fostering communication in an already existing system of the family. Behr concludes that technique has to be considerably modified to meet the needs of two such different situations, and shows how the group-analytic attitude can be valuably incorporated into family therapy. However, many family therapists would strongly disagree with this, just as many analytically minded group analysts would object to using the strategies of a systems approach in the "stranger" therapy group.

The question remains whether these disagreements about practice reflect disagreements about theory. Does each position in the debate rest on a basically different conception of the human being, or can they be reconciled in terms of differences in the context within which human beings are studied? For example, the degree to which the conductor is an outsider can be seen as relative: in family therapy the conductor is more so, providing greater objectivity and power to interrupt established patterns of intervention by interpretation or illustration; in group analysis their position and role are more fluid and flexible—as it were, both inside and outside the circle.

Blackwell takes up the same theme: the difficulties of reconciling a systems approach with group analysis. In a tightly condensed historical overview of systems theory, he isolates four different versions, each of which has demonstrably useful applications to group analysis. He by no means confines group analysis to the therapeutic stranger group, but sees it as a general method, with wide applications to family therapy and organisational consultancy work. However, he recognises a serious limitation of all forms of systems theory in its attempts to remain neutral and objective. Even in its most constructivist forms, it leads to relativism and fails to address itself adequately to a historical or political perspective. He deplores the failure of systems theory to engage with postmodernist thought in the way that psychoanalysis has in the movement initiated by Lacan.

This chapter highlights the points of controversy which rage around the nature of scientific enquiry, the value of a dialectical critique and the fundamental importance of ideology affecting philosophy as well as every other discipline. Blackwell gives his own views at each turn of his argument, and the reader is left to assess to what extent group analysis is a helpful answer to the problems raised or is itself in need of revision in the light of Blackwell's analysis. Some of the difficulties—for example, in his references to a "proper" group-analytic response to the Gulf war—have aroused fierce controversy in the Group-Analytic Society.

Social sciences

John Schlapobersky's chapter makes a clear distinction between monologue, dialogue, and discourse. Though he shows the clinical usefulness of this threefold classification of the modes of speech to be found in the therapy group, his terminology is nevertheless controversial. It is correlated with the distinction between one-body, two-body, and three-body psychology made in object relations theory, but some would not be happy with his use of terms. Monologues and dialogues are distinguished by Bakhtin (see Zinkin's chapter), not in terms of the number of people taking part but in the style of speech or discourse. Monologue expects no answer. In dialogue, the utterance of the speaker is always *incomplete*. Even if only one speaker is present, it requires and expects a response, the response also being incomplete and itself requiring a response. Thus each is also discourse, described as monologic or dialogic. The usual use of the word "discourse" likewise does not depend on the number of participants, but refers to the underlying assumptions (often unconscious or ideological) determining the use of words and the mode of speech. De Mare, in his chapter, uses dialogue not in its generally accepted usage as an interchange between two (which he calls "duologue") but as going on between many people, as in his median groups. The differences are not simply terminological but imply different approaches to the study of language. These remarks do not invalidate Schlapobersky's treatment of the topic, which is helpful to the general reader, but it might cause confusion or disagreement among those who use the words somewhat differently.

In his chapter on group analysis and cultural phenomena, Jaak Le Roy introduces a body of French work which he seeks to integrate with both the group-analytic theory of Foulkes and with Bion. This may create difficulty for those group analysts who see these two approaches as incompatible, though it may satisfy others who are looking for ways of reconciling them (see James's chapter). Le Roy's introductory theoretical outline, drawn from the writings of Kaes, Bleger, Rouchy, and Anzieu, is explicated as though it is non-controversial, but it raises great difficulties in its treatment of the interplay between cultural, individual, and innate developmental factors. The use of the concept of Self (with a capital S), and of individuation and of transpersonal entities, are almost the basic building blocks of Jung's analytical psychology, and it is surprising that Le Roy makes no reference whatsoever to Jung, even though Foulkes did incorporate his ideas. The problem is to account for universal psychic structures which can be regarded as trans-personal, and to decide whether they are culturally transmitted or innate. Although one can speak of primary and secondary groups in the sense that each individual is primarily influenced by the extended family, it is not clear to what extent the family is itself conditioned by culture, and culture itself may be less autonomous than it seems. For example, myths may be understood as cultural products or as structurally independent of culture, as not only Jung but also Levi-Strauss (who rejected Jung's idea of a collective unconscious) have suggested. Furthermore, though mother-infant patterns of interaction are culturally conditioned, how do we account for the highly individual styles observable from the very beginning? These questions are quite complex. Norbert Elias has also dealt with them at some length, and his work too is not considered in this chapter though it had a great influence on Foulkes' thinking. Although Le Roy has valuably extended group-analytic theory by introducing a whole body of sophisticated thinking which is little known outside France, this may not be so easily absorbed into group-analytic theory as he suggests.

Louis Zinkin's examination of the therapeutic function of exchange in the analytic group springs straight from Foulkes' list of therapeutic factors, his emphasis on increasing communication at all levels, and making articulate what was previously unknown or inexpressible. Zinkin's extension of exchange into the spheres of anthropology and morality would not have surprised Foulkes, nor will it surprise our present-day colleagues. Indeed, the idea of group norms and Foulkes' law of group dynamics—that the group represents the norm from which the individual deviates (see Chapter One)—necessitates exchange to arrive at a genuine consensus as opposed to a preconceived and imposed ideas of "normality" and ideal behaviour.

However, some may see Zinkin's proposal of a four-by-four juxtaposition of therapeutic factors and levels of interaction as somewhat contrived—almost too neat to be true—like many prematurely structured, all-inclusive hypotheses. But Zinkin uses the tentative juxtaposition to illuminate rather than close off.

Foulkes himself did not write of projective identification, but of "the level of bodily and mental images" (projective level) "corresponding to primitive narcissistic "inner" object relations in psychoanalysis, other members reflecting unconscious elements of the individual self, where the group represents as outer what are in truth inner object relations" (Foulkes, 1964: 115). Elsewhere he distinguishes between "objective level (mirror phenomena)," in which the group represents inner objects and part objects, and a body level presented by physical manifestations, illnesses, and so on, in which the group represents the body image (Foulkes, 1990: 183). We might see the four-by-four or four-by-five or more—juxtaposition as an invitation to think of process and structure interpenetrating each other.

In so far as psychoanalysts are becoming more interested in interactive exchange at all levels of the personalities of analysand *and analyst*, psychoanalysis is becoming less focused on the "isolated" unconscious of the analysand. In this sense psychoanalysis is moving towards group analysis, where we exchange not only in dialogue, but in listening and in empathic responsiveness, which include allowing and sharing silence.

General, more abstract philosophical theories

The contributions of De Mare, Pines, and Powell, though variously rooted in anthropological observations and psychoanalytic and Jungian theoretical concepts, share a readiness to move beyond the narrow confines of clinically verifiable fact and customary disciplinary boundaries. De Mare adumbrates a "new politics" on the basis of selections from anthropological literature and his own observations of conducting median groups, as though divorced from the small analytic group in which group-analytic theory arose. Pines, retaining his focus on clinical experience in psychoanalysis and group analysis, offers a resonant account of the interaction of individual and group that is dominated by the concept of coherence, itself far from clear. And Powell, boldly— some may say, rashly—moves from the clinical dynamic matrix into the concepts of connectedness that are taken from modern physics and cosmology even to the threshold of theology.

Patrick De Mare's chapter is something of an "odd man out." By starkly contrasting the median group with the small therapeutic stranger group, he makes a number of claims for the specific benefit of the larger number that many would dispute. His view that the small group is more related to the family, that it is more concerned with feeling than with thinking, with insight rather than "out-sight," and is less conducive to dialogue, remains open to question. Many of die problems we have raised in the psychoanalytically based chapters, such as Nitsun's, apply here too. At the other end of the spectrum, Blackwell would surely deny that social and political matters are outside the scope of the small group, and Powell's grand picture of the matrix informs his way of understanding small groups. Dialogue and intersubjective exchange, according to Brown, Pines, and Zinkin, are the very essence of small-group therapy, and even koinonic fellowship is fostered in small-group work. Perhaps the disagreement here could be reduced to the word "therapy," and whether this is narrowly conceived in terms of relief of individual pathology or is more widely seen as a growth process, a raising of the group consciousness.

De Mare's ideas about large, and particularly medium-sized groups, have an implicit prophetic sociopolitical dimension as well as reflecting his experience of their capacity to face the problem of talking freely in dialogue—"on the level," he would say. However, this is not impossible in small or much larger groups, even though in these we first tend to get confronted by family dynamics and "neurotic" transferences in the case of the usual six-to-eight member clinical group, or by "psychotic" fears of annihilation and defences against them in larger unstructured groups. Nitsun and Brown describe the former, for example, in their clinical vignettes. Elliott gives a vivid description of the latter in her description of a large experiential group at the Institute of Group Analysis. It would seem that the size of the group does powerfully influence what happens in it, both in terms of what it stimulates and what it tends to exclude—in that, most group analysts would agree with De Mare.

Malcolm Pines is deeply immersed in both psychoanalysis and group analysis, their history and evolution. Theoretically, one of his major contributions has been to illuminate the complexity of the concept of mirroring, how we discern more of ourselves through others. Here, in developing the idea of coherence, addressed in psychoanalysis by Loewald, he has used a concept which is intrinsically vague. Pines distinguishes group cohesion which he sees as a primitive sticking together, from coherence, which allows differentiation and redrawing of boundaries. In fact, this is a special usage of these terms. According to the *Shorter Oxford English Dictionary*, coherence means cohesion and congruity as well as the "harmonious connection of the several parts of a discourse, system etc. so mat the whole hangs together," and surprisingly context is also given as a definition of coherence. In everyday usage it often implies something is *understandable*, the opposite of incoherent. The very richness and ambiguity of the term thus allows distinctions to be blurred and made. This is in keeping with the allusiveness and resonance of many of Foulkes' profoundest ideas, such as mirroring, explored and extended by Pines (1982) and Zinkin (1983 and 1992); but some, while relishing this aspect of group analysis, might—in another part of themselves— long for clearer concepts with which to grasp the interaction of individual and whole group. Agazarian and Peters (1981) have offered us one set of concepts—distinguishing between individual roles, member roles, and the group-as-a-whole; (Ashbach & Schermer, 1987), in their ambitious Group Analytic Grid, "have attempted to integrate object relations theory and self psychology in intrapsychic, interactive, and whole-group systems at regressed, individuated, and mature levels. Some of us would see such attempts as clarifying, others as too restricting and encouraging premature comprehensiveness and closure." Pines's approach could be seen as that of a skin diver studying the movements of skoals of fish around him, the others' as using a lobster pot or a giant trawling net.

In his chapter, Andrew Powell demonstrates the richness of Foulkes' concept of the group matrix. There are obvious links with systems theory (see Black well's chapter) in the fact that we can speak of several interlinked and often transposed matrices—foundation (forming the cultural bases that permeate all), personal (in which each individual develops and which is embedded in their inner relational world as well as the outer network), and dynamic (developing from the start of each therapeutic group). In Powell's extension of the network of phenomeno-logical and theoretical systems, psychological, physical, and metaphysical, we get a sense of widening horizons that some may find exhilarating, others disturbing; it is as though he is using a universe-sized trawling net. Powell seems to concentrate, in his own terms, more on synthesis than on analysis, or, one could say, on syncretism rather than diacrisis. Carried to extremes it takes us, unapologetically, towards theology, away from the clinical setting where group analysis started and is still most effective. Working with individuals requires the group analyst to recognise and understand differences as well as similarities.

To complete the task described by Jung as "individuation," individuals need to reclaim undeveloped or disavowed parts of the whole self, as Powell fully acknowledges. Only men can the circle of self be completed and enlarged. But completing what you *are* does not include what you are *not*. We believe that what Powell calls "the flowing dynamic course of interaction" requires a *centripetal* as well as a *centrifugal* movement. We need such a balance to maintain relatively stable homeostatic structures between groups, between individuals, within individuals, and between individuals and groups. Our need to allow—perhaps more than we have done—for the importance of boundaries and barriers will be raised in the next section.

Towards an integration

The problems we have discerned are related to the compatibility of some of the contributions with unmodified psychoanalytic theory, itself in the process of revision, and the compatibility with group-analytic theory as laid down by Foulkes of a pseudo-objective approach to systems theory and anthropology. Thus we have questioned the use of unmodified psychoanalytic theory in relation to group analysis because of its bias towards the individual. We believe it is possible to see how what we might call the dialectic between the individual and the social world can take us to a new level of synthesis.

Andrew Powell underlines the fundamental principle of connectedness intrinsic in the idea of matrix. Like Louis Zinkin he emphasises the different levels of the matrix described by Foulkes, and describes how the matrix can function as a transitional space (Winnicott) and a caregiving other (Bowlby). It is a secure place in which to develop because it is not under the omnipotent control of one person. He notes that the matrix has no inherent moral position; that is, it can be used as a waste bin, or for creative containment in which psychic contents can be transformed from a lower to a higher level (Zinkin, 1989a). For Powell, mind and matrix are synonymous as each individual's mind connects with all other minds.

For some, problems might arise when he moves from the psychobiological to the psychophysical, linking with the new physics with its emphasis on pattern and wholeness (Bohm). Whether or not we follow Powell into cosmology and theology, this emphasis on patterns and wholeness is very apposite to our work in group analysis. The bringing together of seeming opposites, so important in Jungian theory, can be vividly enacted in groups where extremes are polarised and personified before they are integrated within the group and often within individuals. Another seeming polarity between mind and body is also resolved at what Foulkes (1990: 175) described as the *body level*, between the projective and the primordial, "in which an individual's unique genetic character interleaves with the principle of connectedness."

Dick Blackwell's chapter on systems theory follows Foulkes in bridging the seeming polarisation in psychoanalytic theory between the individual and society, and pursues Foulkes' aim of locating group analysis in relation to sociology and social psychology. He notes the paradox of the participant-observer position reflected in social science, which is always a part, even a product, of the system it describes within its historical political context. Blackwell sees the dialectical relationship between the individual and the group, in terms of the search for meaning in both personal and sociopolitical life.

Blackwell also uses the idea of a dialectic between reality and language as generating a creative space between them, in Lacan's sense. In applying systems theory to the understanding of individual development—as in Bollas's idea of the ego embodying rules for relating to mother—he points to the need to elaborate this in relation to the family context, to the parental relationship, and relationships between other family members. Recognition of each group member as holding a specific observer position, responding to and different from that of others while retaining its validity, promotes an acceptance and development of diversity and individuality within the group. This is a very good description of what happens during the move towards a greater sense of mature intersubjectivity. It is more than mutually validated "objectivity." It allows for the essential subjectivity of each member's position, and acknowledges their deeper connectedness.

It also links up with Malcolm Pines's ideas about coherency. Pines's approach, leaning on that of Loewald, could be seen as bringing together some of Jung's ideas with those of systems theory. For example, distinguishing between repression and internalisation, he points out how repression works against integration and organisation of the whole psyche, whereas internalisation promotes it. He points out how, in the therapy group, members internalise aspects of the interaction between the therapist, individual members, and the whole group, which become part of the newly coherent self. Increasing communication enhances the coherency of individual members and of the group matrix.

Coherency involves the clarification and redrawing of boundaries. For this to develop there needs to be a safe holding and containing function in the group. A safe space requires clear boundaries. As Colin James describes it, the holding and containing functions of the group allow distress and frustration to be acknowledged, thought about, understood, and shared, so that it moves onto a different level of integration in the whole person and the whole group. Each person has a chance in the group matrix to develop more fully a sense of self in relation to others, through both play and reverie.

Citizenship, James points out, requires being able to take in other people's points of view, drawing on the mature adult's ability to integrate the value of the other, but maintain his own individuality. This is very much part of the coherency that Pines talks about, and links with the issue of ethics and morality that are an important part of social life, as yet insufficiently studied by group analysts (Brown, 1992b).

This ability to see things from another's point of view is also very much part of what Dennis Brown talks of in terms of intersubjectivity.

Empathic mutual responsiveness is internalised as object relations, but so also are failures and blockages. These to varying degrees produce a blockage in relating to and appreciating others as they are. Therapy, according to Brown, therefore involves a re-engaging of the capacity for intersubjectivity, an issue which is becoming increasingly a focus in psychoanalytic writing and practice. We believe, however, that it is particularly well displayed and promoted in a group-analytic context.

The issue of boundaries, important in balancing a centrifugal connectedness with a centripetal ability to differentiate, is taken up by Louis Zinkin. As he puts it, the complex totality of interaction within the boundaries makes the group seem like a living organism. The important therapeutic factor of exchange implies boundaries between people. As he says, while psychoanalysis provides understanding of what goes on inside individuals, it does not concern itself directly with how they are behaving together, or what they understand when in mutual and reciprocal interaction in the context of the whole group. This is very much part of group analysis.

Indeed, Barbara Elliott and Morris Nitsun emphasise the importance of boundaries in earliest development, in terms of both phantasy and interrelationships. Barbara Elliott's exploration of womb phantasies distinguishes between re-enactment in the group of the relationship between the foetus and the mother, not just the infant and the mother, and uses the concept of Communitas adopted by Usandivaras (1989) to describe regression to an undifferentiated state in the group, in which everyone is connected with everyone. Womb experiences contrast with fusional experiences, and require silence in the group. We think that this is an important observation and stresses the importance of allowing silences and encouraging group members to tolerate them. Elliott proposes that memory traces of womb experiences can be internalised by the neonate of both sexes, and have consequences in the course of gender formation, and also might have consequences in terms of people's capacity to tolerate space or containment. One can think of agoraphobia or claustrophobia, and how differently people respond to being in a group.

Morris Nitsun's exploration of primal scene phantasies, in both their positive and negative aspects, puts the primal scene as a bridge between the intrapsychic world and external reality. The primal scene is of significance not only in terms of the Oedipus complex, but also the important move into the social world implied by the third position and the "law of the father," renouncing infantile centrality in finding your place in society. It seems likely that it also plays an important part in coming to terms with being in a group, not always being the centre of attention, and accepting the authority of the conductor, and his or her power to admit new members.

Thus, despite the possibility of theoretical objections to the primal scene as being the "structural centre" of the group, it could be seen as something which group analysts should consider more in developing our understanding of the relationship between the psyche and the social world. Similarly, the objections that one can make from a psychoanalytic point of view about Bowlby's attachment theory seem to be less important in group analysis if one concentrates on the significance of attachment as a source of safety, whether or not it is biologically determined. This includes the safety that a group comes to provide, separation from which plays an important part in the termination phase of therapy. Mario Marrone points out that Bowlby saw the object of study in psychoanalysis as the individual's inner world *together with its interaction with the environment or social context*. Indeed, Bowlby urged that we use many methods to study this, including social psychology and observation of families, as well as ethology and observation of babies. Although Bowlby considered that attachment theory is biologically based, Mario Marrone underlines his view that the quality of primary attachment depends on the degree of empathy and responsiveness of the caregiver, and that this affects personality development and social behaviour.

It is in the family that the developing child does or does not learn to be securely attached in a way that allows differentiation and the development of self-confidence. Within the analytic group a person has a second chance to overcome some of the negative experiences that made this difficult in the first place. As Harold Behr indicates, Foulkes said little about family therapy, but emphasised the importance of the family interview to get an idea of the context in which individuals' problems emerged. The family therapist who is orientated towards the group-analytic model has a problem. The family group is in some respects the exact opposite of the group-analytic group. As the family is an established group, it needs more vigorous intervention to produce change, and a shorter time scale, according to Behr, who talks of the dialectic between psychoanalysis and systems theory. He emphasises the family therapist's loneliness— his need to come in but largely stay out, and to embody the whole group himself. The family therapist is an "outsider," but "adopts the system" using mirroring and resonance, listening to stories and occasionally translating them to other members. This contrasts with group analysis, which encourages the circulation and redistribution of "outsider" characteristics, in order to discourage scapegoating. In group analysis what is alien to the self is ultimately owned, contained, and shared by the group, so the conductor helps the affirmative and supportive mode of communication to allow more painful feelings and disturbing phantasies to surface. It is clear that Behr's experience of family therapy and standard group analysis enables him to get a clearer picture of both, as if using a dialectic between group analysis and family therapy.

Families, clans, classes, and nations all draw on and contribute to the cultural foundations of personality, as Jaak Le Roy describes. He analyses the complex structure of Foulkes' foundation matrix, and points to the importance of its disruption in causing psychopathology. He uses the work of French and South American authors to explore individuation and non-individuation in the primary family, and sees primary and secondary groups as intermediary structures linking the individual to culture. He draws attention to Bleger's idea that an organised and stable frame—whether the setting of analysis, a partnership, or an institution—can act as a repository for the psychotic part of the self, which he calls the not-self. This non-differentiated and undissolved part of the primitive symbiotic links, as he sees them, could perhaps explain the use of foreignness, otherness, and the need for enemies, an endemic problem in social life.

Le Roy distinguishes between the containing and the transitional functions of secondary groups (Rouchy), and in contrast to Bleger's bleak view -describes how a stable frame can also provide transitional space for the development of the individual to "receive, tolerate, elaborate and restitute" (Kaes). This clearly links with James's views on containing and Pines's ideas on coherence, as well as much of what has been developed from a group-analytic perspective, which tends to emphasise the positive potential of groups.

Patrick De Mare's ideas about the median group might seem rather simple, as he concentrates on its ability to develop dialogue in a group insufficiently small to resemble the nuclear family, but large enough to produce anxieties about loss of identity. From experiences in such groups, however, de Mare has been able to develop a theory about frustration creating hatred, which then becomes channelled and neutralised in dialogue. This becomes a model for a form of citizenship that can tolerate differences within a sense of fellowship. The ability to engage in dialogue with people who are seemingly different is an important part of citizenship and toleration.

As John Schlapobersky describes it, the group-analytic approach is distinguished from other methods by including monologue and dialogue in which respectively the individual first encounters him or herself in soliloquy, and searches for intimacy through the dialogue of two. However, true discourse, Schlapobersky claims, is by definition group communication, because the complexity of communication between two people is transformed when a third is introduced and a group is formed. This perhaps reflects the momentousness for social development of the recognition of the parental couple and the father, and illustrates what Foulkes called the model of three (Foulkes, 1964: 49): each member of a group, including the conductor, can be observed in relation to others from a third, outside position. Each member of a group has the opportunity to see each of the others in relationship and with the group-as-a-whole, as well as with himself or herself.

We believe that group analysis has so far tended to neglect the distinction between boundaries and barriers, though the 9th European Symposium in Group Analysis in Heidelberg in 1993 is on that very topic.[2] In structured situations such as a therapy group, a family or an institution, group analysts will very much keep their eyes on boundary issues. But the need for containment and identity will often produce illusory boundaries that Anzieu (1984) calls "psychic envelopes."

A distinguished French psychoanalyst with a special interest in groups, Anzieu's view from outside the narrow "group-analytic envelope" provides a welcome stimulus to think more about the nature of boundaries and barriers. His ideas and those of his compatriots Kaes and Rouchy have been used extensively by Jaak Le Roy in his chapter to explore the containing function of cultural groups. In a valuable analogy, Anzieu compares the group, ego-like, to a two-sided mirror, sensitive to unconscious individual phantasies internally and to collective representations externally. This accords with the ideas of many group analysts, including Earl Hopper (1982), and is directly illustrated in this volume by Colin James's reference to "social dreaming." Anzieu believes that in the absence of a group ego, the group constructs an overarching "psychical apparatus" to protect itself, cope with its members' wishes and drives, and respond to external stimulation. Would we call this "the matrix"? Or is it something more?

In searching to understand the complex relationship between psyche and social world, "psychic envelopes" could be a useful concept. They can be presumed to be based, to varying degrees, on wishful and fearful phantasy, reality that binds mutual identification and concern, and intersubjective recognition of diversity within unity. At times of great upheaval and stress, old envelopes—ethnic, religious and national—can become illusory refuges, not only because of the allure of illusion, but because of their confusion with the real bonds of personal and family ties developed within them, as we see in the rise of nationalisms in Eastern Europe today.

Concluding comments

We shall end with some preliminary thoughts about the psyche and the social world, individual and group, mind that is individual, group, and transpersonal:

• The group and the individual are ultimately indivisible and yet mutually interacting; each acts as a container *of and for* aspects of the other: individuals personify aspects of the group, and the group or aspects of it (including other individuals) can contain parts of each individual, as in a hologram (Zinkin, 1987). This takes us beyond Freud's idea of an instinct-driven Man inevitably pitted against a repressive Society (Freud, 1930), and doomed to seek illusory consolations (Freud, 1927).

• As a field of coherence and valency, the psyche or "superordinate self" has a homeostatic function balancing stability and change, and encompasses individuals, groups, social worlds, and ultimately the cosmos. Its study needs to take account of both our biological nature and our search for meaning in relation to others, society, culture and the cosmos.[3] It requires dialogic discourse (see above, Bakhtin 1981).

• Boundaries between individuals are to varying degrees permeable. The more rigid and seemingly impermeable the boundaries—that is, the more they become barriers—the greater the use of projection and projective identification to supplement them, and maintain an exclusive identification based on "myths" of purity and homogeneity, rather than plurality (Samuels, 1989).

• In both small and large groups, including ethnic and national groups, "otherness" can become threatening. It challenges identity based on restricted identification and too much projection. These produce fear of groups in individuals, and fear between groups that blocks the experience of intersubjectivity. As well as collectively embodying the norm from which each deviate (Foulkes), members of a group also embody the diversity of which they are all afraid (Blackwell, Chapter Three).

The individual develops and always exists within a social matrix. Group analysis seeks to explain and use the figure-ground dialectical relationship between the two. To comprehend it fully, we go beyond learning from the psychoanalytic study of infantile development (and the analyst-analysand dyad), important as these are, to studying families and various social groups, where individuality and identities are formed, deformed, and sometimes broken. We take account of many resonating dialectics—between conscious and unconscious levels of experience, between body and mind, between individual and group, between the personalities of analyst and analysand(s) in both individual and group analysis, between social and family groups, between conflicting cultures, between alternating figures and grounds up to a global level, even to the cosmos. Our contributors have all had something to say about these interacting elements.

Where do we go from here? The writing of this book represents only a small part of the work being done in developing the theory of group analysis. We believe, though, that the exercise of writing the book as a group has helped to establish a consensual view which, despite its areas of healthy controversy, points to the future growth of a distinctive group-analytic theory.

The overall tendency has been the incorporation of allied disciplines so that group analysis takes its place among the generally recognised category of human sciences, as distinct from natural sciences. In this respect, it follows the trend of postmodernist culture, where the search is not for some absolute compendious total system, nor the establishment of a standard text setting out the received wisdom of the experts in the field. This is neither possible nor desirable. Instead, there is great value in partial and provisional insights. We are not seeking the kind of relativism where all ideas are of equal validity, but we do recognise that all observations and all formulations are limited by their subjectivity, and that there is no such thing as the detached and impartial observer. Nor can any "truth" be uttered which is not, in any way, subject to the contingency of the time and place in which it occurs.

So, looking into the future we can predict that processes of confrontation with the findings of other allied disciplines will continue to have an impact on group-analytic theory. This impact will threaten to disrupt some of our ideas but will gradually be absorbed and integrated, and we hope that group analysis will also influence the thinking in those other fields which constitute the human sciences.

A case could be made for entitling this book, more modestly and less grandiloquently, *Psyches and Social Worlds*. This would have been more in tune with the plurality of society and the human personality, and allow for changes in their relationship. Not surprisingly, such changes are reflected in the book; for example, in the way modem physics enters conceptualisation of the matrix (Powell), in the way attitudes to sexual orientation are not seen as inevitably fixed (Nitsun), and even in a "feminist" style of writing that does not assume that "he" implies "she" any more naturally than the reverse (Blackwell).

We believe that the team of contributors has developed some ideas that Foulkes only implied or adumbrated—such as further exploration and explication of systems theory, the difference between standard group analysis and family therapy, the nature of intersubjectivity in groups, the wider implications of the concept of connectedness in the group matrix, the complexity of the foundation matrix, and some of the linguistic implications of verbal communication and of exchange.

In addition, we believe we have discerned a deficit in group analysis to date of concepts applicable to boundaries within but particularly between groups, and of ideas not only rooted in psychoanalysis to explain primitive processes and inter-group problems and morality.

So this has proved not to be a textbook or a handbook in the usual sense of these words. It is a statement of where we find ourselves in part of the English-speaking world, in 1994. We hope it gives the idea of a new kind of learning, a dialogic learning-together through a group-analytic process, whose principles have been adumbrated by S. H. Foulkes.

Notes

1. The authors of this chapter, refer to contributions included by the various authors in the book with the same name: The Psyche and the Social World.
2. It will consider political boundaries and barriers in history, boundaries and barriers within and between organisations, between patients and therapists, and trainees and trainers, between men and women, and

the meaning of boundaries and barriers in the development of cultural identity and between cultures.

3. In developing a cross-cultural psychology, Roland (1988) has differentiated familial, individualised, and spiritual selves, each complex, in the different cultures of India, Japan, and the Western world.

References

Agazarian, Y. & Peters, R. (1981). *The Visible and teh Invisible Group*. London: Routledge and Kegan Paul.

Anzieu (1984). *The Group and the Unconscious*. London: Routledge and Kegan Paul.

Bakhtin, M. (1981). *The Dialogic Imagination. Four Essays*. (M. M. Bakhtin, trans). C. Emerson and M. Holquist, Austin: Texas University Press.

Brown, D. G. (1985). Bion and Foulkes: Basic Assumptions and Beyond, in M. Pines (ed) Bion and Group Psychotherapy, London: Routledge and Kegan Paul.

Brown, D. G. (1992). Transcultural group Aanalysis, 2; Use and abuse of cultural differences. *Group Analysis, 25*: 97–105.

Foulkes, S. H. (1964). *Therapeutic Group Analysis*. London: Allen and Unwin; reprinted 1984, London, Karnac.

Foulkes, S. H. (1990). *The Group as Matrix of the Individual's Mental Life*, Chap. 22 in Selected Papers. London: Karnac.

Freud, S. (1927). *The Future of an Illusion, SE21*. London: Hogarth Press.

Freud, S. (1930). *Civilizatiion and its Discontents, SE21*. London: Hogarth Press.

Hopper, E. (1982). Group analysis and the problem of context. *Group Analysis, 15*: 136–157.

Pines, M. (1982). Reflections on Mirroring. *Group Analysis, 15*: supp. 1–32.

Roland, A. (1988). *In Search of Self in India and Japan: Toward a Cross-Cultural Psychology*. Princeton, New Jersey: Princeton University Press.

Samuels, A. (1989). The image of the parents in bed, in A. Samuels, *The Father*, London, Free Association Books.

Usandivaras (1989). Through communitas to individuation, *Group Analysis*, 22(2): 161–170.

Zinkin, L. (1983). Malignant mirroring, *Group Analysis, 16*: 113–126.

Zinkin, L. (1987). The hologram as a model for analytical psychology, *Journal of Analytical Psychology, 32*(1): 1–21.

Zinkin, L. (1989). The group as a container and contained, *Group Analysis, 22*: 201–217.

Zinkin, L. (1992). Borderline distortions of mirroring in the group, *Group Analysis, 25*: 27–31.

PART V

CHALLENGES
TO THE THEORY/EXTENSIONS

The anti-group: destructive forces in the group and their therapeutic potential*

Morris Nitsun

Introduction: the foulkesian tradition

My training as a group analyst and years of experience of running patient and staff groups have left me with the impression that while groups have great therapeutic potential, they can also be volatile, unpredictable and destructive processes which require considerable understanding and very careful handling. Yet I am struck by how the literature on group analysis and therapy, in its generally optimistic, even idealistic terms, rarely explores this aspect in much depth. S. H. Foulkes, I believe, paid insufficient attention to destructive processes in groups, leaving what I consider to be an important gap in the evolution of group analysis.

My own interest has increasingly been in the negative and destructive attitudes that arise in relation to the group itself. This led me to formulate the concept of the "anti-group" (Nitsun, 1988). This is a broad term describing the destructive aspect of groups that threatens the integrity of the group and its therapeutic development. It does not

---

*This chapter was first published as: Nitsun, M. (1991). The anti-group: destructive forces in the group and their therapeutic potential. *Group Analysis*, 24: 7–20.

235

describe a static "thing," that occurs in all groups in the same way, but a set of attitudes and impulses, conscious and unconscious, that manifest themselves differently in different groups. I believe that most, if not all, groups contain an anti-group, but that whereas in some groups it is resolved with relative ease, in others it can undermine and destroy the foundations of the group. Because of this, I consider it important—if not essential—to be able to understand its origins. I also believe that the successful handling of the anti-group represents a turning point in the development of the group. By helping the group to contain its particular anti-group, not only are the chances of destructive acting out reduced, but the group is strengthened, its survival reinforced and its creative power liberated.

Returning to Foulkes, it seems to me relevant to pick up his own emphasis on the wider social environment and to examine the context in which he first developed his concept of group analysis. Foulkes started group analysis in England in the early 1940s. This was approximately 10 years after he left Hitler's Germany and at a time when the Second World War was raging. I am puzzled about the impact of this social backcloth on his view of group behaviour. On the one hand, we are indebted to him for providing us with an optimistic and valuable therapeutic tool, at a time when we needed optimism. On the other hand, I doubt whether his early formulations of group analysis took adequate account of the dark, very dark, side of the social reality of the time—specifically the massive extent to which groups could be destructive and self-destructive. This can be contrasted with Sigmund Freud, whose experiences at roughly the same time, in roughly the same place, contributed a vein of deep pessimism to his view of human conduct, a theme crystallized in his paper "Civilisation and its Discontents" (Freud, 1930).

My intention here is not to extol pessimism in itself—or for that matter to denigrate optimism—but to raise the question of *realism*, that is, the extent to which a therapeutic model is in touch with both the wider social reality (a point Foulkes insisted on, particularly in his introductory text of 1948; (Foulkes, 1948) and the available clinical data. Yet it would be wrong to suggest that Foulkes was unaware of destructive forces. In a paper originally delivered as Chairman's Address to the Medical Section of the British Psychological Society in 1961, he virtually went as far as to endorse his belief in some form of death instinct:

Personally, I have become more and more convinced in the course of years of the truth and usefulness of the concept of a primary self-destructive force. Nothing is more certain than the ubiquity of destruction—a fact difficult to accept.

(Foulkes, 1964: 138–139)

Realizing the significance of destructive forces in groups, Foulkes attempted to give this a major focus in his view of group relationships. Foulkes saw the neurotic or psychotic individual as an isolated part of his social group and related this to destructive tendencies in the individual:

The particular form which the neurotic position assumes is in its very nature highly individualistic. It is group disruptive in essence because it is genetically the result of an incompatibility between the individual and his original group. *It is at the same time an expression of aggressive and destructive tendencies.*

(Foulkes, 1964: 89; my italics)

Pines (Pines, 1983), commenting on Foulkes' statement, clarified it further by adding that what was in the healthier individual a social situation, where he or she represents a nodal point in a healthy and openly communicative social structure, becomes in the neurotic individual a focal point for aggressive and destructive tendencies. This was thought to originate in the family group and to spread to relationships within the wider social network.

Foulkes had positive and optimistic views about the transformation in group therapy of aggression and destructiveness into healthy forms of aggressiveness and assertiveness: This disruptive, anti-social, destructive aspect of neurotic behaviour is forced to come out into the open and does not receive the sanction of the group' (Foulkes, 1964: 89). A process follows whereby aggressive tendencies in the individual are used to attack and shift the neuroses of other members while constructive tendencies are used to support each other and build up the group: In a word, one could say that disruptive forces are consumed in mutual analysis, constructive ones utilized for the synthesis of the individual and the integration of the group as a whole' (Foulkes, 1964: 90). This view links with Foulkes' socio-biological orientation in so far as the constructive tendencies, once liberated, are seen as slowly leading the group towards the norms of the community of which it is part.

I see this as a worthy but limited and to some extent misguided attempt to relate aggression to the core of group-analytic psychotherapy. I take issue with it on several counts:

1. Aggression is essentially located in the individual: it is the individual's destructive tendencies which make him or her a deviant in an otherwise healthy social group. There is no sense that the group itself, or the community, may be deviant or destructive—in fact, that the group can adversely influence the individual, rather than the other way round. This seems to me ironic in view of Foulkes' consistent emphasis on the social context of the group. It also represents, in my view, the loss of an important opportunity to relate group analysis to wider social pathology.

2. The attempt to equate aggressive energies in groups with analysis and constructive energies with synthesis is an oversimplification. It attempts to reduce complex and challenging issues to a rather mechanical formula.

3. Foulkes' socio-biological orientation has an optimistic but naive ring. The notion of the deviant therapy group moving slowly towards the norms of its community assumes both a stability within social norms and a form of ethical superiority over the therapy group: both assumptions are questionable. The contemporary history of social and family groups—and this is a significant feature of the twentieth century—is that of frequent disruption and destabilization of norms. Equally, conservatively held norms (to which the group might move) may be expressions of social resistance and repression, or even oppression, rather than shining beacons to which we should all aspire. In either event, the relationship between our therapy groups and wider society is a complex one, not easily subsumed in a unipolar socio-biological perspective.

I am led to the conclusion that Foulkes' failure to elaborate on the power of destructive processes in groups was linked to his idealism about groups and the wider community. The impression, rather as Foulkes himself suggested in the passage cited earlier, was that "the ubiquity of destruction" was difficult for him to accept, that it did not fit into an idealistic view of groups, and that he made a partial, schematic attempt at including it in his theory, thereby leaving a crucial area of group analysis undeveloped and unresolved.

In terms of Foulkes' intellectual background, it is clear that the Marxist tradition of the Frankfurt School, which flourished in pre-Hitler Germany, contributed to his utopian view of groups. The fact that this was strong enough to survive the evidence of the Second World War is difficult not to see as containing at least an element of denial. His idealism influenced not only his concept of group analysis but also the way he presented his approach and argued its merits. From time to time, in his writings, his claims are overweening, almost omnipotent. For example, in the chapter "Outline and Development of Group Analysis," after describing the strengths of the approach, Foulkes (1964: 76) concludes: "The therapeutic impact is quite considerable, intensive, and immediate in operation. By and large, the group situation would appear to be the most powerful therapeutic agency known to us." Statements of this sort appear with an uncomfortable frequency in Foulkes' writing. There is seldom sufficient clinical evidence to justify his claims, and an absence of clear awareness of counterbalancing and antagonistic factors in group analysis.

There is of course another likely explanation for Foulkes' eulogizing about groups: he was doing a selling job. Numerous statements (for example, Foulkes, 1964, (Foulkes, 1973) reveal that he felt he was fighting, if not losing, a lone battle against the psychoanalytic (and to some extent psychiatric) establishment, and that he felt compelled to argue the merits of group analysis forcefully: "You say that I advocate my own approach. But what else can I do? If I did not think it the right one, I would not adopt it" (Foulkes, 1964: 121).

We can sympathize with these statements, but one wonders whether the sometimes defensive idealization helped or hindered the cause. After all, what Foulkes was picking up was essentially "anti-group" reactions. The objection of the orthodox psychoanalytic establishment to group analysis was no doubt an intolerant reaction to the deviation from the sacred transferential context of individual psychoanalysis, but how much did it also reflect anxiety about the power of group processes, about the transposition of the therapeutic focus from the cosy privacy of the one-to-one relationship to the group arena, with its potential for destructive aggression, rivalry and alienation? I feel that had Foulkes been able to explore these aspects more openly and more fully, rather than emphatically optimizing the process and outcome of group analysis at all costs, he might have made a more convincing impact on his critics. I also feel he would have encouraged an attitude of open doubt and debate, which I sometimes find missing in the group-analytic milieu.

The concept of the anti-group

It was my own doubt about the value of group analysis that led me directly to conceive of the existence of a phenomenon such as the "anti-group." This to some extent preceded my training in group analysis, but strengthened in the first year of my formal training. I had come from an established individual-therapy orientation, and not only did I find the shift of model difficult, but I felt overwhelmed by the faith in group analysis of many people I encountered at the London Institute of Group Analysis. Foulkes' statement that group analysis is "an act of faith" seemed to have gripped their imaginations. I felt confused, anxious and filled with doubt, rather than reassured. My training turned out to be to a large extent a working-through of my own doubts and their gradual replacement by what I hope is a realistic appreciation of both the strengths and weaknesses of group analysis.

The most important influence on my thinking about the anti-group was the clinical experience I encountered or observed in the implementation of a group approach in my work setting. Most of my work as a clinical psychologist over a period of 20 years has been in a large psychiatric hospital. Here the level of psychopathology among patients is considerable and communication within patient-patient, staff-patient, and staff-staff groups is fraught with difficulty. As Kernberg (Kernberg, 1980) pointed out, there are powerful regressive pressures in institutions of this sort. No doubt this setting primed me to the difficulties inherent in small and large groups, and was not entirely countered by favourable outcomes in some therapy groups. I have seen groups flounder badly in training and clinical practice, groups break down, end abruptly or linger on in states of tense, negativistic impasse. In teaching situations (mainly with clinical psychology trainees) where I presented the principles of group work, I found the most commonly voiced anxiety to be that groups can be destructive. In numerous ways I have witnessed and been confronted by anti-group phenomena.

It also seemed to me that these more generalized anti-group attitudes translated into specific occurrences in the focused task of starting and running an analytic group in a psychiatric outpatient context. I find some of these patterns quite consistent. The first is that I pick up anti-group attitudes at the very start. This happens in the selection process, well before patients actually join the group. I find that many if not most patients referred *do no want* group therapy. They want individual therapy. The suggestion of a group is often met with surprise, anxiety and suspicion. Numerous patients reject the offer of a place in a group. Others can be persuaded to join a group, but do so reluctantly. Patients who actually come asking for group therapy are, in my experience, a minority.

When the group starts, there is, for several months at least, prevailing mistrust *in* the group and *of* the group. Often, this takes the form of attacks on the group; it is not good enough; it is second best; it is because the National Health Service provides so little; it is directionless; there is no guidance; the presence of others with problems is a liability rather than an asset; it is an artificial situation; it gives too little time to the individual; it feels unsafe. These are familiar strains to anyone who has run groups in a similar setting, but they seem to me too often passed over as "teething troubles," as inevitable frustrations on the way to something better, as resistance. As I see it, these complaints form the elements of the anti-group and should be recognized and addressed as such.

Still in the early phases of the group, drop-outs begin to occur. Drop-outs, in my view, are symptomatic of an anti-group process, not just in the individual drop-out, but in the group-as-a-whole, which may unconsciously select a member of the group to enact the rejection of the group. Drop-outs have a disturbing and demoralizing effect on the group and can produce a chain reaction. Despair sets in and questions arise about whether the group can or will survive. In my experience, most groups survive, but as indicated above, by no means all do. Even in groups that continue, the impact of early traumas in the group's development may be so profound that the group never quite recovers. In groups of this sort, communication is usually extremely difficult or disordered and the group may continue, but in a state of severe impasse.

Even in well functioning groups, underlying anti-group attitudes, possibly not previously addressed, may suddenly flare up. A new member joins, an emotional conflict or clash erupts, or some other change occurs, and the group suddenly becomes very negativistic. Breaks, I find, have a particularly strong effect on groups, and in my experience can produce an anti-group backlash both before and after the break. Often, this is a way of denying the value of the group and so avoiding painful feelings of separation.

The anti-group tends to evoke considerable despair and feelings of failure in the conductor. He or she readily feels to blame for the group not working properly. A sense of hopelessness in the conductor may in fact be an important signal of an anti-group at work. Of course, such a situation will also trigger the conductor's own anti-group tendencies—and in turn his or her ability to tolerate and deal with anti-group phenomena will influence the way in which the anti-group is or is not resolved.

Difficulties in running outpatient groups are paralleled in my experience by the problems of running inpatient groups and staff groups in the psychiatric setting. Unless a group culture is already well established, as in certain therapeutic communities, the attempt to establish such a culture can be fraught with difficulty. Recently, I was asked to consult to a psychiatric unit attempting to set up patient and staff groups on an admission ward. My initial point of contact was with the consultant psychiatrist, who valued groups and believed in their therapeutic potential in the ward situation. However, her efforts met with every form of resistance. The patient groups started operating routinely but there was such a degree of misunderstanding and consequent acting out in one of the groups that a cohort of patients refused to return to the group and for a period instigated an anti-group culture on the ward. The staff group (intended to be a sensitivity-type group) has still not got off the ground. Efforts to establish a time and a place for the group to meet are continually sabotaged. When individuals are questioned about their reactions to this, it appears that there is considerable fear of the entire staff group coming together. The threat of angry challenge and confrontation, of a humiliating sense of difference in hierarchical relations, and of unwanted personal exposure, appears to outweigh in people's minds the potential benefits of increased understanding and co-operation that might be a product of the group. The group process is not trusted. Although not surprising that in the disturbed setting of a psychiatric admission ward any attempt at therapeutic work would invite intense expressions of psychopathology, it seemed to me that in this instance the challenge of a group culture triggered particularly strong anxiety and anti-group reactions.

Theoretical explanation

This brings me to the all important question, why? How does the anti-group come about? The answer is complex, explored in greater detail elsewhere (see Nitsun, 1988).[1] Here, because of limitations of space,

I look at it from one particular angle, and this relates to the preference (previously mentioned) that many people have for individual over group therapy. As I said before, I believe this is vital information. The reasons for it are not difficult to come by: in general, people want individual therapy rather than group therapy because they believe it will be safer, more containing, more personally focused and more rewarding. Part of this is realistic, as not only does emotional disturbance originate in the early mother-child relationship, but states of severe emotional distress in later life often generate a wish to restore the primacy of the early one-to-one relationship. This is based on an idealized fantasy of "total togetherness" (Balint, 1968) of a perfectly containing relationship. This is often needed to compensate for profound early disappointment in emotional development, with consequent rage and emptiness. The prospect of group therapy in various respects runs counter to these expectations: the therapist is there for the group and not just for the individual; the space has to be shared by several others in need, strangers who bring their own powerful and unfamiliar agendas, introducing the very note of difference, danger and uncertainty which the patient wishes to avoid and which threatens the fantasy of ideal containment. This is reinforced by the frequently frustrating, painful and bewildering experience of actually being in a group, particularly in the initial stages. The individual's loneliness and alienation may be heightened rather than assuaged by being in the group, and the gap between what is longed for and what is available widens. The discrepancy between the ideal and the actual leads to a form of splitting in which all that is good is associated with the fantasy of the individual relationship (not uncommonly focused on the group conductor) while all that is bad is projected on to the group. The group becomes the bad object, frustrating and depriving, and it unleashes primitive hostility and rage that is directed at the group in the form of anti-group attacks.

In this model, it is important that the group is seen, in part, as a construction of the fantasies and projections of its members, that is, it develops through projective identification. If the projections are influenced by good object experiences, the group becomes, like a good mother, dependable, nourishing, resilient. If, on the other hand, the projections are dominated by bad object experiences, the group will acquire the characteristics of the bad object, undependable, unsafe, persecuting.

The plural nature of the group, that is, the fact that there are several members, increases the possibility of dangerous fragmentation.

The group is, after all, not a whole: it is in parts. This is particularly the case at the start of the group, when it is not yet an integrated unit, a point I have explored elsewhere in greater detail (see Nitsun, 1989a). The fragmentary nature of the group, particularly in a situation of poor, inconsistent attendance and a high dropout rate, renders it a fragile container. This is frightening and disturbing, and the threat of internal fragmentation in the patient is mirrored in the fragmentation of the group. As this reinforces disbelief in the holding and therapeutic function of the group, anti-group attitudes escalate. The wish to attack and destroy the group, combined with actual attacks on it, may become confused with the fragmenting process in the group: destructive impulses appear to have had a disintegratory impact on the group. A vicious circle sets in: the group is perceived as a weak and/or dangerous container; this provokes anxiety and attack; the attack weakens and fragments the group; this invites attack, and so on.

Where the psychological unity of the group develops and deepens, as in most good groups, its plurality may not be a problem—indeed, it may be its strength—but where an anti-group culture predominates, the multiple nature of the group may act as host to a malignant form of projective identification.

My analysis of the destructive threat in groups emphasizes primitive levels of emotional development, mainly the anxiety-defence systems that operate intrapsychically and within the early mother-child relationship. But it should also be recognized that the multiple nature of the group constitutes a threat precisely because it challenges and impinges on this early, vulnerable constellation. It presents the oedipal challenge, of mother, child *and father*, of difference, of competition and of sexuality. It represents the hated family that impinged too early on and that failed to nurture the child.

Once the group is established as the bad object, it becomes the siphon for a whole host of destructive fantasies and impulses. Envy, sadistic hatred and perverse fantasies are all projected into and on to the group. This allows members to disown responsibility for these phenomena in their own lives, and to avoid dealing with them interactionally in the group. In this way, the anti-group has a defensive function. By agglomerating aggressive fantasies and impulses into one collective whole, it protects members from having to face up to crucial difficulties in their inner and outer worlds, and in the group. Envy is a particularly important part of this process. It must be remembered that for all its frustrations, the group *does* offer the promise of containment, of nurturance and of emotional development. Even if in the minds of its members it fails totally to provide this, the experience accentuates the longing for a powerfully dependable and transforming object. The difficulty is that this longing also stimulates envy. This is the primary envy of the breast as the source of life, so cogently described by Klein (1957), and associated with hatred of any potential dependence on the object. In order to rid the self of the painful state of envy, the object must be spoiled and denigrated. In the anti-group scenario, this combines with splitting and fragmenting impulses to extinguish the therapeutic capacity of the group. This is analogous to Bion's (Bion, 1967) "attacks on linking." In this, all meaning, coherence, connectedness, indeed the very capacity for thinking, are undermined.

The ultimate expression of the anti-group is to destroy the group. The tragedy is that the individual(s) are dependent on the object for sustenance, the infant on the parent, and so when a therapy group breaks down, with it collapses the opportunity for emotional growth.

Of course, what I am describing is an extreme picture—that of a group annihilated by the anti-group. I have done so in order to dramatize the impact of the anti-group and to explore its most extensive effects. Fortunately, in reality such devastation rarely happens. Usually there is sufficient good projected on to the group to counteract the ravages of the anti-group. But the two forces are often closely matched. In fact, I believe it is the conflict between on the one hand members' wish to construct a therapeutic group and, on the other, their wish to destroy the group that is pivotal to the development of the group. It leads, in my view, to a situation akin to the depressive position. In this, ambivalence has to be faced fully and a process of mourning endured. In the case of the group, the mourning may have to be for the loss of the fantasy of ideal, passive containment—Balint's "total togetherness." In its place may come an acceptance of the considerable but, nevertheless, *partial* satisfaction provided by the group and an awareness in members that through reparation they can contribute actively to the therapeutic function of the group. Without this happening, I believe that the group as an entity with intrapsychic significance (as contrasted with a supportive but superficial experience) is not fully established. In this sense, the anti-group, paradoxically, has a therapeutic function. It tests the strength of the group and generates the elements of ambivalence that eventually deepen and enrich the group. Foulkes made a statement highly pertinent to the above. In this, he expressed a view that I believe is insufficiently realized in his model of group analysis, but one that is important to note and to consider: "Strangely enough, the acknowl-edgement of the forces of self-destruction and their agencies helps us and makes us therapeutically far more powerful" (Foulkes, 1964: 145).

To summarize, I believe that there is a widespread and fundamen-tal resistance to groups, arising partly from the wish for the fantasised, idealized containment of the two-person relationship and the threat that the group poses to this fantasy. The group acquires the negative, destructive components of the early bad object, which makes it a frus-trating and persecutory experience, and which provokes attacks against it, producing an anti-group process that can lead to the undermining of the group. This may express itself in the clinical progress of the group, and it may also be reflected in the suspicion and hostility towards groups not infrequently encountered in the wider organizational set-ting. In spite of its destructive potential, the anti-group is an important component of group psychotherapy in that it provides access to power-ful, deep-rooted experiences of gap, loss, disappointment and ensuing hatred, and also points the way to the origins of ambivalence, which can be utilized constructively in the development of the group.

Concluding comments

I need to clarify an aspect of the anti-group that may be troubling the reader. This concerns the nature of the concept and the extent to which I see it as a thing that exists in its own right, a sort of group devil that rises from the murky unconscious depths to darken the group with evil. I referred briefly to this at the start of the essay, but it is important to confirm here that I am using the term in a more abstract way, as a con-struct describing a constellation of destructive fantasies and impulses that may impinge on the group in varying ways and degrees. The term is a bit like a group "fable," akin to the way Menzies-Lythe (Menzies-Lythe, 1981) described some of Bion's (Bion, 1959) later theories of group functioning, a metaphor that dramatizes and pictorializes the essence of the group.

In terms of the theory underlying the concept of the anti-group, I am aware of having moved from a group-analytical model to an object-relations model, influenced by Klein, by Bion (1961) and also by Anzieu (1984), in France. It seems to me significant that theoretical developments concerning destructive forces in groups have been made *outside rather than within* the group-analytic model. This is not surpris-ing given the forcefully optimistic emphasis in the Foulkesian approach, whereas object-relations theories have tended to concentrate strongly on destructive intrapsychic and interpersonal phenomena. This difference has to some extent produced a split. Although it is often argued that the group-analytic model is a flexible one with sufficient width to embrace other theories, the fact is that this has happened only to a limited extent, with group-analytic theory remaining for the most part curiously underdeveloped. My concern, however, is not just with theory: it is as much, if not more so, with the practice of group analysis, which I believe benefits from a full recognition of the impact of constructive *and* destructive group energies.

I am aware of certain omissions in this paper. Partly because of constraints of space, partly because this is essentially a theoretical essay, I have excluded detailed clinical illustrations of the anti-group and its therapeutic possibilities: this is the subject of a separate paper (Nitsun, 1989b). I hope, nevertheless, that my description of the anti-group has conveyed something of the flavour of its expression in clinical group work. I have also not considered the implications of the anti-group for some crucial aspects of group-analytic practice, for example, selection, the group matrix and the role of the conductor. These require detailed consideration. Particularly important is the role of the conductor in identifying the anti-group, in handling and harnessing destructive forces in the group, and in recognizing his or her position in the conflict between defensive idealization and repudiation of the group.

Finally, I wish to return to the social perspective with which this essay began, specifically the sociohistorical context in which group analysis originated. My ideas about the anti-group stem more from the clinical world of the psychiatric setting than from a wider consideration of social forces. However, I find it necessary to try and relate the one to the other. Bringing the social perspective up to date in contemporary terms, it seems to me that in the second half of the twentieth century, we have been preoccupied with two major themes concerning our self-destructiveness. The first was—and, to a lesser extent, still is—the danger of a nuclear holocaust. The second, and more recent, is our anxiety about the destruction of the global environment. These preoccupations both reveal a deep sense of the fragility of our civilization as well as of our potential to destroy ourselves. In this era, it seems to me all the more important to be in touch with our destructive potential and for us as group analysts to be aware of the links that exist between the wider social sphere and the microcosmic world of the therapy groups we run.

Note

1. Nitsun refers to his unpublished paper; Since then, he has published a book on the subject which readers can easily access (Nitsun, 2002).

References

Anzieu, D. (1984). *The group and the unconscious*. London: Routledge and Kegan Paul.

Balint, M. (1968). *The basic fault: Therapeutic aspects of regression*. Tavistock Publications: London.

Bion, W. R. (1959). *Experiences in groups*. Tavistock: London.

Bion, W. R. (1967). *Second thoughts*. Aronson: New York.

Foulkes, S. H. (1948). *Introduction to group-analytic psychotherapy*. Heinemann: London.

Foulkes, S. H. (1964). *Therapeutic group analysis*. Allen & Unwin: London.

Foulkes, S. H. (1973). The Group as matrix of the individual's mental life in group therapy. In *Group Therapy—An Overview*, (ed. L. R. Ed. Wolberg & E. K. Schwartz), Stratton: New York.

Freud, S. (1930). *Civilization and its discontents'*. Hogarth: London.

Kernberg, O. F. (1980). *Internal world and external Reality*. Jason Aronson: New York.

Klein, M. (1957). Envy and gratitude, in *Envy and gratitude and other works (1946–1963)*. Reprinted London: Hogarth Press, 1975.

Menzies-Lythe, I. (1981). Bion's contribution to thinking about Groups. In *Do I dare disturb the Universe?*, (ed. J. S. Grotstein), Caesura Press: Beverly Jills, CA.

Nitsun, M. (1988). The Anti-Group: Destructive forces in the group and their Therapeutic Potential', unpublished theoretical Paper presented on IGA Qualifying Course, Year II.

Nitsun, M. (1989a). Nippets and Imps: The transformational processes in a psychotherapeutic group, unpublished clinical Paper presented on IGA Qualifying Course, Year III.

Nitsun, M. (1989b). Early development: Linking the individual and the group, *Group Analysis*, 22(3): 249–260.

Nitsun, M. (2002). *The anti-group: Destructive forces in the group and their creative Potential*. Routledge: London.

Pines, M. (1983). The contribution of S. H. Foulkes to group psychotherapy. In *The evolution of group-Analysis*, (Anonymous), Routledge and Kegan Paul: London.

CHAPTER SEVENTEEN

Specialists without spirit, sensualists without heart: psychotherapy as a moral endeavour*

Farhad Dalal

Terminology and methodology

In what follows, I will use the terms ethics and morality interchangeably, in part because there is no agreement in moral philosophy about the distinctions between them.

The article speaks to the generic field of psychotherapy, to the fundamentals of our profession and is not limited to specific schools or modalities; it concerns itself with the philosophy behind the psychology. In this sense the article focuses on ideas about practice rather than the practicalities of practice.

Further, I will not try to speak from an objectivist position, "the view from nowhere" as Thomas Nagle (1986) has called it; instead, I will speak from a subjective viewpoint, from within an ongoing journey rather than from outside it. The danger in proceeding this way is that at the end it might turn out that all I will have accomplished is to reinvent a number of well-known and well-worn wheels. And in some senses this is indeed true. But it is ever thus. We continually find things

---

*This chapter was first published as: Dalal, F. (2012). Specialists without spirit, sensualists without heart: Psychotherapy as a moral endeavour. *Group Analysis*, 45: 405–429.

afresh "for yet another first time" as Garfinkel (1967) once said—be it an insight, a taste, an idea, or the first smell of spring—as though we have never known these things before. In this process something comes alive for yet another first time. So in speaking to you in this way, I hope to bring alive for you, for perhaps yet another first time, something that has come alive for me.

And finally, given that I will be touching on terms like soul and love, I should flag up my attitude to these notions. Some might presume that having moved to the town called Totnes (recently twinned with Narnia) where crystal and angel therapy abound, that I have literally gone off with the fairies. This is not so. I will speak as a secularist and material-ist. I will not be calling on higher powers. What I have to say is firmly grounded in the material, in the everyday, in the ordinary.

Preamble

In a book called The Philosopher's Dog (2004), the moral philosopher Raimond Gaita said this about their family dog Gypsy,

> We did not discipline Gypsy to make her predictable. We did it to make her trustworthy.
>
> (Gaita, 2004: 42)

The word pair "predictability/trust" literally knocked the wind out of me. It crystallized many of the questions I had been circling around for the last few years to do with organizational life, as well as our profession of psy-chotherapy; and particularly as the profession tries to come to terms with the powerful arrival of CBT—the Cognitive Behavioural Tsunami.

In what follows, one of the things I want to urge, is not to succumb to the panic being generated by this tsunami and rush into manualizing our ways of working. But nor do I want to advocate for a return to the arrogant complacency of the old status quo. It seems to me that here is an opportunity to really re-think what we are about.

Like many of you, I continue to ruminate about my practice: What do I think I am doing? What am I actually doing? What do I publicly admit to about what I am doing? Over the last few years my ruminations have been fed by the repeated appearance of the theme of forgiveness in vari-ous guises in the clinic. It was in the midst of this sort of rumination that I stumbled across Gaita's work, which triggered the thought in me that the practice of psychotherapy is actually a work in ethics. I do not just mean that morality features in the content of the work, rather the activity of psychotherapy is in itself a profound moral endeavour, a practice in ethics.

But the thought of going public about this epiphany generated considerable anxiety in me as it goes against the grain of the ruling paradigm: this being that psychotherapy is a scientific treatment, and as such is concerned with matters of fact rather than of value. When matters of value enter the clinical arena—politics and morals say—then in the main we have been trained to think of them as expressions and symptoms of internal dramas, and for them to be reductively interpreted as such.

The first assertion

My work to date has drawn on Norbert Elias to champion the views of Radical Foulkes over those of the Orthodox (Dalal, 1998, 2002). Like many others, I have been arguing against an idea of an individualistic, asocial and pre-social internal psychological world. This work may be summarized by the maxims that the "we" is prior to the "I," and that the "I" is a conflictual entity constituted out of the varieties of "we" that one is born into. The fact that the region of the "we" is constituted by power-relations, leads to the first assertion: that the psyche is constituted and patterned by the field of power-relations one is born into.

In taking this stance, I recognize that I have already parted company with many colleagues whose allegiance lies with the internalist account of classical psychoanalysis. But this is where I am bound to begin.

If my first assertion has relied on the sociology of Norbert Elias, then my second assertion will lean heavily on the writings of the moral philosopher Raimond Gaita. And to confess this at the start—I am even more of a novice when it comes to moral philosophy than I am of sociology.

The second assertion

I begin with Foulkes' notion of belonging, which he said is critical to psychological well-being. Belonging means that we have a place in the world, but it also means that we find ourselves placed in the world. The fact that we find ourselves placed, reminds us that power relations are intrinsic to notions of belonging and community.

Anyhow, as soon as one starts talking of belonging and community, then one is immediately precipitated into the territory of morals and ethics. At the very least, this is because communities define themselves in part, by the meaning worlds they sign up to. And of necessity these are moral considerations—what is a good life, and what is a bad life? What is right and what is wrong? These distinctions—these ways of life—form the boundaries of community.

To say that we live in the social world is also to say that we live in a moral universe; to say that the psyche is patterned by power relations is to grant that it is constituted by a profound sense of good and bad. And to speak of good and bad, is to speak of ethics, of meaning and meaningfulness. The second assertion then is this: the psyche is not only constituted by power-relations, it is also constituted by moral-relations. As Gaita says,

> We cannot radically rescind from the ethical constitution of our inner lives without becoming unintelligible to ourselves.
>
> (Gaita, 2008: 53)

In other words one cannot conceive of a Self outside, beyond or devoid of ethics, because ethics and morals constitute the self. Without them there would be no self to speak of, consequently the lives we lived would no longer be recognizably human, as they would have been rendered meaningless.

I now find myself somewhat bemused. Why does the idea that the self is ethically constituted feel so new to me, given that at the very beginnings of psychoanalysis we find Freud's vision of the superego, given that Klein's collected works are entitled Love, Guilt and Reparation (1998) and so on. Surely, all this speaks directly into the moral domain. And yet, despite these works and ideas being familiar, for me this felt like a new thought; I have to say "for me" because it might not be "for you."

Meaning and morals—how do they arise?

I know that my importance to the world is very limited, and soon enough for all the difference it will make, it will be as though I had never existed. As someone called Martin Myers once said: "First you're an unknown, then you write one book and you move up to obscurity' (http://quotedb.net/martin-myers/). More significantly, in a few billion years our entire solar system will be cosmic ash. From this perspective, our lives and preoccupations are utterly pointless as they make not one jot of difference to the future of the larger picture. This realization can lead to nihilistic despair about the present. One way out of this despair is to ask "what is the universe for?" Or "what is the purpose of existence?"

This attempt to give meaning to our brief and haphazard lives by imagining that we are part of some larger cosmic plan was closed off by Wittgenstein when he asked.

> Why people think that an after-life should solve the problems of life or give meaning to life. Why should the meaning of the next life not be as problematic as the meaning of this one?
>
> (Wittgenstein in Gaita, 2004: 74)

And yet, despite recognizing my utter insignificance, my life nevertheless feels more or less meaningful to me. Is this hubris on my part? Or am I in the grip of a grandiose delusion?

I think it neither.

My view is this: we are meaning-making beings in a meaningless universe.

So how do we make meaning? And is the meaning we make meaningful?

To ask these sorts of questions is actually to ask, where does our moral sensibility of right and wrong come from? This is because, as I hope it is already becoming evident, moral frameworks are intrinsic to meaning schemas. But how do they arise?

Socio-genetic morality—the Eliasian and Radical Foulkesian account

It is the case that ethical capacities are innate in all human beings. However, much like the innate capacity for language, the socialization processes come to give our innate ethical capacity particular shapes and forms, creating cultural norms and so forth. These internalized conventions become aspects of the social unconscious. This is one aspect of the "I" being formed out of the "We-s" one is born into. Elias and Radical Foulkes would say that these processes not only penetrate, but also create the deepest corners of the psyche. This describes something very important: how pre-existing systems of conflicting moralities come to be established in individuals; but it has little to say about how and why those moral schemas should arise in the first place.

Instrumental morality—the internalist account

The instinctivist streams within psychoanalysis, specifically Freud and Klein, derive the moral sensibility out of internal psychological mechanisms. An instance of this is Freud's derivation of the sense of social justice: he begins with the jealous older child's murderous feelings towards the younger sibling. The child solves the difficulty by identifying with the younger sibling. Next, Freud says, "If one cannot be the favourite oneself, at all events no one else shall be favourite" (1921: 120). Freud tells us that it is this sort of dynamic which forms the basis for our desire for equality and justice. If I cannot have all the cake (which is what I would really like) then I will make sure that we all have exactly the same amount of cake. "Social justice means that we deny ourselves many things so that others may have to do without them as well" (1921: 121). This is not a version of social justice that I find particularly inspirational.

In both the Freudian and Kleinian account the moral attitude is a structural psychological solution. It is a way of managing internal difficulties to enable us to live with other people. This sort of account renders morality instrumental. This sort of morality is a means to an end, the "end" being the wellbeing, safety and survival of the self and the species.

This sort of account of how morality comes to be established in the self does not touch me, and nor does it move me. In contrast, when Gaita says "we are ethically constituted" (Gaita, 2008: 53), I find myself moved and come to hear something for "yet another first time."

Does it matter whether I am moved or not? And ought I to trust that which moves me? I will attend to these important questions shortly. But first, I want to describe the account that does move me.

Empathic morality—Gaita's account

Gaita's derivation of morality fits well (in different ways) with aspects of the world views of Winnicott and Bowlby. And because this derivation of morality is relational, it is also deeply congenial to the group analytic sensibility. Gaita says that the seeds of our moral attitudes are to be found in the deep attachments we form with each other, and specifically, through the attachment called love. And it comes about in the following way:

As infants, the persons we attach to start to matter to us. And because they matter to us, we come to feel concern for their wellbeing. It is this concern for them that makes us want to act in kindly and decent ways towards them and generates in us a sense of obligation to them. It these sorts of considerate attitudes and behaviours, that are the basis of those that we end up calling moral. And it is this that makes our lives feel meaningful.

Although obvious, the point I want to emphasize is that meaning is constituted by the kinds and quality of relationships one finds oneself embedded in. It is the presence or absence of our attachment objects, and the ethical quality of those relationships, that make our lives feel more or less meaningful.

It is as ordinary, and as profound as that.

Two (false) problems of altruism

But even here, there is a reductive and cynical understanding regarding our capacity for concern. This cynical viewpoint comes about because of the radical split made by Kant between duty and desire. According to his way of thinking, if an act makes me feel good, then because I will have benefited from it, by definition it therefore cannot be altruistic.

But why should I not feel good about doing a good deed? Surely the fact that I come to feel good is in part what motivates me to do the right thing. The cynic, and perhaps the psychoanalyst, might continue to insist that the apparent act of generosity is in fact disguised self-promotion: doing good in order to be seen-to-do-good and admired for it. This is often true. But to tar all acts of generosity with this Machiavellian, narcissistic brush is to radically distort things. By no means do these perverse versions of kindness and generosity speak to the entirety of the territory.

If the first difficulty of altruism is caused by the split between duty and desire, then the second difficulty is caused by the split between the external and internal worlds. The fact that some acts of goodness are in the Machiavellian service of eliciting the approval of others, led Kant to suppose that the approval of others is always corrupting. He said that it was the responsibility of each person to work out right from wrong themselves, and to do so internally, without reference to others (reference).

But this kind of radical exclusion of others is only possible in a solipsistic individualistic conceptualization of human life. The fact that we humans are social beings means that we both need and desire the approval of our belonging groups. Approval and disapproval are the means by which we calibrate our beings with others in our belonging groups. This after all is the import of Foulkes' claim that belonging is necessary to psychological well-being. In contrast, Rudyard Kipling's poem. If (1895) valorizes the man who is indifferent to the opinions of others. To my mind, such a person is not to be admired but feared, because indifference to others is the stuff that psychopaths are made of.

The fact that at times the desire for the approval of others is for Machiavellian or narcissistic ends, should not be used to obscure the fact that the approval of others is intrinsic to our well being and something we can never do without. And this is the point: the grounds for approval and disapproval are intrinsically moral.

Gaita is arguing that that there are versions of obligation, civility, kindness and generosity that are ends in themselves, the basis of which are to be found in our responsive capacity for empathy and love. Here, we do good because we desire to do good to others, because we feel for them, because we want them to feel good. This capacity too is part of the human condition, a capacity that is common enough, in the love between some parents and their children, and in the love of some individuals for other individuals.

In sum, love, empathy and attachment are the generators of our ethical sensibilities and the attitudes and behaviours that we come to describe as moral. This is how Gaita puts it:

> Attachments and the joy and grief, which they may cause, condition our sense of the preciousness of human beings. Love is the most important of them.
>
> (Gaita, 2008: 27; italics added)

Interim summary

There are several ways of capturing the bones of the discussion so far. The first is to say that there are two kinds of morality, one of which is an instrumental morality of the Freudian kind that is essentially self-serving; whilst the other is an empathic morality and is other-serving. There are echoes here with Freud's distinction between Eros and Agape.

Whilst registering the distinction between the two, it is important not to create a major split between them and hold onto a more nuanced position. As Gaita says:

> Fidelity and justice are not reducible to the material or psychological advantages they bring [but] neither are they separable from them.
>
> (Gaita, 2008: 8)

Another way of encapsulating the prior discussion is through a distinction between the Hobbesian idea that "human nature is the enemy of ethics" (Alford, 2002: 22) in which ethical frameworks are a way of controlling a savage human nature; and Gaita's vision in which ethics are an aspect and expression of human nature. Once again the distinction is not to be taken as an opposition. Rather I want with Gaita to emphasize the second of these, which says that there are versions of obligation, civility, kindness and generosity that are ends in themselves, the basis of which are to be found in our responsive capacity for empathy and love.

I am not for a moment wanting to deny the darker side of human life. Of course adults, infants and children are also self-centred, devious, hateful, demanding and difficult. But on what basis is it claimed that these aspects of the human condition are more real and fundamental than those of love, compassion and generosity?

The final way of characterizing the territory is to collate the three routes through which three versions of morality come to be established in each of us.

First is the process in which we unconsciously imbibe the pre-existing moral norms of the communities that we are born into. This is the "social unconscious."

Second is the morality of rules and regulations. Here, one learns to say please, sorry and thank you in the right places at the right times, and useful though this might be as a social lubricant, in itself it can remain empty etiquette. This kind of morality is in conflict with desire, embodied as it is in the conflict between the Superego and the Id.

The third source of morality arises out of one's responsive feelings; here, actions construed as moral are driven by one's desires and are not in conflict with them. Here, there arises in one's body a genuine impulse to say sorry and thank you, because they give expression to feelings of remorse and gratitude that arise in response to the other.

It is clear then that we are neither fully determined as excessive social construction might suggest, and nor do we have unfettered free will as Kant conceived.

Individuation through guilt, love and gratitude

If we put the moral emotions in the centre of the picture, then some surprising things follow out of it. For one, it leads to differentiation and individuation. This happens in several ways, the first of which has to do with guilt.

The classical psychoanalytic thesis proposes that guilt is only possible after individuation, at the point one realizes that the hated and loved objects are one and the same. Gaita (following a Wittgensteinian line) reverses the sequence to say, that it is the experience of remorse that shocks one into wakefulness to realize that it is me that has injured this particular person. In this moment one becomes painfully conscious of self and other as beings, as distinct beings.

This reversal is resonant with the Fairbairn's enduring and telling critique of Freud and Klein: he said that they had mistaken techniques for causes (Reference).

The next differentiating mechanism is driven by the effects others have on us. Our attachment and dependence on specific others means that our wellbeing, comes (in part) to rely on their good will. Our attachments make us vulnerable to the whims of those we attach to. It is this combination, that we cannot control them, and yet our wellbeing is in part reliant on them, that also painfully forces on us the realization these individuals have an existence that is separate from us, and yet we remain ever connected and dependent upon them.

This is how Gaita summarizes it:

> Our sense of the reality of others is partly conditioned by our vulnerability to them, by the unfathomable grief they may cause us. It is also conditioned by our shocked and bewildered realisation of what it means to wrong them. Remorse is that realisation.
>
> (Gaita, 2008: 34)

Perhaps the most critical of drivers in the individuation process is love; the persons we love become irreplaceable in our affections, and therefore individuated. No other child can replace this child, no other friend this friend, no other lover can replace this lover. Each is truly unique to me, and no other will do. Iris Murdoch puts it beautifully: "Love is the extremely difficult realization that something other than oneself is real" (Murdoch, 1999: 215).

A small experience led me to realize something similar about gratitude. Whilst on holiday, on a singularly hot and sticky morning, we were suddenly bathed in a deliciously soft breeze. I noticed arising in myself a feeling of gratitude. But then, I became aware that there was no object for this gratitude—there was no where to put it as it were. In one sense I felt gratitude to the breeze itself, but in so doing I animated it, even more, I humanized it. You could say that I was falling into the error of anthropomorphizing the breeze. Maybe so. But what struck me through this entirely trivial experience, was the realization that I needed something or someone to receive my gratitude, and without it, the experience was somehow incomplete. So in a sense, gratitude creates a need for the other, and it too comes to render the other "real." And perhaps this is also why when there is no receptacle for gratitude (or blame), we find it necessary to invent gods or the fates in whom we can place these feelings.

This then, is Gaita's claim: that the moral emotions come alive when people are individuated, and the converse, that it is the evocation of the moral emotions, which individuates both self and other.

It follows, and we know it to be true, that it is easier to act ruthlessly against those not individuated, the faceless generic "them," because here, there is no direct purchase for empathic morality. This is where rule-based morality becomes necessary, but not in a straightforward way. Gaita argues that we are only able to meaningfully employ rule-based morality by the device of remembering that the stranger is irreplaceable in someone else's affections, and so has a face for them, and it is this realization that humanizes them in our eyes.

I now want to turn to questions of "practice," but in order to do that I need to step back and set up a frame within which to have the discussion. To this end, I start with Kant because although some of the problems we are mired in could be said to begin with him, so do some of the solutions to those self same problems.

Kant, Appiah, Buber

One of the key questions that Kant (Reference) tussled with was that of human responsibility. He could see that much of the natural world operated as though it were mechanically following rules of cause and effect in a more or less predictable way.

It was critical for Kant that we did not think of and treat human beings as belonging entirely to the natural world. Because if we proceeded in this way, then humans would not have to take moral responsibility for their actions; their decisions would simply be the "effects" of certain prior "causes."

The philosopher Appiah put it like this: to understand events in the natural world one looks for causes, but in order to understand human behaviour, we look for reasons (Appiah, 2005).

There is a deep resonance between Gaita's word pair predictability/trustworthiness, and Appaiah's cause/reason. A resonance that is perfectly encapsulated by another word pair, Martin Buber's I-Thou and I-It (Buber, 1958).

Predictability and cause, speak to the world of things, the I and "it." Meanwhile reason and trust speak to the world of human interaction, of I and Thou. It is these terms, trust and reason, more strongly than anything else, that shows that humans reside in a moral universe; and to say that humans reside in a moral universe is to say that they reside in the realm of meaning.

Kant →	Things	Persons
Appiah →	Cause	Reason
Gaita →	Predictability	Trust
Buber →	I-It	I-Thou

Figure 1. The philosophers.

Having set up the frame, the purpose of which has been to sharpen the distinction between things and persons, I move onto discussing clinical practice.

The attitude of the natural scientist

The attitude that our profession is still in thrall to, is that of the natural scientist, with its ideals of objectivity, of reason purged of emotion, of impersonal detachment. This is why we grant more status to those designated as analysts over those designated as therapists. The scientific sounding languages of psychoanalysis and group analysis feed this view point: projection, matrix, nodes, networks, resonance, splitting, transference, dynamics, and so on. We garner for ourselves the prestige of physics departments by calling our clinical discussions "scientific meetings." Indeed, this Foulkes Lecture has been organized by the Scientific Committee of the Group Analytic Society.

When it comes to the study of things, the detached impersonal attitude of the natural scientist makes good sense. But even here, as the natural scientists themselves came to realize, their investigations were never entirely impersonal nor fully detached. This is why they came to invent investigative protocols like randomized control trials and double blind experiments—the intention of which is to remove the experimenter from the experiment. But now, when this same impersonal attitude comes to be utilized in the clinic, then it is no longer a scientific attitude, but scientistic. This is Wittgenstein's term for pseudo-science. The problem with the adoption of the scientistic attitude in the clinic, is that it achieves the exact opposite of its intentions: it actually distorts what it seeks to reveal. Let me explain:

When one studies a human face with an impassive eye, then, unlike inanimate things, the face that is being studied is affected by the impassivity, and reacts to it.

As is well known, if a mother were to keep her face impassive, her infant will first make efforts to enliven her, then if that fails it becomes distressed, and if that too fails, it falls into a kind of depression. Similarly, an impassive face causes adults to feel uncomfortable no less than infants. So when a patient gets anxious when faced with an analyst's impassivity, the easy mistake is to think that as the analyst is not doing anything, the anxiety must belong to the patient as it is emerging from "inside" them. It is in this way a conceptual error has been built into the heart of classical psychoanalytic theory.

The point, although a truism, is nevertheless worth stressing: humans are ever-responsive beings. The patient is influenced as much by what the analyst does as much as by what she does not do.

Gaita puts it like this:

> If our understanding of our inner life and its actuality are interdependent, if the concepts with which we identify and explore our

inner life partly determine the character of that inner life, then a scientistic distortion of those concepts will not only distort our understanding, it will distort the inner life itself.

(Gaita, 2008: 247, italics added)

The nature of the distortion created by the impassivity is this: the
"Thou" is distorted into an "It." If the one-who-comes-for-help is primarily thought of as a diagnostic category then they are rendered "it."
"Itification" fits well with the paradigm of therapy as scientific treatment. Most powerful is our seemingly innocuous itifying category,
"patient." In the mouths of some colleagues, the term is saturated with
haughty condescension.

And the one-who-comes-for-help is also prone to render the helper
an "it" called expert or therapist. The realm of the "it" is less about
"being with," and more about "doing to" and being "done to." To this
way of thinking the actual relationship is of no account, and if it is, it is
only instrumental.

This is quite a thing to say: that the impersonal, detached attitude of
the analyst that is so highly prized in our profession, actually distorts
the clinical field. This of course is no surprise to the inter-subjectivists,
who would concur with Gaita to say that clinical phenomena are being
co-created by all those who are present, and not just "found" by an
observing analyst.

But I am not here arguing that we should not use categories—which
is both nonsensical as well as impossible. As Buber says more poetically: "This is the exalted melancholy of our fate, that every Thou in our
world must become an It" (Buber, 1958: 21).

This is the problem I am now faced with:

If the categorization process is necessarily a detaching and distanc-
ing process, and I cannot not categorize, then what is to be done? If the
scientistic attitude is distortive, if "Thou" is bound to become "It," then
where should I turn?

Wittgenstein: an attitude towards a soul

To begin attempting an answer, I have to start seemingly a long way off
for reasons that will quickly become apparent, with a question that has
engaged philosophers over the ages: how do I know that other people
have conscious minds like me?

The positivist Descartian answer is that first, I observe behaviours, from which I infer and deduce that the other might also have a conscious mind like me. And it is only then that I decide to respond to them on this basis, as if they had minds like me. Here we have hypothesis and inference taking place in an isolated mind.

Wittgenstein reverses the sequence to say that first come our spontaneous responses to others. He says that these responses, which are spontaneously called out of us, are the condition rather than the consequence of ascribing states of consciousness in others (Gaita, 2004: 54).

> Out of such unhesitating interactions between ourselves and between us and animals, there developed—not beliefs, assumptions and conjectures about the mind—but our very concepts of thought feeling, intention, doubt, and so on.
>
> (Gaita, 2004: 61; italics added)

The key term in the above is "unhesitating." For example, the philosopher David Hume raised many grave philosophical doubts about what we can logically know with any certainty about the world, but he found that in day to day life these

> ... doubts dissipated when they were overtaken by the pleasures of convivial conversation with ... friends over a game of backgammon.
>
> (Gaita, 2004: 46)

Something is just called out of us, and when it is, there is no hesitation, no doubt. Wittgenstein puts it like this:

> What gives us so much the idea that human beings can feel? Nothing gives us so much as the idea, for it is not a matter of having an idea. It is not an assumption, a conjecture, or a belief, or even knowledge.
>
> (Wittgenstein, 1963: 283)

If it is not any of these things, then what is it?

It is that which is unhesitatingly called out of us, which Wittgenstein calls "an attitude towards a soul."

The word soul is not being used here for an entity in the religious sense. What soul means here is that the being has the capacity to suffer "and with the possibility of ... [the suffering] going deep" (Gaita, 2008: 239).

At its simplest, soul means the capacity to feel, to feel deeply, and for the feelings to be meaningful.

Another way of talking about this attitude is to say that one finds oneself moved.

This is key: It is the response that is called out—say pity—that reveals the sentient nature of the other. One does not feel pity for a stone, however hard it is kicked. This attitude towards a soul is akin to Buber's notion of I-Thou, and both are ethically constituted. I speak here of nothing more mysterious than empathy.

On being moved: responsivity

We are still mired in the ideological battle between the rationalism of the Enlightenment and the emotionalism of the Romantics, of head versus heart, of thought versus feeling. The cognitive and analytic schools tending to privilege thought over feeling, and the humanistic, feeling over thought.

According to classical psychoanalytic ideology, it is the interpretation, delivered by the detached analyst that is the key to change. In his later years Foulkes himself was not much for making interpretations, still less transference interpretations.

> The modern tendency to put transference interpretations totally and explicitly into the centre of the analytic procedure is open to grave doubt. This can be overdone and in fact reinforces the neurosis. It seems to me that the transference phenomenon, thought essential for human relationships and for analysis to take place, is nevertheless in a certain sense the victory of the neurosis over both the therapist and patient alike. Thus I cannot agree with the monopoly conceded in certain techniques to the transference and its interpretation.
>
> (Foulkes, 1978: 116, italics added)

In contrast to the values of detachment, I have been arguing for the values of responsivity and its interconnectedness with meaning and ethics.

Critical to the interconnectivity are the emotions as they are the vehicle through which we come to register our ethical responses. Our emotions move us. And the ways that we are moved—towards or away, opening or closing off, are in themselves expressions of our ethical response to what is moving us. I am not by any means advocating that we dispense with our rational faculties, which are also deeply responsive. Here is the thing: both faculties, the rational and the emotional, do cognitive work. But the cognitive work of one is not fully explicable, nor reducible, to the other.

Pascal captured the sentiment perfectly in his aphorism (paraphrased) "The Heart has its reasons which Reason does not understand" (Pascal, 1958: 79). But in order not to collapse into anti-rationalism, we ought to remember that "Reason has its reasons which the Heart cannot always follow."

The clinic

I am now going to recast the reasons why people come for psychotherapy into the language being developed in this paper, as having to do with responsivity and meaning. Mostly people come because something has gone awry in their responsive capacities. This they commonly describe symptomatically as difficulties of living with other people, be it shyness, panic attacks, fear, anger issues, and so on. But they also come because of ruptures in their meaning schemas. This they commonly describe symptomatically as suffering from depression, anxiety, low self-esteem, and so forth.

They come because they feel bad—and often enough they think that they feel bad because they are bad.

We have arrived at the heart of the issue. I will try now to describe as carefully as I can, why I think what I have come to think. If our responsivity is integral to our humanity, then it is exactly this capacity that has atrophied or been damaged in the one-who-comes-for help. Further the damage has come about precisely because of being treated as an "it" by significant others during the developmental processes. It follows then that the detached attitude of an unresponsive therapist will necessarily reproduce and reinforce this self same experience of being an "it." It is for this sort of reason that I think the therapist needs to be responsive rather than removed. Wittgenstein famously said that some things cannot be said, but only shown. To this I would add: some things cannot be explained but only experienced, and it is only then that they can be metabolized and become meaningful. And for this to be possible, it requires the therapist to come out of their analytic bunker to be responsive, and be responded to.

In the to-and-fro dance of gesture and response between protagonists, each comes progressively to be attuned to the other. With hard work and some luck, on occasion each finds, and is found by the other.

It is in this moment of finding and being found, that meaning comes alive. Moments like these, few and far between, are at the heart of therapy.

And when this happens, I think it is an experience of love. I do not say that the experience is akin to that of love. I say that it is love. If the therapist is able to risk being present as an ethical being with their values and sense of right and wrong intact, then they are bound to be present as a responsive being because our responsivity is integral to our ethical sensibilities. If only on this basis, it can be seen that the ideal of the therapist's detached neutrality is unsustainable.

Foulkes himself was well aware of this, when he said "what I mean by "following the group's lead" is following with discrimination" (Foulkes 1948: 139, italics added).

To discriminate is to make choices, and these, however scientific and objective they might seem are always ethically constituted.

> Aside: take these two statements:
> Psychotherapy should be evidence based.
> The only evidence that should count is quantitative evidence.
> Are these scientific claims, or moral injunctions?

In arguing for responsivity I am arguing against the convention which makes not-responding a virtue. Many therapists have turned not responding into an art form, of finding elegant ways of not answering questions and so forth, because they think that in responding they will be acting out in some way. And sometimes that is of course true. But it is also the case that this way of being reproduces and reinforces earlier experiences of being not responded to, of being treated as an "it."

It is for these sorts of reasons, over the last years I find myself becoming increasingly transparent in the clinic. By transparent I do not mean speaking about my own life issues, but transparent in regards to what is arising in me in response to what is taking place in the consulting room. This then results in aspects of me being much more visible. In effect, by putting myself on the line in this way, I am continually risking myself. And that seems perfectly fair to me, as I am expecting, inviting and requiring the ones who come for help (singular or group) to also risk being present in the room in all their complexity.

The attitude I am describing (with the help of Gaita) is somewhat different to the way the analyst's emotions are conventionally understood in our field, this being primarily as counter-transference and as being "caused" by the patient. The convention is that the analyst keeps these feelings to themselves, whilst they analyse them for their informational content regarding the state of mind of the patient. And following this, if the analysis has got somewhere, the analyst makes an interpretation. I think this sort of process sensible, but if this is all that takes place, then it is devoid of spirit and I think it entirely sterile.

On love

I have been arguing that the moments we find ourselves being moved are important and ought to be attended to because they reveal something. What is revealed, particularly through the movement called love, is the humanity of the one who is loved. And this is the important thing: it is revealed to both, the one who loves and the one who is loved. This shows just how wrong is the sanctimonious injunction that you first have to learn to love yourself, before anyone else can love you. The reality is otherwise. It is through being loved by others (if we are lucky enough) that we come to know that we are loveable. This surely is the significance of parental love: it reveals the child's humanity to itself, and so it comes to think of itself of value. If love is absent then something never comes alive, and perhaps it is killed off entirely. And let us not forget the power of the child's love to transform the parent. For many an adult, this is their first real experience of being loved.

Similarly, in the clinic, I think that it is the therapist's attitude of love that is critical to the therapeutic endeavour.

Trust in the face of uncertainty

I have been arguing all this while that we ought to give more weight to our emotional responses in the consulting room, but in doing so I am not arguing that it is the only thing we ought to give weight to. Just because something feels right does not make it so. This was the crucial error of the Romantic vision, an error repeatedly reproduced by many a humanistic and person-centred therapist.

It is because the emotions are not entirely to be trusted that Kant privileged the reasoning processes over emotional ones. But no certainty is to be found in the rational realm either. This is readily demonstrated by the fact that despite utilising the reasoning process, intelligent individuals continually arrive at different conclusions.

But there is a more fundamental problem with positivist claims of objectivity, and it is this: all rational systems (even mathematics) have to build on something that they cannot prove: axioms. Axioms are deemed to be self-evident truths not requiring proof. But when axioms are stripped of their scientistic clothing, they turn out to be nothing other than an experience, perhaps even just a feeling, but always something subjective. Every rationalist objective edifice is built to some degree on subjective sands, and so, as with the emotional realm, there is always room for doubt.

For example, there was a famous occasion when Bertrand Russell (Reference) became utterly exasperated by the fact that despite his best efforts, he was unable to get Wittgenstein to concede that it was certain that there was no rhinoceros present in the study that they were having their argument in.

So we need not be all that perturbed by the unreliability of our emotional lives, because uncertainty and ambiguity are intrinsic to the human condition.

Having said that, the problem remains: given that there is no certainty, how do I decide when and whether I ought to trust the response arising in me? Gaita answers:

> When we are moved we trust what moves us and trust that we are rightly moved. We trust wisely however, only when trust is disciplined.
>
> (Gaita, 2008: xxxvii)

I was perplexed: what does it mean to discipline trust? Then I read Fred Alford who echoes Gaita in saying this about pity:

> Pity is an intense experience of attunement ... [but] pity needs to be educated ... to feel pity towards the right person to the right extent...
>
> (Alford, 2002: 138–42)

I came to think that both of them are actually speaking of the cultivation of wisdom and thoughtful reflection.

Each of them addresses the difficulty in making decisions when one is mired in subjectivity, of knowing how to proceed when one is "in the thick of things." Bion famously spoke of the difficulty of "thinking under fire," which I would reframe as the difficulty of "responding with authenticity in the heat of the moment." One anxiety reducing strategy utilized for decision making in these turbulent subjective waters, is to fall back on rule making and rule following. For example: only speak in and through the transference; never gratify a patient's wish but always interpret it, and so on.

Rules and expertise are indeed helpful when trying to navigate the turbulent subjective waters of the clinic, but by themselves they are not nearly enough. I am not of course advocating mindless rule breaking as the answer to mindless rule following. As a character in a comic novel by Terry Pratchett says: "Look, that's why there are rules, understand? So that you think before you break them" (Pratchett, 2001: 251).

On this point there was a telling and crucial study conducted by Dreyfus and Dreyfus (1988). They showed films of three groups of people (novices, teachers, and experienced practitioners) doing resuscitation work, to members of each of these groups. Each was asked to rate the skill level of what they observed. The interesting thing for our purposes, is that the teachers rated the novices most highly. It turned out that this was because the novices being novices, proceeded mechanically by following the rules they had just been taught (if A then do X). Whereas the experienced practitioners were continually breaking rules, and improvising (even though A, I think it better to do M). I would say that they are exercising the wisdom (rather than expertise) that they have accumulated over years of practice, and in so doing they turn out to be more efficient than pedestrian rule followers.

Similarly, in this regard, there is a danger that our trainings capitulate to the demands of positivist efficiency ideologues to train therapists in the impoverished language of skill sets and competencies. And even when they are not doing this, it seems to me that in the main our trainings foster the cultivation of expertise over that of wisdom. But of course, wisdom cannot be taught, it can only be shown.

Returning to the clinic, if I remain convinced that what is arising in me is meaningful, even though I might not be able to articulate the entire what and the why of it, then I think that I am ethically bound to give expression to it in some way. This view point is in sharp contrast to the person-centred therapist and the classical analyst, both of whom think that they should do their utmost to keep themselves out of the picture.

But it is also the case that I give expression to my response, not as unassailable truth, but as a gesture into an ongoing conversation. In doing this I am both modelling and inviting the ones who come for help to do the same. What happens next is that which is voiced is tested and transmuted in the forge called "conversation." It is in this sense that I think of the activity of therapy as responsive ethical conversation rather than as analysis.

The reality is this: we cannot help be moved, we cannot help but feel. Thought is always passionate.

Gaita again:

> A dispassionate judgement is not one which is uninformed by feeling, but one which is undistorted by feeling.
>
> (Gaita, 2008: 89)

Elsewhere he cautions

> if we fear that our thought has been distorted because we have been sentimentally moved, then instead of trying not to be moved, we should strive to being not sentimentally moved.
>
> (Gaita, 2008: 252)

In responding, we are being called upon to trust something in the face of uncertainty. And in doing so we trust something that might well turn out to be false. That in itself is not a problem, if one has trusted and acted with sincerity, and if one remains open to dialogue and revision. Protocols and manualized decision-making process are of no help in this sort of situation because they drive the process down pre-determined lines, rather than staying open to the present and venturing into the unknown. The trust that is required to go forward as an ethical being, is disciplined trust, which we might even call wisdom.

To conclude

At the conclusion of this article, we are left with two anxieties that we can never escape and nor can we resolve. The Enlightenment anxiety is that feelings ought not to be trusted because they are so fickle, instead one should trust Reason. The Romantic anxiety is that the approval of others ought not to be trusted as it is corrupting of one's true opinion—instead one finds truth by looking inside to one's feelings.

The first is an anxiety about our subjectivity and the second about our capacity for objectivity. What is true is that neither should be entirely trusted, because the discourses we are born into to some degree pre-empt not only what we are able to think but also what we will tend to feel about certain things, as well as the sorts of people we will look to for approval—generally the more powerful. But we are not entirely determined, cultural sheep. We are also to some degree Kantian beings, capable of questioning and inquiring into the conditions of our exis-tence and transforming them. I say "to some degree" because we are not as free as Kant supposed us to be. Nevertheless, these compromised capacities are all I have at my disposal, which is why the problematic notion of discipline becomes so very important.

There are many things I have not been able to attend to in this article, for example shame and justice which make a bridge between politics and psychology. Nor have I had the space to make links with others who have spoken on similar matters, Farenzi, Sullivan, Frankl, Levinas, Bollas, the intersubjectivists, the phenomenologists, and so on. I have focussed on the loving emotions and made almost no mention of hate-ful ones. I have concerned myself entirely with the activity and attitude of the therapist and not attended to the contribution of the ones-who-come-for-help. I have spoken at the level of ideas and not fleshed these out with clinical material as is usually the case in our profession. I have left out these and other valuable elements in the service of clarity and brevity and not because I think them unimportant.

What I *have* done in this paper is to place ethics at the centre of the human condition, and at the centre of our work as psychotherapists. I have said that this requires the therapist to be a responsive presence. But this responsivity needs to be a thoughtful and "disciplined" one. I have also followed Kant to say that because human beings are not things, it is unethical to treat them as such. To my mind this is one of the key charges to be made not only against the cognitivists but also certain streams within the analytic schools: that their forms of treatment are unethical precisely because they conceptualize and treat the ones-who-come-for-help as things—despite their rhetoric asserting otherwise.

There is an apocryphal story of desperate soldiers lost in enemy ter-ritory. They find a map, which they use to find their way to safety. They then discover that the map they had used was for another territory altogether. The moral of the story being that even when one gets to where one was hoping to get to, it is not necessarily because of the reasoning that was utilized in the process.

In my view, whatever the school, cognitive, analytic or humanistic, the therapies that prosper do so, not so much because of the rationales endemic to each of the schools, but because of the therapist's ability to bring to the work an attitude towards a soul.

I think that at this historical moment we can draw moral courage from Gaita's fighting words (aimed at philosophers but also pertinent to us):

> We should cease to look for [reductive, positivist] justification while at the same time refusing to concede that this is intellectual dereliction.
>
> (Gaita, 2004: 50)

He urges us not to succumb to the demand that we subject our work to the impoverished version of evidence that is prized by policy makers in today's world, and to argue why this is not an intellectual cop out, and nor is it negligence on our part.

This article then is my attempt at swimming against the mechanistic tide prevalent in the cognitivist therapies, as well as the scientistic tide prevalent in some of the analytic therapies, and trying to do so without succumbing to the anti-rationalism promoted by sections of the humanistic traditions.

I have been arguing for the privileging of a certain version of fluidity, subjectivity, responsivity, engagement and authenticity in which not only is our work grounded, so is our very humanity.

Acknowledgement

I need to thank Malcolm Pines for publishing my first book, and my group analyst, Liesel Hearst, without whose help I would not be where I am today. About the work itself: this turn in my thinking has in part emerged from the preoccupations of my recent book, Thought Paralysis. But it has also been heavily influenced by ongoing conversations with my wife, Angelika Gölz, her interests and her ways of thinking. And finally, in this moment, I also want to remember three colleagues and friends who were important to me, and who sadly, are no longer with us—Dennis Brown, Tom Hamrogue and Marisa Dillon Weston. A video to the lecture can be found at: https://vimeo.com/43760107#.

References

Alford, F. C. (2002). *Levinas: The Frankfurt School and Psychoanalysis*. London: Continuum.

Appiah, K. A. (2005). *The ethics of identity*. New Jersey: Princetown University Press.

Buber, M. (1958). *I and thou*. London: Continuum International Publishing.

Dalal, F. (1998). *Taking the group seriously: Towards a post-Foulkesian group analytic theory*. London: Jessica Kingsley Publishers.

Dalal, F. (2002). *Race, colour and the processes of racialization*: New Perspectives from Group Analysis, Psychoanalysis, and Sociology. Hove: Brunner-Routledge.

Dreyfus, H. L. & Dreyfus, S. E. (1988). *Mind over machine: The power of human intuition and expertise in the era of the computer*. New York: The Free Press.

Foulkes, S. H. (1948). *Introduction to group analytic psychotherapy*. London: William Heinemann Medical Books. Reprinted London: Karnac, 1983.

Foulkes, S. H. (1978). *Group analytic psychotherapy—methods and principles*. London: Karnac.

Freud, S. (1921). *Group Psychology and the analysis of the ego*. SE XVIII: pp. 67–144. London: Hogarth Press.

Gaita, R. (2004). *The philosopher's dog*. London: Routledge.

Gaita, R. (2008). A *common humanity; thinking about love, truth and justice*. Oxon and New York: Routledge.

Garfinkel, H. (1967). *Studies in ethnomethodology*. Englewood Cliffs: Prentice-Hall.

Kipling, R. (1990). *"If" in Rudyard Kipling: The complete verse*. London: Kyle Cathie Ltd.

Klein, M. (1998). *Love, guilt and reparation*. London: Vintage Classics.

Murdoch, I. (1999). *"The Sublime and the Good"* in Existentialists and Mystics: Writings on Philosophy and Literature, Peter Conradi (ed.), pp. 205–20. New York: Penguin Books.

Nagle, T. (1986). *The View from Nowhere*. Oxford: Oxford University Press.

Pascal, B. (1958). *Pascal's Pensées*. New York: Dutton & Co.

Pratchett, T. (2001). *Thief of Time*. London: Corgi Books.

Wittgenstein, L. (1963). *Philosophical investigations*. Oxford: Blackwell.

CHAPTER EIGHTEEN

Complexity and the group matrix*

Ralph Stacey

I n his last paper on the group matrix (Foulkes, 1973), Foulkes says of a group-analytic group:

> What an enormous complexity of processes and actions and inter-
> actions play between even two or three people, or these people and
> myself, or between two in relation to another three, and so on. What
> enormous complexity, quite impossible to perceive and disentangle
> even theoretically all at the same time. How is it that they can nev-
> ertheless understand each other that they can to some extent refer
> to a shared common sense of what is going on?
>
> (1973: 227)

His answer to this question is the existence of a "suprapersonal matrix"
(1973: 227). He sees this as an alternative to the view that what is happening in a group is due to the interaction of individual minds. He
makes it clear (1973: 226) that he is talking about a psychic system, one

---

*This chapter was first published as: Stacey, R. D. (2001). Complexity and the group matrix. *Group Analysis*, 34: 221–239.

of interacting mental processes, not individuals interacting to form a superimposed social system.

Communication and the group matrix
as suprapersonal psychic system

According to Foulkes, when people come together in a group they create a new phenomenon. A suprapersonal psychic system, which Foulkes describes in a number of different ways as: the context of the group, that is, the background in which the individual is figural (1973: 230); a total unified field of mental happenings of which the individual is a part ((Foulkes, 1971): 214); transpersonal processes that go right through individuals like X rays, but which those individuals can modify, elaborate and contribute to in their own way (1973: 229); interacting mental processes that transgress the individual (1973: 229). By mental processes, Foulkes seems to mean communications such as "acts, active messages, movements, expressions, silent transmissions of moods ..." (1973: 213) both conscious and unconscious. In the latter category, he includes resonance, transference, projection and so on.

Although earlier he had referred to the matrix as a group mind, in his last paper on the matrix he rejected that terminology and talked about "the mind" as an interacting transpersonal mental process, or "mind" as a multiperson phenomenon (1971: 225). As I interpret this, he is saying that an individual mind is the trans personal processes that penetrate him or her through and through to the core so that individual mind is a multiperson phenomenon. This dynamic formulation begins to suggest a view of causality in which interaction is perpetually constructing the future when in their coming together people create the new phenomena of suprapersonal psychic systems. This conceptualization of mind is surely a significant departure from classical psychoanalytic formulations in which mind is located in the individual. Foulkes's view had its critics (for example, Van der Kleij, 1982) who felt that it either removed the individual altogether or presented a picture removed from the ordinary experience of individuality.

However, Foulkes repeatedly argued that he was not removing or reducing the individual because, as I understand it, part of the psychic suprasystem consists of the foundation matrix that individuals bring with them to the group. In my view, this development of his argument takes him right back to locating the mind in the individual in the way that classical psychoanalytic theory does. My argument here is essentially the same as Dalal's (Dalal, 1998) broader analysis of Foulkes's thought. To explain this further, consider the steps in Foulkes's argument. First, he defines the nature of the suprapersonal psychic system as follows:

> I have accepted from the beginning that even this group of total strangers, schemas of the same species and more narrowly of the same culture, share a fundamental mental matrix (foundation matrix). To this their closer acquaintance and their intimate exchanges add consistently, so that they also form a current ever moving, ever-developing dynamic matrix.
>
> (1973: 228)

> This pre-existing and relatively static part we call the "foundation matrix." On top of this there are various levels of communication which are increasingly dynamic. They develop under our eyes. This is called the "dynamic matrix."
>
> (1971: 213)

He makes it clear that the various levels of matrix in the suprasystem operate at the same time in various admixtures but says that for reasons of clarity one can distinguish between the

> ... relatively static and unalterable genetic foundation matrix. and the rest, which is to a greater or lesser extent, subject to change within the group-analytic group.
>
> (1971: 213)

Of course, the foundation matrix changes through biological and cultural evolution but such evolution takes a long time. It seems clear to me from these quotes, that as far as a specific group-analytic group is concerned, the theory postulates a suprapersonal psychic system having stable, static aspects and dynamic ever-changing ones, to be thought of as intertwined with each other as interacting mental processes. However, there has been an important shift in the argument in the way in which the relatively static processes called the foundation matrix are linked to genetics. Foulkes confirms this shift when he says that mental processes cannot interact *per se* because it is ultimately whole persons who interact with whole persons:

> What I mean by saying that mental processes interact is the selective interaction that goes on impersonally, instinctively, intuitively, basically unconsciously, in accordance with the inner constellation and predispositions of those concerned and which determine their interaction. The total interactions of the individuals are in fact the result of affinities or disaffinities of individual instincts, emotions, reactions of all sorts, character predispositions, for example. There is at the same time an unconscious interpretation of these reactions on the same basis.
>
> (1973: 228–9)

> ... The individual's behaviour has been decisively shaped by the original family group.
>
> (1973: 231)

Through the notion of the foundation matrix, Foulkes has brought the individual back to the central position because now mental processes interact in a way determined by instincts, predispositions and inner constellations and decisively shaped by early family life. This determination and decisive shaping clearly refers to the individual mind. Instincts, predispositions and so on, constitute causative factors operative before the individual comes to a group to create the new phenomenon of the suprapersonal psychic system. In fact, if their minds are determined and decisively shaped in the way just described, what is the causative role of this newly created suprasystem of transpersonal processes that pass through individuals? The argument has moved from a dynamic multiperson interactive process in the living present that is potentially constructing the future to one in which the future is the unfolding of individually enfolded instincts, predispositions and unconscious inner constellations. How these two are to be understood as processes in one newly constructed suprasystem is far from clear. Despite Foulkes's insistence that the notion of the individual is retained, it is retained in what seems to me to be unconvincing ways, either as transpersonal processes passing through an individual, or as the unfolding of instinctual and culturally determined behaviour, or by both in some way not made clear.

For me, the notions of a psychic suprasystem, on the one hand, and the foundations of inherited instincts and early predispositions on the other, are two mutually inconsistent explanations in a number of ways. One privileges the group as a psychic system transgressing the individuals and the other privileges the genetically/culturally determined individuals as constructing the group. One implies transformative causality in which the future is schemas constructed in the living present, while the other implies a formative causality in which the future is unfolded from what is already there. One emphasizes the possibility of the unknown and the other the likelihood of the known.

However, in his insistence that the total psychic suprasystem must be understood as one intertwined system consisting of foundation and dynamic matrices, Foulkes ends up with a "both/and" explanation On the one hand, there is the dynamic matrix understood as a jointly created suprasystem, above or across individuals, penetrating or transgressing them as their minds. This is a multipersonal phenomenon and thus a notion very different to classical psychoanalytic theory. On the other hand there is the foundation matrix, suggesting something below or before individuals which is explained in terms of biological determinism and decisive shaping by early family experience, fully in accord with classical psychoanalytic theory of mind as a single-person phenomenon. Foulkes does not choose between these explanations but quite explicitly states his "both/and" position (1973: 227, 230–1), He argues that, against the background of the total field one can focus on the group as a whole or on the individual, in which latter case psychoanalytic formulations apply. It all depends upon what one wishes to observe. He sees both as abstractions in terms of figure (group, individual) and ground (total field or psychic suprasystem) and regards both as schemas true from the position from which the observation is made. However, he does express a preference for the multiperson view of mind (1973: 227).

For me this is an unsatisfactory position that diminishes Foulkes's important insight about the centrality of relating and communicating between people in understanding the nature of the group and the individual. It also diminishes his insights about the arbitrariness of defining some processes as inside the individual and others as outside. Simply accepting both positions, it seems to me is an easy way out of having to live with the paradox of the individual and the group. Foulkes's explanation provides the relief of retaining two contradictory theories by looking at them sequentially, keeping one for one purpose and one for another, in so doing, the theory loses the dialectic, the paradox of groups and individuals simultaneously forming and schemas formed by each in communicative processes. A similar point was made by Van der Kleij (1982), who also criticized the conceptualization of individuals as nodes in a matrix, through whom transpersonal processes passed. He proposed a "dialectical" formulation in which attention moves back and forth between individual and group, which in the end is not much different to Foulkes because it too is a "both/and" sequence rather than the paradox, or dialectic, of behaviour as simultaneously individual and group.

I propose a way of understanding the relationship between individual and group not in terms of systems above or below people but as processes of a paradoxical nature in which, in their communicative interaction, individuals form groups and are formed by them simultaneously. I suggest that this approach might be a means of developing Foulkes's important insight on the centrality of communication in a way that focuses on the communicative interaction between individuals rather than the interaction between mental processes in a psychic suprasystem. The approach I suggest draws on the thoughts of G. H. Mead about mind, self and society and upon some analogies provided by the natural sciences of complexity.

Mead on mind, self and society

Mead (Mead, 1934) argued that all social animals communicate with each other through a conversation of gestures: movement, touch, sound, visual display and odour. Each gesture by one animal calls forth a response from another, and gesture and response together constitute a social act that is an act that is meaningful to those gesturing and responding. This is what the social, in general terms, meant to Mead: responsive processes in which animals communicate meaningfully in a continuous cycle of cooperative and competitive interaction with each other.

However, although there is meaning in such a process there may be no mind or consciousness. Mind is a process in which a gesture can call forth the same bodily response in the one making it as in the one to whom it is made. It is only through the capacity that the one making a gesture has to call Forth in him/herself a similar attitude to those schemas called forth in the other, that the maker of a gesture can be aware of what they mean. For example, this capacity enables one to be aware that the gesture of shouting at someone may arouse fear or anger in that someone. That awareness is possible because the gesture of shouting arouses the potential of fear or anger in oneself. Such a gesture is what Mead called a significant symbol. It is significant because it means the same thing, in a bodily sense, to the maker of the gesture and to the recipient.

Mead, like Foulkes, is concerned with the nature of communication in a group but his formulation suggests another answer to the question posed by Foulkes, as quoted at the beginning of this article: how is it that strangers coming together in a group can immediately understand each other? Foulkes's answer is the foundation matrix. Mead's answer is the biological capacity to call forth in oneself a similar attitude to one's gesture as that called forth in the other. The role of the biological here is completely different. Biology is not acting as a causal determinant in the form of instinct but as a capacity, namely, the capacity to relate to others in a particular way. Instead of having to posit the existence of a psychic suprasystem it is enough that humans have central nervous systems enabling them to communicate in significant symbols. This is an explanation based on experience-near communicative interaction not on an hypothesized psychic system above, across, beneath or behind those communicating.

For Mead, the elaboration of vocal gestures into language enables a more sophisticated development of mind. Language enables the maker of a gesture to be aware, in advance, of the likely response of the recipient and enables the maker of the gesture to signal to the recipient how the act is likely to unfold. The maker of the gesture is thus, conscious and can think, that is, hypothesize likely responses to a gesture in a kind of role-play. To have a mind means to be aware of the possible consequences of actions, as those actions emerge, by means of silently conducted conversations in the pauses between gestures and responses. Mind is silent, private role-playing of gesture-response conducted during the vocal, public interaction of gesture-response that is social cooperation (Bakhtin (Bakhtin, 1981) 1962; Elias, 1970, 1989; Vygotsky, 1986). This is a view of individuals in a relationship continuously evoking and provoking responses in each other, responses that each paradoxically also selects and chooses on the basis of their previous histories of interaction. The private, silent conversation of a body with itself is the same process as public, vocal conversation between bodies and in this sense mind is always a social process even though it is an individual conducting the private silent conversation. This is an experience-near interpretation of what it means to say that the individual is social through and through to the core, one that does not require the postulate of a psychic suprasystem. Mead's theory of mind is firmly linked to the body because mind as silent conversation of gestures requires a living, biological body. The conversation involves more than words; it is always interwoven with feelings and direct communication between bodies in the medium of feelings, a point Foulkes clearly makes in his notion of resonance.

The individual mind is then logically the same process as social relating, in that both are cooperative communicative interactions of living bodies. The only difference is that one is silent and private while the other is vocal and public. It is impossible to have a mind in advance of vocal, public interaction, just as it is impossible to have that vocal, public interaction, that sophisticated human social ration, in the absence of minds. Neither form of conversation is primary or prior to the other. They must both arise together, simultaneously. This immediately renders problematic the labelling of one as more or less fundamental and suggests that the individual and the social are at one level of explanation, not two. This is also Elias's view (1989); he said that the individual was the singular of relating and the group the plural. Meaning is not something that is going on in a mind as thought before action but, rather arises, and continually re-arises in the conversation of gestures, in the action and interaction, through social relationships conducted in significant symbols. There is no need to postulate a separate psychic or social level, or any kind of transpersonal processes, or any notion of a group mind.

Mead takes the argument a step further with his concept of the generalized other. By this he means that one does not simply call forth in oneself the attitude to one's gesture of a particular other but comes to call forth in oneself the collective attitude towards one's gesture. In other words, in the private role play of silent conversation the attitude of one's group towards one's actions finds a voice. This is a social form of control, arising simultaneously in the group and the individual; Mead then proceeds to suggest what it means to be self-conscious. One is self-conscious when, as a subject, one becomes an object to oneself. To be an object to him/herself an individual must experience him/herself from the standpoint of others; he or she must talk to him/herself as others talk to him or her. This happens as an individual learns to take up the roles of others to him/herself, as a unique identity, in a form of role-play with him/herself. The silent conversation then involves a "me," that is, an identity, which is the attitude of one's group towards oneself. The individual's response to this "me," is the "I," that is, the action that an individual takes in response to the perceived community view of him/herself. The "I" response is potentially novel and hence unpredict-able. The "I" response has the potential to change others, opening up the way for simultaneous individual/group evolution.

In this process, an individual takes the attitude of the whole com-munity towards him/herself, as well as the attitude of individual others towards him/herself and the attitude of others towards each other. It is through this process that individual and community display controlled cooperative behaviour. This sophisticated human social process is pos-sible only in language. It follows that the self is a social construction emerging in relationships with others and only animals that possess language can possess a self that they are aware of. Mind and self do not emerge out of a clash between something that is already there in the indi-vidual and social constraint as in the classical Freudian view. Mind and self emerge in social relationships. Individuals are forming and schemas formed in the group all at the same time. Mind and self arise between people rather than as schemas located in an individual. Change in the group and in the individual is the same process, namely, change in pat-terns of communicative interaction. An individual changes when his/her private role-play/silent conversation with him/herself changes.

However, if there is no psychic or other system above, below or behind the ongoing flow of communicative interaction between bodies in the living present just what is it that imparts pattern or coherence to that communicative interaction? Mead did not address this question and it is here that insights from the natural complexity sciences (see Stacey et al, 2000; Waldorp, 1992) developed over the last few decades have, I believe, some important analogies to offer.

Analogies from the natural sciences of complexity

Natural complexity scientists (e.g. Allen, 1998a, 1998b; Goodwin, 1994; Kauffman, 1995; Prigogine, 1997) are interested in explaining how vast numbers of interactions between entities in nature can produce coherence in the absence of any blueprint or programme determining that coherence. Vast numbers of entities, such as the neurones in a brain or ants in a colony, interact with each other according to their own local principles of interaction—that is, they self-organise. In certain conditions of a paradoxical nature, sometimes called the edge of chaos and sometimes called complexity, this kind of self'-organisation exhibits the capacity to produce emergent coherence that none of the entities "intended" or "knew about in advance." Emergence is thus a different notion of causality, one that does not depend upon a blueprint or any system outside interaction itself. In other words, emergent coherence is not due to anything above, below, behind or anywhere else. Emergence is coherence arising in the interaction itself. By analogy, it seems to me to be quite plausible to argue that human interaction also has intrinsic pattern-forming properties. It follows that Mead's concept of continuing social acts as gestures/responses has intrinsic pattern-forming capacities, making it superfluous to postulate any kind of psychic suprasystem.

It is worth noting at this point that complexity here is a theoretical construct, sometimes specifically meaning a paradoxical dynamic of stability and instability at the same time and sometimes referring to a collection of other constructs to do with self-organisation and emergence. Clearly, in the passage previously quoted, Foulkes (1973: 227) was using the word "complex" as a descriptive adjective, not a theoretical construct. Notions of self-organisation and emergence, therefore, offer an alternative way of understanding his insight about the importance of communicative processes in a group. The following paragraphs briefly outline, some of the theorizing of Prigogine, based on his work in chemistry and other areas. For me, they are suggestive of how one might think about human groups.

At the beginning of his hook The End of Certainty, Prigogine poses what he sees as a central question: "Is the future given, or is it under perpetual construction?" (Prigogine, 1997). His answer is clear: he sees the future for every level of the universe as under perpetual construction. He says that nature is about the creation of unpredictable novelty where the possible is richer than the real. For him life is an unstable system with an unknowable future and human creativity is essentially the same process as nature's creativity. Central to Prigogine's approach, at all levels, is the distinction between individual entities and populations, or ensembles, consisting of those entities. He takes the ensemble as fundamental and argues that change in whole ensembles emerges over long periods, through the amplification of slight variations in individual entities, that is, the variability of individuals in the case of organisms or microscopic collisions in the case of matter, it is this variability that is amplified to reach bifurcation points where a system spontaneously self-organizes to take completely unpredictable paths into the future. Self-organization is the process in which a system "chooses" a path at a bifurcation point as a result of individual variability, or fluctuations. Prigogine is arguing, therefore, that even at the most fundamental levels of matter, it is the individual variability of entities and the interactions between them that lead to emergent change in populations of ensembles. He sees this process as extending to every level including that of human action.

The possibility of the evolution of novelty depends critically on the presence of microscopic diversity. When individual entities are the same—that is when they do not have any incentive to alter their patterns of interacting with each other, there is only stability. When individual entities are different and thus do have incentives to change their patterns of interaction with each other, they display change of a genuinely novel kind. The "openness" of the individual entities to the possible leads to a continuing dialogue between novel individual "experiments" and (almost certainly) unanticipated collective effects. Here, the future is under perpetual construction through the micro interactions of diverse entities. The "final" form towards which a phenomenon moves is not given beforehand, nor is it schemas "chosen" from outside. The forms continually emerge in an unpredictable way as movement into the unknown. However, there is nothing mysterious or esoteric about this. What emerges does so because of the transformative cause of the process of the micro interactions, the fluctuations themselves.

What emerges, then, is always a potentially transformed identity: the identities of the whole and of the entities constituting it at the same time. Therefore, the differences between the entities themselves and their collective difference from others, also emerge at the same time. Micro interactions transform themselves in a paradox of forming while schemas formed and an explanation of what is happening requires an understanding of these micro interactions (Stacey et al, 2000).

Mead's explanation of mind, self and society is a similar expression of this view of causality, one in which the process of interaction between biological bodies is the transformative cause of that interaction. In this explanation, it is in the detailed interaction between people, their ongoing choices and actions in their relating to each other, that their minds and selves arise. They arise as patterns that display both continuity and potential transformation. At the same time, the social, the cooperative interaction of humans is also formed as continuity and transformation. The movement here is paradoxical in that it is both continuity and transformation at the same time, the known and the unknown at the same time, the individual and the social at the same time, that all arise in the micro detail of interaction.

This means that there is no need to postulate a suprasystem or to posit a foundation matrix that unfolds what is already unfolded. Human communicative interaction could have the intrinsic capacity to pattern itself and Mead suggests how this might actually happen in an account based entirely on communicative interaction itself. I now want to turn to more recent studies of human relating that seem to me to point to the transformative potential of communicative interaction between people.

Developing the notion of the group matrix as process

Using detailed research on infant behaviour. Stern (Stern, 1985, Stern, 1995) explains how an infant's self emerges in the mutual relationships between him/her and his/her family members. In effect he presents a family as an evolving process in which family members relate to each other in accordance with principles that organize their experience. Stern calls these organizing principles *schemas-of-schemas-with*:

1. A *schema-of-schemas-with* is based on the interactive experience-of-schemas-with a particular person in a specific way, such as schemas hungry and awaiting the breast or bottle or soliciting a smile and getting no response ... a way that is repetitive in ordinary life.
2. A *representation-of-schemas-with* is a network of many specific schemas-of schemas-with that are tied together by a common theme or feature. Activities that are organized by one motivational system are frequently the common theme for example, feeding, playing, or separation. Other representations are organized around affect experiences; they might be networks of schemas-of-schemas-sad-with or—happy-with for example. Yet other representations are assemblies made up of many representations that share a commonality

such as person (all the networks that go with a specific person) or place or role. (Stern, 1995: 19–20)

Stern is here describing an individual psyche in terms that are quite consistent with the functioning of the brain. Just as neurones trigger other neurones, so one schema of-schemas-with triggers others. Although he uses the terminology of representations, which may be problematic, he is postulating that the psyche is a process of interacting schemas rather than some mental apparatus or psychic system above them. He describes how an infant's schemas-of-schemas-with evolve in the interactive experience with the mother and the father and other family members and how an infant self emerges in this evolution. He talks about how the mother has many schemas of-schemas-with, for example, her schemas-of-schemas-with her infant, her mother, her husband, herself, and about how they interact with her infant's schemas-of'-schemas-with her. He illustrates in some detail how both the normal and the pathological development of a personality emerge from the continuous interaction between all of these schemas-of-being-with and how indeed, the infant's arrival contributes to the further evolution, normal and pathological, of all other family members' schemas-of-being-with. Although he does not use the terminology of complexity theory, it seems to me that he is describing complex processes in which each family member's relational schemas are interacting with those of others to producing emergent patterns of family relationship (the group) that constitute the further evolution of their relational schemas (individual minds). These relational schemas are continuously replicated or recreated and as this happens there is the possibility of novel emergent relational patterns.

Those writing from an intersubjective psychoanalytic perspective adopt a similar formulation:

> ... recurring patterns of intersubjective interaction within the developmental system in the establishment of invariant principles that unconsciously organise the child's subsequent experiences. ... It is these unconscious ordering principles, crystallized within the matrix of the child-caregiver system, that form the essential building blocks of personality development...
>
> (Stolorow et al, 1993: 5)
>
> Thus the basic units of analysis for our investigations of personality are *Structures of experience*—the distinctive configurations of

self and other that shape and organize a person's subjective world. These psychological structures are *not* to be viewed simply as "internalisations" or mental replicas of interpersonal events. Nor should they be regarded as having an objective existence in physical space or somewhere in a "mental apparatus." Instead, we conceptualise these structures as systems of ordering or organising principles … through which a person's experiences of self and other assume their characteristic forms and meanings. Such structures of subjectivity are disclosed in the thematic patterning of a person's subjective life
(Stolorow et al, 1994: 23–4)

Consider how these formulations might be used to think about a therapy group as complex processes of communicative interaction. I use the term organizing "theme" rather than organizing "principle" or "schema" because it captures for me the narrative and motivating nature of the process through which humans interactively organize their ordinary, everyday experience in narrative-like patterns (Brune, 1990; Stacey, 2001). Terms such as "principle" and "schema" convey a sense of propositions, or rules, and in doing so fail to be suggestive of the fluidity in the organization of ordinary, everyday experience. As members of a group communicate with each other publicly and vocally, that is, as they act bodily towards each other, their interaction patterns itself in an emergent way as one communication triggers others. Public communicative interaction is thus being patterned as narrative themes patterning the experience of being together. As they communicate with each other, each also simultaneously engages in a private role play/silent conversation, which is the action of the body directed towards itself. This private communicative interaction is also patterning itself as personal organizing themes reflecting personal histories of relating to others.

These organizing themes, both public and private, are not, however, to be thought of as constituting a suprapersonal system because they are the acts of bodies. Furthermore, they are not to be thought of as models or inner worlds that are stored in brains, waiting to be brought out of storage as it were, and shared. Some neuroscientists are now arguing that changes in the brain in response to stimuli are transient and do not last for more than a few hours (Rose, 1995) and others, working from a complexity perspective, argue that it is inappropriate to describe the brain as storing anything (Barrie et al, 1994; Freeman, 1994, 1995; Freeman & Barric, 1994; Freeman & Schneider, 1982; Kelso, 1995; Skarda & Freeman, 1990). for example:

The patterns of activity are created by dynamic neural interaction in the sensory cortex, not by registration and filtering of stimuli. There is no evidence for storage, retrieval, cross-correlation or logical tree search,

(Freeman, 1994: 332)

... the brain is *fundamentally* a pattern forming, self-organized, dynamical system poised on the brink of instability. By operating near instability, the brain is able to switch flexibly and quickly among a large repertoire of spatio-temporal patterns. It is, I like to say, a "twinkling" system, creating and annihilating patterns according to the demands placed on it.

(Kelso, 1995: xvii)

It seems therefore to be inappropriate to think of storing psychic organizing themes, either uniquely individual or shared with others and more appropriate to think of themes triggering other themes, sometimes along routes that have become habitual and sometimes along novel routes. These themes are most obviously expressed in language, in the to and fro of ordinary conversation, but they are also no less importantly expressed in non-verbal cues and emotional resonance.

So, as soon as members of a group meet each other, they all actively, albeit largely unconsciously, select and so organize their own subjective experience of being in that place with those people at that time and they do this according to some personal organizing themes formed in their own individual histories of relating. However, what those particular themes are at that particular moment will depend just as much on the cues being presented by others as upon the personal history of a particular individual. Each is simultaneously evoking and provoking responses from others so that the particular personal organizing themes emerging will depend as much on the others as on the individual concerned. Put like this, it becomes clear that no one individual can be organizing his or her experience in isolation because they are all simultaneously evoking and provoking responses in each other. Together they constitute intersubjective, reflexive processes *of* emergent themes patterning their experience of being together in which further themes continuously emerge.

The group matrix can then be defined, not as a system or a network, but as process that is continuously replicating and potentially transforming patterns of *intersubjective narrative themes that organize the experience of being together*. These themes emerge, in variant and invariant forms, out of the interaction between individual group members as they pattern that very interaction. However, these processes are embodied. Although themes patterning the experience of being together emerge in the interaction between people and therefore cannot be located "inside" any individual, the experience that is being so organized is always a bodily experience, that is, changes, marked or subtle, in the feeling tones of those bodies.

The following clinical material illustrates how themes organize group members' experience of being together. This is an illustration, not evidence of the veracity of the theoretical points I have made. I do not believe that such accounts could constitute evidence in any traditional scientific sense because each group meeting is unique and open to many different interpretations.

Clinical illustration

> In a session some 20 months into the life of a group, "Bill" repeated a consistent complaint about the group not addressing feelings or members' relationships with each other. As usual "Diane" and "Helen" took his comments as a direct criticism of them and aggressively suggested that there was nothing stopping him from talking about his relationships. "Fred"—as usual—supported Bill and complained about not being able to express anger in the group. "Jane" said that she found Bill's long silences frightening and felt that he did not like her. "David" attacked Bill for adopting a superior attitude. By this time Bill had slumped back into his seat in a kind of silent, analytic pose. He announced that the remarks of the others had simply confirmed what he already knew, namely, that people in the group did not like him. Diane said that occasionally she saw flashes of his personality that she liked. He replied that he did not care what she thought and told her that she was very self-centred.

So, remarks by one person evoke feelings and remarks from another, which in turn trigger other remarks and feelings in others in a self-organizing way. The private role play/silent conversation of each proceeds simultaneously with their public communicative interaction. There is an invariant and therefore largely predictable strand in the themes that emerged here as continuity with the past. On many occasions before Fred, Helen or Diane would recount some difficulty they were having and this would evoke complaints from either or both Bill and Fred that feelings were not being expressed. This would be denied and taken as a criticism. However, the particular form this sequence would take and when it would occur was quite unpredictable: there was always the potential for transformation. Also, the communicative process organizing itself as themes of being together does not mean that all share the same theme. Each member is responding differently around a theme that has to do with dissatisfaction with the group and each other, of being liked or not liked. For example, Jane is organizing Bill's silence into an experience of not being liked while Diane organizes her experience of Bill's remarks into a criticism of her. Bill organizes whatever they all say or do as further confirmation of their not liking him.

I suggest that group communication is processes patterned as many themes that organize the experience of being together in the group. These interacting themes are simultaneously arising between people and being experienced in their individual bodies. Thus, in the case given above, Bill's remark about people in the group being considerate is evoked by Diane's prior comment and his remark in turn evokes a statement from her. But, as he makes his remark he slumps in his chair while she stiffens in hers signalling her apprehension. Even where there is no apparent change in posture, I suggest that there will always be subtle changes in body rhythms as changes in feeling stales accompany the emergent themes organizing experience. Communicative interaction is self-organizing as emergent pattern in itself. These patterns are changes in the themes organizing local interaction as group members seek to fit in with each other in some way. These organizing themes are continually re-creating themselves in a self-reflexive way as people continuously experience the changes in their bodies. Note how the explanation runs entirely in terms of communicative interaction, having conscious and unconscious aspects, in a way that does not require any notion of a suprasystem or transpersonal processes. The explanation is action-based with nothing behind, above or below the action itself.

Paying attention to themes organizing the experience of being together

From the perspective I suggest, the group conductor seeks to understand the group in terms of his or her perceptions, feelings about and resonance with, the emerging themes organizing the experience of being together. As a participant in the construction of these themes, the group conductor may articulate some of those themes, particularly those that the group members seem unconscious of, in the interest of assisting the group to take the next step. In the Foulkesian tradition, the conductor seeks to facilitate communication, particularly when it is stuck in repetitive patterns or when the group's pathology is located in one of its members.

Here again I find an analogy from the complexity sciences helpful. Complex systems generally display three classes of dynamic. In some conditions the system dynamic takes the form of repetitive patterns of regular predictability. In other conditions, the same system displays patterns of randomness and disintegration. But at intermediate conditions between those producing regularity and those producing disintegration, the system displays the dynamic-known as the edge of chaos, or what others call complexity. Here the system dynamic is paradoxically patterned as stability and instability at the same time. Researchers have shown that the healthy heart functions in the dynamic at the edge of chaos and that disease is the loss of complexity (Goldberger, 1997). This, it seems to me, is analogous to Foulkes's notion of a healthy group as one characterized by free-flowing communication while the unhealthy group is one that loses this "complexity" and gets stuck in repetitive interactions.

There is another implication too. If an individual mind is thought of as a private role-play or silent conversation, it is useful to ask group members to recount what they say to themselves, particularly when they are depressed, about to panic or experiencing other distressing moments. This question, I have found, is immediately understood by group members and elicits useful material that seems to move the member forward in the sense of participating more fully in the group. The aim is to encourage shifts in patterns of silent conversation, to introduce new voices and greater variety into silent conversation with oneself, as relief from the repetitive silent conversations of mental distress.

Conclusion

I argue that the group matrix is not a system but processes of interaction in which intersubjective narrative themes pattern the members' embodied experience of being together. I have suggested that these are self-organizing processes that emergently reproduce themselves as bodily actions, always with the potential for transformation. In other words, themes produce further emergent themes patterning the experience of being together in potentially transformative ways.

From a complexity perspective there is no need to postulate a suprapersonal psychic system or any transpersonal processes. Nor is there any need to postulate an individual mental apparatus. Instead, there is a notion of psychic phenomena as emergent narrative themes that form while being formed by patterns of communicative interaction between human bodies.

References

Allen, P. M. (1998a). Evolving complexity in Social Science. In: C. Altman & W. A. Koch (eds) *Systems: New Paradigms for the Human Sciences*. New York: Walter de Gruyter.

Allen, P. M. (1998b). Modeling Complex Economic Evolution, in F. Schweite & G. Silverberg (eds) *Selhstorganization*. Berlin: Dunker and Humbolt.

Barrie, J. M., Freeman, W. J. & Lenhart, M. (1994). "Cross-modality Cortical Processing: Spatiotemporal Patterns in Olfactory, Visual. Auditor)" and Somatic EEGs in Perception by Trained Rabbits.' *Society for Neuroscience Abstracts*, 414(10).

Bakhtin, M. M. (1986). *Speech genres and other late essays*. Austin: University of Texas Press.

Bakhtin, M. (1981). *The dialogic imagination: Four essays by Bakhtin M. M.*, trans. Emerson, C. & Holqusit M., Texas University Press: Austin.

Brunner, J. (1990). Acts of meaning. Cambridge, MA: Harvard University Press.

Dalal, F. (1998). *Taking the group seriously: Towards a post-Foulkesian group analytic theory*. Jessica Kingsley: London.

Elias, N. (1970). *What is Sociology?* New York: Columbia University Press.

Elias, N. (1989). *The Symbol Theory*. London: Sage Publications.

Foulkes, S. H. (1971). Access to unconscious processes in the group-analytic group. *Group Analysis*, 4: 4–14.

Foulkes, S. H. (1973). The Group as matrix of the individual's mental life in group therapy. In *Group Therapy—An Overview*, (ed. L. R. Ed. Wolberg & E. K. Schwartz), Stratton: New York.

Freeman, W. J. (1994). Role of Chaotic Dynamics in Neural Plasticity, in J. van Pelt, M. A. Comer, H. B. M. Uylings & F. H. Lopes da Silva (eds) *Progress in Brain Research, vol. 102*. Amsterdam: Elsevier Science.

Freeman, W. J. (1995). *Societies of brains: A study in the neuroscience of love and hate*. Hillsdale, NJ: Lawrence Erlbaum.

Freeman, W. J. & Barrie, J. M. (1994). Chaotic oscillations and the genesis of eaning in cerebral cortex', in G. Buzsaki, R. Llinas, W. Singer, A. Berthoz & Y. Christen (eds) *Temporal Coding in the Brain*. Berlin: Springer.

Freeman, W. J. & Schneider, W. (1982). Changes in the spatial patterns of rabbit olfactory EEC with conditioning to odors. *Psychophysiology, 19*: 45–56.

Goldbergcr, A. L. (1997). Fractal variability versus pathologic periodicity: Complexity loss and stereotypy in disease. *Perspectives in Biology and Medicine, 40*(4): 543–561.

Goodwin, B. (1994). *How the leopard changed its spots*. London: Weidenfeld and Nicolson. Kauffman, S. A. (1995). *At Home in the Universe*. New York: Oxford University Press.

Kelso J. A. Scott, (1995). *Dynamic patterns: The Self-organization of brain and behavior*. Cambridge, MA: MIT Press. Mead, C. H. (1934) Mind. *Self and Society*. Chicago: University of Chicago Press.

Mead, G. H. (1934). *Mind, self and society*. Chicago University Press: Chicago: .

Prigogine, I. & Stengers, I. (1984). *Order out of chaos: Man's new dialogue with nature*. New York: Bantam Books.

Prigogine, I. (1997). *The end of certainty: Lime. Chaos and the new laws of nature*. New York: The Free Press.

Rose, S. P. R. (1995). Memory formation: Its molecular and cell Biology. *European Review, 3*(3): 243–256.

Skarda, C. A. & Freeman. W. J. (1990). Chaos and the New Science of the Brain. *Concepts in Neuroscience, 1*(2): 275–285.

Stacey, R. (2001). *Complex responsive processes in organizations: Learning and knowledge creation*. London: Routledge.

Stacey, R., Griffin. J. D. & Shaw, P. (2011). *Complexity and management: Fad or radical challenge to systems thinking*. London: Routledge.

Stern, D. (1995). *The motherhood constellation: A unified view of parent-infant psychotherapy*. Basic Books: New York.

Stern, D. N. (1985). *The interpersonal world of the infant*. In (Anonymous), Basic Books: New York.

Stolorow, R., Atwood, C. & Brandchaft, B. (1994). *The intcrsubjective perspective*. Northvale, NJ: Jason Aronson.

Vygotsky, L. S. (1986). *Thought and language*. Cambridge, MA: MIT Press.

Van der Kleij, C. (1982). About the matrix. *Group Analysis, 15*(3): 219–234.

Waldorp, M. M. (1992). *Complexity: The emerging science at the edge of chaos*. Englewood Cliffs, NJ: Simon and Schuster.

INDEX